Privacy and Data Protection Law in New Zealand

Privacy and Data Protection Law in New Zealand

Paul Roth
Blair Stewart

This book was originally published as a monograph in the International Encyclopaedia of Laws/Privacy and Technology Law.

Founding Editor: Roger Blanpain
General Editor: Frank Hendrickx
Volume Editors: Jos Dumortier, Pieter Gryffroy, Ruben Roex & Yung Shin Van Der Sype

Wolters Kluwer

Published by:
Kluwer Law International B.V.
PO Box 316
2400 AH Alphen aan den Rijn
The Netherlands
E-mail: lrs-sales@wolterskluwer.com
Website: www.wolterskluwer.com/en/solutions/kluwerlawinternational

Sold and distributed by:
Wolters Kluwer Legal & Regulatory U.S.
7201 McKinney Circle
Frederick, MD 21704
United States of America
E-mail: customer.service@wolterskluwer.com

ISBN 978-94-035-1616-5

e-Book: ISBN 978-94-035-1516-8
web-PDF: ISBN 978-94-035-1526-7

The Authors

Paul Roth, BA (Brown), LLB (Hons) (Otago), MA, PhD (Bryn Mawr).

Paul Roth is Professor Emeritus in the Faculty of Law at the University of Otago, Dunedin, New Zealand. He is an enrolled Barrister and Solicitor of the High Court of New Zealand, and formerly practised part-time in the areas of privacy law and employment law. Prior to becoming a lawyer in New Zealand, he taught Greek and Latin at several universities in the United States. At the University of Otago, he taught courses in Privacy Law, Employment Law, and International Human Rights Law. He has also given seminars for the New Zealand Law Society on privacy law and employment law. He has been on the editorial boards of *Human Rights Law and Practice*, *Privacy Law and Policy Reporter* (Australia), the *New Zealand Law Review*, and the *Employment Law Bulletin*.

Paul has published widely in the areas of privacy law and employment law. He has been the sole author, from 1995 to 2018, of the loose-leaf legal text *Privacy Law and Practice* (LexisNexis), and is co-author of *Access to Information* (first edition, 2014; second edition, 2017). He has also written chapters on Privacy Law and Employment Law for *International Human Rights Law in Aotearoa, New Zealand* (Thomson Reuters, 2017). He has written commentary on New Zealand's Privacy Act for *Mazengarb's Employment Law (Butterworths/LexisNexis,* 1994–2021) and on the Human Rights Act for *Human Rights Law* (Thomson Reuters, 2008–2012). He was one of the editors of the *Global Encyclopaedia of Data Protection Regulation* (Kluwer, London, 1999–2003). Other publications include: 'Privacy and the Human Rights Challenges of Technology and Globalisation', in *Universal Human Rights*, (Macmillan, 2000); 'What Is "Personal Information"?' *New Zealand Universities Law Review* (2002); 'Data Protection Meets Web 2.0: Two Ships Passing in the Night', *University of New South Wales Law Journal* (2010). He has also reviewed reports on privacy for the New Zealand Law Commission (2004, 2007–2009), and was a member of the Law Commission's reference committee on privacy (2007–2011).

The Authors

Blair Stewart BA, LLB (Hons) (Auckland)

Former Assistant Privacy Commissioner, New Zealand (1993–2018), Enrolled barrister and solicitor of the High Court of New Zealand.

Blair Stewart was an Assistant Privacy Commissioner for twenty-five years in New Zealand until 2018. Throughout that period, he was responsible within the Office of the Privacy Commissioner for codes of practice and international policy and, for various periods, for information matching oversight, legislation and policy, litigation, and special projects. In the context of codes of practice, Blair was responsible for developing one of the world's earliest comprehensive health information privacy laws in 1993. In relation to policy, Blair was a pioneer in the theory and practice of privacy impact assessment in the 1990s and ran several influential international workshops on the subject in the early 2000s. He also led a major review of the Privacy Act 1993 and wrote the review report which was influential in the eventual replacement law. Within the international realm, Blair was particularly active in regional and international groupings of privacy regulators playing a leading role in establishing the Asia Pacific Privacy Authorities Forum, APEC Cross-border Privacy Enforcement Arrangement (CPEA), and Global Privacy Enforcement Authorities Network (GPEN) as well as serving for a period as Secretariat for the Global Privacy Assembly. Blair was a New Zealand representative to several international governmental privacy committees, particularly within APEC and OECD. Blair served on APEC's Data Privacy Subgroup from its inauguration from 2007 to 2018, being closely involved in the preparation of the APEC Privacy Framework in 2005 and leading the work to revise and reissue the Framework in 2015.

Blair has been published in relation to Human Rights, Freedom of Information and Privacy over many years, beginning with editing, and co-authoring, Auckland Lesbian & Gay Lawyers Group, *Out Law: A Legal Guide for Lesbians & Gay Men in New Zealand*, August 1994, the first book of its kind in New Zealand. Blair was on the editorial panels for the New Zealand journal *Human Rights Law and Practice*, from its inauguration in 1995, and the Australian journal, *Privacy Law and Policy Reporter*, also from 1995, both journals discontinued after many years of publication. In more recent years, Blair has published on regulatory topics in two volumes in Springer's Law, Government and Technology Series, 'Privacy Impact Assessment: Optimising the regulator's role' in Wright and De Hert, *Privacy Impact Assessment*, 2012, and 'Cross-border breach notification' in Wright and De Hert, *Enforcing Privacy: Regulatory, Legal and Technological Approaches*, 2016. Since 2018, Blair has jointly edited the Lexis Nexis publication, *Privacy Law and Practice*, covering developments in New Zealand privacy law.

Prior to joining the Privacy Commissioner, Blair worked in legal practice in Auckland, New Zealand, and in legal and regulatory roles in London, UK. From 2018-22, Blair was a committee member of the Privacy Foundation New Zealand. In 2022, Blair was appointed as a Professional Teaching Fellow by the University of Auckland.

The authors would like to acknowledge and thank the editorial team at Kluwer. For this title, Paul Roth wrote Part I, Chapters 1 and 4; Part II, Chapters 1, 2, and

3; Part III, Chapters 1, and 2; Part IV, Chapters 1, 2, 3, 4, 5, 6, and 7; Part VIII, Chapters 4, 5, and 6; and Part IX, Chapters 1, 2, and 4. Blair Stewart wrote Part I, Chapters 2 and 3; Part III, Chapter 3; Part IV, Chapter 8; Part V, Chapters 1, 2, 3, 4, and 5; Part VI; Part VII, Chapters 1 and 2; Part VIII, Chapters 1, 2, and 3; Part IX, Chapter 3 and 5; and Part X, Chapters 1, 2, 3, and 4.

The Authors

Table of Contents

List of Abbreviations

AC	Appeal Cases (UK)
Act	Privacy Act 2020
CA	Court of Appeal
CBPRs	APEC Cross-Border Privacy Rules System
COE	Council of Europe Modernised Data Protection Convention
DC	District Court
DOC	Department of Conservation
ER Act	Employment Relations Act 2000
GCSB	Government Communications Security Bureau
GDPR	General Data Protection Regulation: Regulation (EU) 2016/679 of the European Parliament and of the Council on the protection of natural persons with regard to the processing of personal data and on the free movement of such data
HC	High Court
HR Act	Human Rights Act 1993
HRNZ	Human Rights Reports of New Zealand
HRRT	Human Rights Review Tribunal
INZ	Immigration New Zealand
IPP	Information Privacy Principle
IRD	Inland Revenue Department
ISA	Intelligence and Security Act
JOP	A Joint Oversight Panel
LGOIM Act	Local Government Official Information and Meetings Act 1987
NCSC	National Cyber Security Centre
NHI	National Health Index
NSN	National Student Numbers
NZAR	New Zealand Administrative Reports
NZBN	New Zealand Business Number
NZCA	New Zealand Court of Appeal Decisions
NZCRT	New Zealand Complaints Review Tribunal Decisions

List of Abbreviations

NZERA	New Zealand Employment Relations Authority Determinations
NZHC	New Zealand High Court Decisions
NZHRRT	New Zealand Human Rights Review Tribunal Decisions
NZLC	New Zealand Law Commission
NZPrivCmr	New Zealand Privacy Commissioner (in relation to citation of case notes)
NZSIS	New Zealand Security Intelligence Service
NZULR	New Zealand Universities Law Review
PRN	Person Record Number
SC	Supreme Court
TFN	Tax File Number
TICSA	(Interception Capability and Security) Act 2013
TLR	Times Law Reports (UK)
1993 Act	Privacy Act 1993

Preface

General Background to New Zealand's Privacy Act

The legislative protection of privacy in New Zealand has resulted from both international influences and national developments from the 1970s onwards. Moreover, alongside the legislative track, common law protection of privacy interests led to the acceptance of an invasion of privacy tort by the 1990s. The period was clearly ripe for the introduction of privacy protections. The chief international influences that accelerated and expanded the development of privacy legislation in New Zealand were the 1980 OECD Guidelines,[1] which thoroughly informed the information privacy principles (IPPs) of the Privacy Act 1993; the 1995 European Union Personal Data Directive,[2] in terms of which New Zealand was found to have an 'adequate level of data protection' in 2012;[3] and the GDPR,[4] which had an important role in expanding privacy protections in the replacement Privacy Act 2020, particularly in relation to coverage of overseas agencies that have some New Zealand connection.

The legislative background to New Zealand's Privacy Act

In 1971 the government asked the Law Revision Commission to carry out a study of privacy in relation to computer databanks. While the study was ongoing, the earliest parliamentary move towards more comprehensive privacy legislation in New Zealand was taken. This was an unsuccessful private member's measure entitled the Preservation of Privacy Bill, introduced into the House of Representatives in 1972. The long title of the bill was 'An Act to preserve individual privacy and to prevent storage and distribution of incorrect personal information in and from computer memory banks.' It would have established a Privacy Commissioner and a Register

1. Recommendation of the Council concerning Guidelines Governing the Protection of Privacy and Transborder Flows of Personal Data, adopted 23 Sep. 1980, amended 11 Jul. 2013.
2. Directive on the Protection of Individuals with Regard to the Processing of Personal Data and on the Free Movement of Such Data, Directive 95/46/EC of the European Parliament and the Council of the European Union, 24 Oct. 1995.
3. Commission Implementing Decision of 19 December 2012 pursuant to Directive 95/46/EC of the European Parliament and of the Council on the adequate protection of personal data by New Zealand, 2013/65/EU.
4. Regulation on the protection of natural persons with regard to the processing of personal data and on the free movement of such data, and repealing Directive 95/46/EC, Regulation (EU) 2016/679, 27 Apr. 2016.

of Computer Installations. Although the proposal for a Register of Computer Installations was the last time computer registration was ever seriously considered in New Zealand, the bill's proposal for a Privacy Commissioner successfully endured with the creation (or continuation) of a statutory privacy commissioner in every subsequent government bill.

A Privacy Commissioner Bill was introduced by the Minister of Justice in 1975, but it did not survive a change of government at that year's general election. However, a statutory Wanganui Computer Centre Privacy Commissioner was established two years later and some general functions from the 1975 bill did find their way to the newly established Human Rights Commission established in 1977.

Major steps along the road towards privacy legislation during the 1980s included work of Tim McBride, an academic lawyer, and the Information Authority, a body temporarily established under the Official Information Act 1982 that was charged with review and recommendatory functions. In November 1984, McBride published an extensive resource paper for the Human Rights Commission entitled *Privacy Review*, and in December 1987 he authored an influential paper commissioned by the Department of Justice entitled *Data Privacy: An Options Paper*.

Work on privacy legislation was undertaken prior to the 1990 general election by the outgoing government, which, having lost the election went into opposition. After the election, the Department of Justice briefed the incoming minister on the importance of putting privacy legislation in place and the government introduced the Privacy of Information Bill to Parliament in August 1991. The measure was divided into two separate bills by a Select Committee so that certain clauses of the Bill could be enacted relatively quickly as the Privacy Commissioner Act 1991. The reason for this was the government's wish to proceed with its plans for implementing information matching as a matter of urgency. Information matching is a procedure by which one set of information may be compared with another set of information, so that discrepancies may be discovered and the appropriate corrective and enforcement steps taken. Action was aimed particularly at detecting fraud and abuse by beneficiaries under the social welfare system. The Privacy Commissioner Act was enacted in December 1991. It provided for the office and functions of the Privacy Commissioner, and it contained provisions relating to information matching among government agencies.

In the meantime, the Privacy of Information Bill remained before the Select Committee and was given further impetus and importance by planned public health reforms and the 1992 publication of the European Community's proposed Council Directive Concerning the Protection of Individuals in Relation to the Processing of Personal Data, which, if adopted, would have placed restrictions on the flow of personal data out of the European Community to countries that did not have adequate data protection measures in place. The title of the Bill before the Select Committee was subsequently changed from the Privacy of Information Bill to the Privacy Bill on its second reading, and it was enacted as the Privacy Act 1993 on 17 May 1993. It came into force six weeks later on 1 July. The 1993 Act was to last for more than twenty-seven years before being replaced by new privacy law. During that period the Act was substantively amended several times. The three principal amendments to the 1993 Act were the inclusion of new parts in 2010, 2013 and 2017 that collectively added about an extra third to the length of the Act. Some of these changes were made to enable the law to provide an 'adequate level of data protection' to meet European Union standards.

It proved difficult to comprehensively or substantially change the statute in a timely way once the privacy law had been enacted. Accordingly, despite major recommendations for reform from the Privacy Commissioner, from 1998 onwards, and the Law Commission in 2008-2011, it was not until 2018 that a replacement Bill was introduced to Parliament. In November 1998 the Privacy Commissioner submitted a 422-page report *Necessary and Desirable: Privacy Act 1993 Review* to the Minister of Justice recording findings and offering 154 recommendations. The Commissioner's report under s. 26 was duly tabled in Parliament but unfortunately matters stalled at this point. The Law Commission eventually received a reference to review privacy law in October 2006. This resulted in a report in June 2011 *Review of the Privacy Act 1993: Review of the Law of Privacy Stage 4* (R123). As with the Commissioner's review a decade earlier, the Law Commission's review of the Privacy Act was rigorous and transparent. Its principal report was 364 pages long with 126 recommendations (and further recommendations in relation to information sharing and public registers). The Law Commission decided that an entirely new Act, rather than an amendment, was warranted.

A replacement Privacy Bill was introduced to Parliament in March 2018. The bill was referred to the Justice Committee, which reported back a year later in March 2019 and a Second Reading followed in August 2019. On 17 March 2020 the Minister of Justice released a Supplementary Order Paper (SOP 482) indicating the government's intended amendments and a 1 November 2020 commencement date, from which it could be inferred that the bill was expected to be enacted in late-April. However, a week later a State of National Emergency was declared in response to the COVID-19 pandemic and Parliament was adjourned. However, on 3 June it was back to business and the bill completed the Committee of the Whole House stage. Three weeks later the bill completed its third reading and the Royal Assent was received on 30 June 2020. A mere two months further delay had resulted from one of the most severe global disruptions since the Second World War which was a fairly impressive late burst of speed after a sluggish law reform pace over the preceding decades.

The sources of Privacy Act jurisprudence

The Privacy Act has had an active jurisprudence since its first enactment in 1993. The cases deal with 'interferences with the privacy of an individual' through breach of one or more of the IPPs in the Act. Most of the cases can be found online on the NZLII website (New Zealand Legal Information Institute, http://www.nzlii.org/databases.html). At the lowest level, there are Privacy Commissioner case notes (NZPrivCmr), which, although numerous, by no means deal with all of the cases investigated by the Privacy Commissioner. They record the Privacy Commissioner's conclusions on selected investigations that may be of practical or public interest. These cases have no legal force, but are for the benefit of the parties involved and are intended to provide the potential basis for the settlement of complaints. There are also numerous decisions of the Human Rights Review Tribunal

(NZHRRT) and its predecessor, the Complaints Review Tribunal (NZCRT, 1994-2002). These decisions, unlike the Privacy Commissioner's case notes, have legal force, but the Tribunal is not bound by the doctrine of precedent, though Tribunal decisions have persuasive value for subsequent decisions by the Tribunal. Tribunal decisions may be appealed to the High Court (NZHC), the Court of Appeal (NZCA) and the Supreme Court (NZSC). Such appellate decisions create legally binding precedents.

A good deal of the jurisprudence relating to access and correction of personal information had been previously covered under New Zealand's freedom of information legislation (the Official Information Act 1982 and the Local Government Official Information and Meetings Act 1987). The findings of the Ombudsmen on complaints about withholding personal information and refusals to correct were published in the *Compendium of Case Notes of the Ombudsman* (CCNO). These were issued periodically in the early years of the Ombudsmen's jurisdiction, and individual case reports have been subsequently published online on the Ombudsmen's website (https://www.ombudsman.parliament.nz). While the Ombudsmen's views carry great moral weight, aimed as they are at government agencies by an independent officer of Parliament, the views are not, strictly speaking, legally binding, but there is a high expectation of compliance. A small number of cases have gone on to be judicially reviewed in the High Court and, exceptionally, the Court of Appeal.

The Privacy Act 2020 is available online at: https://www.legislation.govt.nz/act/public/2020/0031/latest/LMS23223.html?src=qs.

General Introduction

§1. General Background of the Country

Geography

1. New Zealand/Aotearoa is located between the Tasman Sea and the South Pacific Ocean, approximately 1,600 km south-east of Australia. There are two principal islands, the North Island (Te Ika-a-Maui, 133,729 sq. km) and the South Island Te Waipounamu, 150,437 sq. km). The archipelago also encompasses 700 smaller islands, most of which are uninhabited. The small size of most these islands, together with the lack of close neighbours, has given New Zealand the world's fourth largest exclusive economic zone. New Zealand has a total area of 270,500 sq. km, roughly the same as Great Britain or Japan. The climate is predominantly temperate.

History

2. Given its geographical isolation, New Zealand was not discovered and settled until about 1,000 years ago. The original settlers were the Māori, a Polynesian people who lost contact with the Pacific Islands from where they had come and adapted to the New Zealand environment. The country was subsequently settled by immigrants from Great Britain and other European countries in the nearly nineteenth century. In 1840, it became a colony of Great Britain after the signing of the Treaty of Waitangi. The population of settlers from Britain grew dramatically in the course of the nineteenth century, but the Māori population fell severely as a result of epidemics. In the twentieth century, the Māori population grew substantially, and there was further large-scale immigration, particularly after the Second World War.

3. New Zealand is a socially progressive country. It was the first country in the world to give women the right to vote (in 1893). It established a state-sponsored structure for conciliation and arbitration of labour matters, slightly before Australia (in 1894), and it created a 'welfare state' in the 1930s, as well as a no-fault accident compensation scheme (in 1974).

4. New Zealand is also a human rights compliant country. It has ratified many international human rights treaties. It has an independent Human Rights Commission (since 1977), and has numerous laws implementing human rights, such as equal pay (1972), race relations (1971), equal employment opportunities commissioner, and disability rights commissioner, health and disability commissioner (1994).

Demography

5. In 2021, New Zealand had a population of approximately 5,000,000 people. Of these, Māori made up about 16.5%; Asians, 15.3%; and non- Māori Polynesians (Pasifika), 9%. Just over three-quarters of the population live in the North Island.

Legal System

The New Zealand Constitution

6. New Zealand is a former British colony. It became an independent dominion in 1907, but did not formally sever its constitutional ties with Great Britain until 1947.

7. New Zealand is a unitary state and does not have a written constitution in the conventional sense of an entrenched constitutive document.[5] The country is a constitutional monarchy and parliamentary democracy on the Westminster model, with the Queen of New Zealand as the Head of State.[6]

Judicial system

8. New Zealand has an independent judiciary. The independence of judges is a highly guarded constitutional value. In a system of law operating under the doctrine of Parliamentary supremacy, however, the effect of a judicial decision may always be overridden by an Act of Parliament if the legislature wishes to change the law in light of court decisions relating to the application of the common law or the interpretation of a statute.

9. In addition to the judiciary of general jurisdiction (civil and criminal), there are also a number of specialist courts and tribunals, such as the Environment Court and the Employment Relations Authority and Employment Court.

10. In so far as is relevant to the privacy and data protection regulation context, the judicial institutions of first instance are the Human Rights Review Tribunal for Privacy Act matters, and the District Court for common law and criminal law matters.

11. Cases that are not settled through conciliation by the Privacy Commissioner may be brought to the Human Rights Review Tribunal, which is established under the Human Rights Act 1993.[7] This Tribunal also has jurisdiction over complaints about discrimination under the Human Rights Act, and about the provision of health and disability services under the Health and Disability Commissioner Act 1994.

---

5. Although there is a statute entitled the Constitution Act 1986, it is largely descriptive of existing constitutional arrangements and is not constitutive.
6. The Queen of New Zealand is Elizabeth the Second, also Queen of the United Kingdom of Great Britain and Northern Ireland, and Head of the Commonwealth.
7. Section 93.

12. The District Court, currently established under the District Courts Act 2016,[8] is the first instance court of general jurisdiction.[9] It has a civil jurisdiction over claims up to $350,000. Cases may be transferred to the High Court if the matter involves a claim over $90,000,[10] or if an important question of law or fact is likely to arise,[11] which is not uncommon in privacy-related cases.

13. The High Court has jurisdiction over civil matters where the claim is over $350,000, established under the Senior Courts Act 2016.[12] Appeals from decisions of the Human Rights Review Tribunal and the District Court are heard in the High Court.

14. There is a right to seek leave to appeal to the Court of Appeal, also established under the Senior Courts Act,[13] and thence to the Supreme Court, also established under the Senior Courts Act.[14]

§2. Telecommunications Infrastructure

Brief history of New Zealand telecommunications from 1840 to 1990

15. New Zealand is an island country surrounded by ocean and distant from most other countries and markets. Its three largest islands stretch 1,600 km in a long and narrow archipelago, with a maximum width of 400 km. Much of the country is hilly with up to a third being mountainous. The challenging terrain hampered development of communications following the country's founding under the Treaty of Waitangi in 1840.

16. Traditionally, the indigenous Māori people travelled by foot and canoe (waka) over a network of traditional routes crossing the country. Throughout the nineteenth century coastal shipping continued to be a major means of connecting the main settlements although railways began being constructed from 1863 by provincial governments.[15] The provinces were abolished in 1876 and the national government consolidated and accelerated railway construction with a national network, delayed by war in the North Island, largely complete by 1920.

17. The provincial governments also initiated telegraph construction from 1862 although the national government took charge from 1865 with the first enactment of

8. Section 7.
9. Where the claim is higher, the High Court has first instance jurisdiction.
10. Section 86(1)–(3).
11. Section 87(2)(a).
12. Section 6.
13. Section 45.
14. Section 65. It was first constituted under the Supreme Court Act 2003.
15. The dates given in this account of historical developments are generally taken from, A.C. Wilson, *Telecommunications*, Te Ara: the Encyclopaedia of New Zealand, http://www.TeAra.govt.nz/en/telecommunications (accessed 12 Jun. 2022).

Electric Telegraph Acts. A telegraph cable was laid across the Cook Strait to connect the North and South Islands in 1866 and, partly funded by the New Zealand and New South Wales governments, an international telegraph cable connecting New Zealand to Australia was laid in 1876 which connected New Zealand to a growing global telegraph network.

18. In 1877, news of the development of telephony reached New Zealand and the following year the government began to test the new invention. In New Zealand the state monopolised the development of telephone exchanges and the network from the very beginning with the first telephone exchanges being set up in 1881 in Auckland and Christchurch.

19. A government Telegraph Department was set up in 1864 and later joined the Postal Department to become the Post and Telegraph Department (P & T) in 1881 (known as 'the Post Office' after 1959). Following the Second World War telephone use increased substantially and in the 1970s and 1980s new services, such as fax and pagers, arrived while use of telegrams declined. International submarine cables using improved technology were laid, notably the COMPAC (Commonwealth Pacific) system linking Commonwealth countries (opened in 1962).

20. The 1960s saw the arrival of the first worldwide satellite links. These were in large part American-funded and overseen by the International Telecommunications Satellite (INTELSAT) Organization. New Zealand joined INTELSAT in 1965, the same year satellite calls to the UK began. In 1971, New Zealand's first earth-based satellite station was opened north of Auckland.

21. Mobile phones were first available in the 1980s. Expensive and relatively large, the phones were used by a small minority. With the introduction of smaller, reasonably priced, digital mobile phones in the 1990s, use became commonplace. The price and size of mobile phones continued to drop and use increased. The introduction of the short message service (SMS), or texting, in 1998 prompted an explosion in the rate of use.

22. In 1989, New Zealand's first link to the Internet was established by the University of Waikato to the University of Hawaii. New Zealand's first commercial ISP was also established in 1989.[16] New Zealand's first website was launched in 1992.

23. Under reforms to state-owned enterprises in the 1980s the telecommunications role was, in 1987, split from the Post Office to become a standalone corporation known as Telecom New Zealand run as a business for profit. The telecommunications market opened fully to private competition in 1989 and, in 1990, Telecom was privatised.

16. Internet New Zealand, *History of the Internet in New Zealand*, http://old.internetnz.net.nz/aboutnet/history/ (accessed 12 Jun. 2022).

Infrastructure developments since 1990

24. Since the deregulation of telecommunications, privatisation of Telecom and the enactment of the Privacy Act 1993 the telecommunications landscape transformed entirely. The traditional 'tyranny of distance' was upturned with New Zealand's connection to the world through the Internet. Digital telephony in the 1990s allowed for transformative data services. A few selected infrastructure-related developments from the period since 1990 are noted here.

Domestic and cross-border fibre networks

25. Demand for data, particularly from Internet use, from the 1990s put growing strain on the traditional telephony 'copper network' and the 'pipes' – underwater cables – connecting New Zealand to the world. Fibre optic cable is now used.

26. There are now three international submarine cable connecting New Zealand to the world with a fourth to be commissioned in 2022.[17]

27. The Southern Cross Cable Network (SCCN) made the first international submarine connection in New Zealand and was commissioned in 2000. SCCN forms a protected ring network among nine cable landing stations (two each in Australia, New Zealand, Hawaii and the US mainland, and one in Fiji) and an access point in San Jose, California. SCCN was followed by Tasman Global Access (TGA) which is a 2300 km submarine cable system connecting New Zealand and Australia and commissioned in 2017. The third, commissioned in 2018, was the Hawaiki Cable which spans 15,000 km, linking Australia, New Zealand, American Samoa, Pacific Island, Hawaii, and Oregon, on the US West Coast. The 14,000 km Southern Cross Next cable is expected to connect New Zealand in 2022. This links Australia and the USA with a branch to New Zealand.

28. Additionally, there is domestic submarine cable, the Aqualink cable system.

29. The domestic demand for faster internet broadband outpaced what the existing networks could deliver. Accordingly, in 2009 the New Zealand Government rolled out a nationwide Ultra-fast Broadband (UFB) initiative.[18] This was later joined by an associated Rural Broadband initiative (RBI).

30. These and related initiatives, continued by successive governments, have been very successful in extending fibre access across the country and increasing

17. *See* 'Cable Landing Stations in New Zealand' at https://www.submarinenetworks.com/stations/oceania/new-zealand (accessed 13 Jun. 2022).
18. *See* Murray Milner, *Ultra-Fast Broadband: The New Zealand Experience*, 8(2) J. Telecomm. & Digit. Econ. 31 (Jun. 2020).

broadband uptake and data speeds. Some 30,000 km of fibre optic cable were laid between 2011 and 2022 covering roughly 83% of New Zealand.[19]

31. The policy objectives of UFB included:

- to cover 75% of the population by end of 2019;
- to cover all schools and hospitals and 90% of businesses by the end of 2015;
- to provide services of at least 100 Mbps downstream, upgradable to 1000 Mbps;
- open access network with non-discrimination.

32. All of the above policy objectives were met by the end of 2019.[20]

5G mobile

33. Another piece of important telecommunication infrastructure in New Zealand, is the radio spectrum, defined as electromagnetic energy of frequencies lower than 3000 GHz. It is managed by the Crown, through the Ministry of Business Innovation and Employment (MBIE), on behalf of the public. Frequency bands are planned for various uses depending on the purpose and technology. The government licences and auctions frequency bands for periods of up to twenty years allowing telecommunication services to be provided.

34. In 2019, the government gave the go-ahead for the 3.5 GHz band to be used for 5G networks, with spectrum rights being allocated in 2020 though auction. Due to Covid-19, the auction was cancelled, and a direct allocation process followed. This resulted in the offers of 40 MHz to Dense Air, 60 MHz to Spark, and 60 MHz to 2 degrees, with Vodafone having long-dated existing ownership of a 3.5 GHz spectrum band.[21]

35. The government has allocated part of the 3.5 GHz spectrum for Māori use. This relates to the Crown's obligations under the Treaty of Waitangi.[22]

36. The roll out of 5G has begun in New Zealand. The 5G roll-out sees the government's Mobile Black Spot (MBS) infrastructure on track. The MBS investment

19. New Zealand Infrastructure Commission, *State of Play: Telecommunications*, 2022, 10, at https://www.tewaihanga.govt.nz/assets/Uploads/Telecommunications-State-of-Play-December-2020.pdf (accessed 13 Jun. 2022).
20. See Statement by Hon Kris Faafoi Minister of Broadcasting, Communications and Digital Media, 'NZ a top 10 connected nation with stage one of ultra-fast broadband roll-out completed' 24 Nov. 2019 at https://www.beehive.govt.nz/release/nz-top-10-connected-nation-stage-one-ultra-fast-broadband-roll-out-completed (accessed 13 Jun. 2022).
21. New Zealand Infrastructure Commission, *State of Play: Telecommunications*, 2022, 20, at https://www.tewaihanga.govt.nz/assets/Uploads/Telecommunications-State-of-Play-December-2020.pdf (accessed 13 Jun. 2022).
22. See statement by Hon David Clark, Minister for the Digital Economy and Communications, 'Māori recognised as telecommunication sector leaders' 2 Feb. 2022 at https://www.beehive.govt.nz/release/m%C4%81ori-recognised-telecommunication-sector-leaders (accessed 14 Jun. 2022).

is part of a bigger $270m infrastructure package announced in August 2017 that should be completed by 2022. New cell towers to manage 5G are expected throughout the country as coverage continues.

Network security

37. The Telecommunications (Interception Capability and Security) Act 2013 establishes obligations for New Zealand's telecommunications providers in two main areas affecting infrastructure – interception capability and network security.

38. First, all telecommunications providers must help fulfil interception warrants (or use ongoing statutory authority). In addition, a smaller group of network operators must pre-invest in the necessary equipment and technical resources to carry out interceptions over their networks.

39. Second, the Act sets out a path to identify, and if necessary, address network security risks which may arise from network operators' proposed investments in network equipment. Network operators must engage with the Government Communications Security Bureau (GCSB) about changes to their network equipment where such changes could have an impact on national security.

40. Part 3 of the Act, which relates to network security, establishes a framework under which network operators are required to engage with the GCSB (through the National Cyber Security Centre) about changes and developments with their networks where these intersect with national security. The legislation sets out a path to identify and address, prevent, mitigate, or remove network security risks which may arise. Pursuant to this procedure the GCSB turned down a telecommunications network provider's proposed use of Huawei equipment in a new 5G network because GCSB considered it would raise significant network security risks.

§3. The Information and Communications Technology Market

41. For a substantial period since 1990 New Zealand had one of the most deregulated telecommunications sectors in the world. While substantial private sector competition was stimulated there were problems related to the behaviour of dominant players placing barriers to the entrance of new players and new services. Gradually regulation, usually of a light touch, was reintroduced to promote competition and provide consumer protection.

42. While the state had sold its own telephone company it once again became an investor in telecommunications through its Ultra-Fast Broadband (UFB) programme and Rural Broadband initiative (RBI) (noted above). These had implications for the market requiring, for example, Telecom to restructure itself as two independent companies (Spark and Chorus) to participate in the UFB roll-out. The Crown's Treaty of Waitangi obligations in relation to allocation of radio spectrum (noted above) also encouraged Māori participation in the mobile telecommunications market.

Principal telecommunications industry players

43. New Zealand's telecommunications sector dates to the 1800s, when the government's first telegraph network emerged. The New Zealand Post Office became the lead agency for telecommunications and would remain responsible until the 1980s, at which time Telecom New Zealand was created as a separate government-owned entity. In 1989, the sector was one of the first in the world to be deregulated leading to the privatisation of Telecom. Today, New Zealand's telecommunications sector includes a number of privately owned companies.

44. In 2008, Telecom was split forming the separate companies of Spark and Chorus. Spark became a provider of services (a retail service provider) and retained the mobile network, with Chorus becoming a wholesale provider taking the majority of the existing infrastructure, including Telecom's copper network. Consequently, New Zealand's copper network, which reaches 98% of premises and forms the basis of fixed-line phone, dial-up, and ADSL and VDSL Internet, is owned by Chorus. The network is open for unbundling and open access, meaning other service providers can rent lines and obtain services from Chorus in order to provide their own retail broadband service.

45. The existing mobile networks are wholly owned by Spark, Vodafone, and 2degrees. In addition, there is the Rural Connectivity Group (RCG) which is a joint venture subsidiary of the three mobile network operators.

Market regulation

46. The Commerce Commission seeks to ensure broadband and mobile markets are competitive through regulation of wholesale telecommunications services and our monitoring of how the retail market is performing. Under the Telecommunications Act 2001 the Commerce Commission has two primary functions.[23] The first is to regulate certain fixed-line and mobile services by setting the price and/or access terms for that service. The second is to monitor and report on competition, performance, and developments in telecommunications markets. Both of these functions are focused on promoting competition and transparency in telecommunications markets for the benefit of consumers. In addition, the Commission is also responsible for allocating the exact amount telecommunications providers must pay in government levies each year.

23. Commerce Commission, 'Commission's role in telecommunications' at https://comcom.govt.nz/regulated-industries/telecommunications/commissions-role-in-telecommunications (accessed 13 Jun. 2022).

47. Given the risk of monopolistic behaviour in pockets of the telecommunications sector, the Commerce Commission plays an important regulatory role.[24] The regulatory regime has evolved in recent years to reflect technological changes and has regulatory frameworks dedicated to particular subject areas such as fibre wholesale services or copper line wholesale services.

48. For copper line services, the Commerce Commission enforces a wholesale regulatory framework with service determinations, which includes setting the maximum price Chorus may charge retail service providers (RSPs) and the minimum service quality standards to be met. Pursuant to the Telecommunications Act 2001 wholesale prices are set by the Commerce Commission. For several years, the network has been open for unbundling, which is where retail service providers instal their own equipment in the network and only rent the bare copper lines.

49. In 2018, there were changes in the regulatory environment providing for the deregulation of the copper network from 1 January 2020 in those areas where fibre is available, and the right for Chorus to withdraw copper services subject to a number of consumer protections being in place.

50. For fibre connectivity, a wholesale regulatory framework has been introduced that will replace the price controls through contracts that Local Fibre Companies and Chorus have with the Crown through CIP.

51. Chorus is subject to price/quality regulation which sets out the maximum allowable revenue they can earn. However, within that revenue cap there are no regulatory controls on Chorus' price discrimination ensuring consumers are protected from monopoly powers. The other Local Fibre Companies are subject to information disclosure.

52. Targeted regulation across mobile infrastructure has enabled competition to develop and facilitate the entry of the third mobile network operator (2Degrees) into the market. The Commerce Commission monitors performance, development, and competition in the telecommunications market and conducts inquiries/reviews where appropriate.

53. Regulation specifically governs the auctioning of spectrum bands under the Radiocommunications Act 1989, overseen by MBIE. Under the Act, property rights were established for spectrum bands. Following a review in 2005, there is a defined spectrum auction design that ensures a competitive allocation.

24. New Zealand Infrastructure Commission, *State of Play: Telecommunications*, 2022, 20–22, at https://www.tewaihanga.govt.nz/assets/Uploads/Telecommunications-State-of-Play-December-2020.pdf (accessed 13 Jun. 2022).

§4. E-GOVERNMENT

54. The New Zealand Government maintains an active digital government programme to meet people's needs using emerging technologies, data, and changes to government culture, practices, and processes. In 2020, a position of Minister for the Digital Economy and Communications was created.

55. The digital government programme is mainly driven through the Government Chief Digital Officer (GCDO) within the Department of Internal Affairs. The GCDO is responsible for:

- setting digital policy and standards;
- improving investments;
- establishing and managing services;
- developing capability;
- system assurance (assuring digital government outcomes).[25]

56. The New Zealand Government works with other governments to promote best-practice development of digital technologies. It has signed international charters related to transparency and accountability. For instance, it is part of the Open Government Partnership, an international initiative where signatory countries work to be more open, accountable, and responsive to citizens. Using new technologies is a part of this. It has also adopted the International Open Data Charter which reinforces New Zealand's commitment to open data and promoting accelerating the release of open government data. The New Zealand Government participates in Digital Nations, or DN, which is a network of the world's most advanced digital nations with a shared goal of harnessing digital technology and new ways of working to improve citizens' lives. It is also active in the OECD's E-Leaders working group.

57. Functional leads are charged with developing and improving a designated area across government. The roles are delegated to specific chief executives by the Public Service Commissioner.

- Government Chief Digital Officer.
- Government Chief Data Steward.
- Government Chief Information Security Officer.
- Government Chief Privacy Officer.

58. Of particular interest is the position of Government Chief Privacy Officer established in late-2013 following a series of high-profile privacy breaches in the state sector. Two of the significant cross-government accomplishments of the GCPO have been:

25. *See* https://www.digital.govt.nz/digital-government/leadership/government-functional-leads/government-chief-digital-officer-gcdo/ (accessed 14 Jun. 2022).

(1) the Privacy Maturity Assessment Framework; and
(2) guidance on privacy management, privacy risk assessment, and privacy incident response planning.

Part I. Privacy Protection in New Zealand

Chapter 1. Privacy Protection in the Constitution

§1. The New Zealand Constitution

59. New Zealand is a former British colony. It became an independent Dominion in 1907, but did not formally sever its constitutional ties with Great Britain until 1947.

60. New Zealand is a unitary state and like Great Britain, it does not have a written constitution in the conventional sense of an entrenched constitutive document. Although New Zealand has a statute entitled the Constitution Act 1986, it is largely descriptive of existing constitutional arrangements. The country is a constitutional monarchy and parliamentary democracy on the Westminster model, with the Queen of New Zealand as the Head of State. The Queen of New Zealand is Elizabeth the Second, also Queen of the United Kingdom of Great Britain and Northern Ireland, and Head of the Commonwealth. New Zealand operates on the principle of Parliamentary sovereignty.

§2. Statutes Having 'Constitutional Status' That Are Relevant to Data Protection

I. Introduction

61. While New Zealand does not have a written constitution, there are a number of statutes that are of particular constitutional importance and are regarded by convention as 'higher law'. This is in the sense that they form part of the constitutional background or landscape by informing government practice and the enactment of other legislation. Moreover, cross-political consensus would be expected in the event of amendment or repeal of this legislation. Several of these statutes are relevant to data protection.

62. The constitutional importance of this legislation is reflected by the convention that it must be taken into account when developing or proposing new legislation. The *Cabinet Manual*, which provides guidance to the core executive branch of government, states that when ministers are developing and seeking approval of bills, they must ensure that they comply with particular legal principles or obligations.[26] In particular, ministers must draw attention to any aspects of proposed legislation that may have implications for or affect the rights and freedoms contained in the New Zealand Bill of Rights Act 1990; the Human Rights Act 1993 (HR Act); the principles in the Privacy Act 2020; and the guidance contained in the *Legislation Guidelines*.[27]

63. Thus, when a bill is submitted to the Cabinet Legislation Committee for approval for introduction to Parliament, ministers are required to confirm that the draft bill complies with these laws.[28] If proposed government legislation does not conform to the above standards, then the government will be expected to justify any departures when the bill is debated in Parliament or considered by a Parliamentary select committee. Given the doctrine of Parliamentary supremacy, once a bill becomes law, it may not be challenged on legal grounds, but at least there will have been some transparency in the process, with the government having made a deliberate decision to depart from conventional standards that may have to be publicly justified.

64. New Zealand statutes that are regarded as being of constitutional significance and have some relevance to privacy are described below.

II. New Zealand Bill of Rights Act 1990

65. A report containing a draft Bill of Rights was tabled in the House of Representatives in 1985 by the then Minister of Justice.[29] This *White Paper* deliberately omitted to provide for a general right to privacy, but did recognise that the right of individuals to be secure against unreasonable search or seizure gave rise to fundamental privacy interests. The *White Paper* stated:

> There is not in New Zealand any general right to privacy, although specific rules of law and legislation protect some aspects of privacy. It would be inappropriate therefore to attempt to entrench a right that is not by any means fully recognized now, which is in the course of development, and whose boundaries would be uncertain and contentious.[30]

66. In the event, the New Zealand Bill of Rights Act 1990 provides that for the 'right to be secure against unreasonable search or seizure, whether of the person,

---

26. *Cabinet Manual* (2017), at para. 7.65, available at https://dpmc.govt.nz/our-business-units/cabinet-office/supporting-work-cabinet/cabinet-manual.
27. These *Guidelines*, adopted by Cabinet (2018 edition) and available at http://www.ldac.org.nz/guidelines/legislation-guidelines-2018-edition/, have been compiled by the Legislation Design and Advisory Committee, an independent committee established by the Minister of Justice. Chapter 8 of these guidelines is entitled 'Privacy and dealing with information about people'.
28. *Cabinet Manual*, at para. 7.61.
29. *A Bill of Rights for New Zealand: A White Paper* (AJHR A.6A, 1985).
30. *Ibid.*, at para. 10.144.

property, or correspondence or otherwise',[31] but the legislation is not entrenched. Like other New Zealand legislation of constitutional significance, it is able to be repealed by a simple majority in Parliament. Nevertheless, this provision on unreasonable search or seizure has been interpreted by the New Zealand courts as protecting fundamental aspects of the important civil and political right to privacy.[32]

67. However, since the above observations were made in the *White Paper*, the position relating to the legal recognition of a right to privacy in New Zealand has changed significantly, with the right more fully recognised by Parliament consequent to the enactment of a Privacy Act in 1993, the predecessor of the current 2000 legislation, as well as recognition by the CA of a privacy tort at common law.

68. The *Cabinet Manual* requires the Minister of Justice to examine all legislation for compliance with the New Zealand Bill of Rights Act and advise the Attorney-General accordingly,[33] and the New Zealand Bill of Rights Act, in turn, requires the Attorney-General to report to Parliament whenever a bill being introduced appears to be inconsistent with any of the rights in the New Zealand Bill of Rights Act.[34] The New Zealand Bill of Rights Act also recapitulates the protections against discrimination contained in the HR Act (below),[35] which is relevant to the processing of 'sensitive' data, and it affirms the right of individuals to natural justice in respect of decisions that affect them,[36] which is relevant to the regulation of automated decision-making.

III. Human Rights Act 1993

69. The HR Act sets out the various grounds for prohibited discrimination.[37] These are extensive by international standards. As noted above, the various grounds are recapitulated in the New Zealand Bill of Rights Act. The significance of the Human Rights Act in the data protection context is that data may not be used in a manner or for a purpose that amounts to discrimination under the Act. This legislation is relevant to regulating the processing of 'sensitive' categories of data.

IV. Privacy Act 2020

70. The Privacy Act 2020 is New Zealand's primary data protection statute. It amends and re-enacts the earlier Privacy Act 1993. The Legislation Design and

---

31. New Zealand Bill of Rights Act 1990, s. 21.
32. *See*, for example, *R v. Jefferies* [1994] 1 NZLR 292, at 319 (Court of Appeal); *R v. Grayson & Taylor* [1997] 1 NZLR 402, at 407 (Court of Appeal).
33. *Cabinet Manual* (2017), at para. 7.62.
34. New Zealand Bill of Rights Act 1990, s. 7.
35. *Ibid.*, s. 19.
36. *Ibid.*, s. 27.
37. Human Rights Act 1993, s. 21(1).

Advisory Committee's *Guidelines*[38] and the *Cabinet Manual*[39] both advise the government and policy advisers to ensure that new legislation affecting personal information is consistent with the principles and guidelines in the Privacy Act.

V. Freedom of Information Legislation

71. New Zealand has two freedom of information statutes that are regarded as being of some constitutional significance because of the importance placed on the accountability and transparency of public sector decision-making.[40] The Official Information Act 1982 covers information held by the central government and other public sector agencies, and the LGOIM Act covers the local government sector.

72. The Ombudsmen, who oversees the operation of this legislation, have described the Official Information Act as a statute of constitutional importance,[41] and the New Zealand Court of Appeal (NZCA) has observed that 'the permeating importance of the Act is such that it is entitled to be ranked as a constitutional measure'.[42]

73. This legislation is relevant to several aspects of privacy: the protection of privacy when government information is proposed to be disclosed;[43] rights of access to and correction of personal information about individuals (until this function was taken over by the Privacy Act in 1993);[44] and the right to reasons for government decisions that affect individuals.[45] There is an important interplay between the Privacy Act and New Zealand's freedom of information legislation.[46]

---

38. *Legislation Advisory Committee: Guidelines on Process & Content of Legislation*, Ch. 15: Privacy and the fair handling of personal information, available at http://justice.govt.nz/lac/pubs/2001/legislative_guide_2000/chapter_15.html#18
39. *Cabinet Manual*, at para. 7.65.
40. Official Information Act 1982 and the Local Government Official Information and Meetings Act 1987.
41. For the quasi-constitutional status of the Official Information Act, *see* Ombudsmen's own-motion investigation of Department of Corrections in relation to the detention and treatment of prisoners, 2005, http://ombudsmen.govt.nz/cms/imagelibrary/100169.doc
42. *Commissioner of Police v. Ombudsman* 1 NZLR [1988] 385, at 391.
43. The long title to each of the freedom of information statutes provides that one of its purposes is 'the preservation of personal privacy'. *See also* s. 4(c) of the Official Information Act, s. 4(c) of the and the Local Government Official Information and Meetings Act. The Official Information Act, s. 9(2)(a) (= s. 7(2)(a) of the Local Government Official Information and Meetings Act) provides that official information may be withheld if it is necessary to 'Protect the privacy of natural persons, including that of deceased natural persons', and there is no countervailing interest in disclosure.
44. Rights to access to and correction of personal information in the freedom of information legislation is now limited to legal, as opposed to natural, persons.
45. Official Information Act 1982, s. 23; Local Government Official Information and Meetings Act 1987, s. 22.
46. *See* below, at Part IX, Ch. 2.

§3. Fundamental Constitutional Principles and Values

74. In addition to legislation enacted by the New Zealand Parliament, there are a number of fundamental principles and values rooted in equity and the common law and that underlie the legal system. The Legislation Advisory and Design Committee, an independent committee established by the Minister of Justice that produces guidance on the development and scrutiny of proposed legislation, has commented that 'these values and principles can be expressed at differing levels of abstraction', but fundamentally they concern human dignity and liberty.[47] Equity has long protected confidential information and relationships, and the common law has recently developed to give greater protection to privacy interests.[48]

47. *Legislation Design and Advisory Committee: Legislation Guidelines (2018 edition)*, Ch. 4.3, The principle of legality – the dignity of the individual and the presumption in favour of liberty, available at http://www.ldac.org.nz/guidelines/legislation-guidelines-2018-edition/constitutional-issues-and-recognising-rights/chapter-4/
48. *See* below, Part I, Ch. 4.5.1.

Chapter 2. National Application of Regional and International Convention

§1. GENERAL

75. New Zealand is a member of the United Nations and its specialised agencies, such as the International Labour Organisation. It is also a member of the Organisation of Economic Cooperation and Development (OECD) and, at the regional level, Asia Pacific Economic Cooperation (APEC).

76. The OECD Privacy Guidelines of 1980 were the principal influence in shaping New Zealand's 1993 privacy law and the influence continue through the 2020 law. Another significant factor has been the European Union data protection instruments. The APEC Privacy Guidelines have had only a minor effect on the 2020 law.

§2. UNITED NATIONS INTERNATIONAL COVENANT ON CIVIL AND POLITICAL RIGHTS

77. Although the International Covenant on Civil and Political Rights is not particularly explicit on data protection, New Zealand's commitment to respecting human rights represented by the ICCPR does underpin its human rights statutes. Although not acknowledged explicitly in the 1993 Act, the 2020 Act provided in section 3 that the purpose of this Act is to promote and protect individual privacy by, among other things:

> giving effect to internationally recognised privacy obligations and standards in relation to the privacy of personal information, including the OECD Guidelines and the International Covenant on Civil and Political Rights.

§3. OECD PRIVACY GUIDELINES OF 1980 AND 2013

78. The influence of the OECD's Privacy Guidelines of 1980 on New Zealand's privacy law is obvious from the outset where the long title of the Privacy Act 1993 begins:

> An Act to promote and protect individual privacy in general accordance with the Recommendation of the Council of the Organisation for Economic Co-operation and Development Concerning Guidelines Governing the Protection of Privacy and Transborder Flows of Personal Data ...

79. The 1993 Act's 12 IPPs gave effect to the OECD's basic principles of national application. Features that distinguished the OECD approach from the existing Council of Europe and developing EU approaches were mirrored in New Zealand's 1993 Act, such as the omission of 'special categories' of information or data export controls.

80. The OECD updated its 1980 Guidelines in 2013 and encouraged forms of data export controls and breach notification and these changes were reflected in the 2020 Act. However, these new features in the 2020 Act cannot necessarily be attributed solely or principally to OECD influence since they were also features of influential EU data protection instruments of 1995 and 2016.

§4. APEC Privacy Framework 2005 and 2015

81. In addition to the OECD, New Zealand is also a member of APEC which has also been active in privacy policy development. Compared to other international groupings, APEC became active in privacy reasonably late. Its Privacy Framework of 2005 came too late to have any influence on the 1993 Act. The Framework was updated in 2015.

82. APEC's efforts since the adoption of the 2005 framework have largely been devoted to developing cross-border privacy rules that could operate across APEC's heterogeneous set of economies and regulatory regimes. After many years of development, the APEC Cross-Border Privacy Rules system (CBPRs) was endorsed by APEC Leaders in 2011. Several years later, the complementary APEC Privacy Recognition for Processors (PRP) system was added. A network of regulators, the Cross-border Privacy Enforcement Arrangement (CPEA), was established to support these systems and privacy enforcement generally. New Zealand has not yet joined the CBPRs or PRP, although the Privacy Commissioner has joined the CPEA.

83. The APEC CBPRs is an accountability-based system that facilitates privacy-respecting data flows among APEC economies. Participating companies are required to adhere to the standards established by the APEC CBPR system and to domestic laws in the economies in which they operate. All APEC CBPR system certified companies have their privacy policies and practices evaluated by an approved independent third-party verifier (known as an 'Accountability Agent'). Accountability agents monitor and enforce companies' compliance with the APEC CBPR programme requirements. In appropriate cases, they are also required to report non-compliance to Privacy Enforcement Authorities.

84. The APEC Privacy Framework has been implicitly recognised in one aspect of the 2020 Act. IPP 12 anticipates 'prescribed binding schemes' under which an internationally recognised scheme for protecting personal information might be formally recognised for the purposes of cross-border transfers. The APEC CBPRs and PRP appear to be the only internationally recognised schemes for protecting personal information open for New Zealand to join.

85. IPP 12 sets out the requirements for agencies for disclosure of personal information outside New Zealand. The principle allows an agency to disclose personal information to a foreign person or entity only for certain enumerated exceptions. Exception (d) allows an agency to disclose if it believes on reasonable grounds that the recipient is a participant in a 'prescribed binding scheme'. Section 7 defines 'binding scheme' as:

> *binding scheme* means an internationally recognised scheme in which the participants agree to be bound by –
>
> (a) specified measures for protecting personal information that is collected, held, used, and disclosed; and
> (b) mechanisms for enforcing compliance with those measures

86. 'Prescribed binding scheme' is defined in IPP 12(3) to mean a binding scheme specified in regulations made under section 213. Regulations may only be recommended where the minister is satisfied that the binding schemes require a foreign person or entity to protect personal information in a way that, overall, provides comparable safeguards to those in the Privacy Act.

§5. Comprehensive and Progressive Agreement for Trans-Pacific Partnership

87. The Comprehensive and Progressive Agreement for Trans-Pacific Partnership (CPTPP) is a free trade agreement involving eleven countries in the Asia-Pacific region, including New Zealand, Australia, Brunei Darussalam, Canada, Chile, Japan, Malaysia, Mexico, Peru, Singapore, and Vietnam. It was signed and came into effect in 2018.

88. The Electronic Commerce chapter includes obligations on personal information protection in Article 14.8:

Article 14.8: Personal Information Protection

1. The Parties recognise the economic and social benefits of protecting the personal information of users of electronic commerce and the contribution that this makes to enhancing consumer confidence in electronic commerce.
2. To this end, each Party shall adopt or maintain a legal framework that provides for the protection of the personal information of the users of electronic commerce. In the development of its legal framework for the protection of personal information, each Party should take into account principles and guidelines of relevant international bodies.
3. Each Party shall endeavour to adopt non-discriminatory practices in protecting users of electronic commerce from personal information protection violations occurring within its jurisdiction.
4. Each Party should publish information on the personal information protections it provides to users of electronic commerce, including how:

(a) individuals can pursue remedies; and
(b) business can comply with any legal requirements.

5. Recognising that the Parties may take different legal approaches to protecting personal information, each Party should encourage the development of mechanisms to promote compatibility between these different regimes. These mechanisms may include the recognition of regulatory outcomes, whether accorded autonomously or by mutual arrangement, or broader international frameworks. To this end, the Parties shall endeavour to exchange information on any such mechanisms applied in their jurisdictions and explore ways to extend these or other suitable arrangements to promote compatibility between them.

89. Article 14.11 addresses cross-border transfers and provides:

Article 14.11: Cross-Border Transfer of Information by Electronic Means

1. The Parties recognise that each Party may have its own regulatory requirements concerning the transfer of information by electronic means.
2. Each Party shall allow the cross-border transfer of information by electronic means, including personal information, when this activity is for the conduct of the business of a covered person.
3. Nothing in this Article shall prevent a Party from adopting or maintaining measures inconsistent with paragraph 2 to achieve a legitimate public policy objective, provided that the measure:
   (a) is not applied in a manner which would constitute a means of arbitrary or unjustifiable discrimination or a disguised restriction on trade; and
   (b) does not impose restrictions on transfers of information greater than are required to achieve the objective.

90. The CPTPP has not had a direct effect upon the 1993 or 2020 Privacy Acts, as the New Zealand Government considered that both enactments fully complied with the CPTPP requirements.

§6. Regional Comprehensive Economic Partnership

91. The Regional Comprehensive Economic Partnership (RCEP) is a free trade agreement that was ratified by New Zealand in November 2021 and came into force on 1 Jan. 2022. Fifteen countries signed RCEP in 2020. These countries include the ten members of the Association of Southeast Asian Nations (ASEAN) plus five regional countries with which ASEAN has free trade agreements (including New Zealand).

92. Chapter 12 on electronic commerce is in quite similar terms to CPTPP. Article 12.8 provides:

Article 12.8: Online Personal Information Protection

1. Each Party shall adopt or maintain a legal framework which ensures the protection of personal information of the users of electronic commerce.
2. In the development of its legal framework for the protection of personal information, each Party shall take into account international standards, principles, guidelines, and criteria of relevant international organisations or bodies.
3. Each Party shall publish information on the personal information protection it provides to users of electronic commerce, including how:
   (a) individuals can pursue remedies; and
   (b) business can comply with any legal requirements.
4. The Parties shall encourage juridical persons to publish, including on the internet, their policies and procedures related to the protection of personal information.
5. The Parties shall cooperate, to the extent possible, for the protection of personal information transferred from a Party.

93. Article 12.15 addresses cross-border transfers and provides:

Article 12.15: Cross-border Transfer of Information by Electronic Means

1. The Parties recognise that each Party may have its own regulatory requirements concerning the transfer of information by electronic means.
2. A Party shall not prevent cross-border transfer of information by electronic means where such activity is for the conduct of the business of a covered person.
3. Nothing in this Article shall prevent a Party from adopting or maintaining:
   (a) any measure inconsistent with paragraph 2 that it considers necessary to achieve a legitimate public policy objective, provided that the measure is not applied in a manner which would constitute a means of arbitrary or unjustifiable discrimination or a disguised restriction on trade; or
   (b) any measure that it considers necessary for the protection of its essential security interests. Such measures shall not be disputed by other Parties.

94. As can be seen, the exception in Article 12.15.3 is wider than the equivalent exception in CPRTPP (Article 14.11.3) as it expressly includes exceptions for 'any measure that it considers necessary for the protection of its essential security interests' in addition to measures a party 'considers necessary to achieve a legitimate public policy objective'.

§7. European Union Data Protection Directive 1995 and General Data Protection Regulation 2016

95. New Zealand is not, of course, a European Union Member State. However, the EU data protection instruments have had some influence on the shape of New

Zealand's privacy laws. New Zealand has paid some heed to the EU instruments in reforming its own privacy laws for three principal reasons:

(1) New Zealand wished to facilitate the transfer of data from Europe for processing by New Zealand businesses (by having the Privacy Act recognised as providing an 'adequate level' of data protection for EU purposes).
(2) The GDPR has extraterritorial reach that may impact New Zealand agencies that, for example, offer goods to consumers in the EU and thus some alignment of standards may assist the compliance costs for these exporters.
(3) The EU data protection standards have come to be seen as best global practice and New Zealanders have aspired to have higher standards embedded in New Zealand law.

However, New Zealand has not simply cloned the GDPR into its law. It has largely maintained the OECD roots of its law and continued a light-handed regulatory approach. The 2020 Act lacks a number of the features of the EU's GDPR.

The influence of the EU data protection instruments can be seen in several respects:

- The 1993 Act was amended by the Privacy (Cross-border Information) Amendment Act 2010 in several ways to meet EU concerns and to enable the European Commission to find that New Zealand's law was 'adequate' for cross-border transfers: in particular the Act was amended to remove a requirement that foreigners be in the country to exercise subject access rights and to introduce a transfer prohibition notice regime. The European Commission issued its decision recognising New Zealand's privacy law as adequate on 19 December 2012.
- The 2020 Act included new provisions such as mandatory breach notification, cross-border disclosure prohibition, and stronger enforcement powers. These changes cannot be entirely attributed to EU influence but it was undoubtedly a consideration for lawmakers.
- The EU GDPR is expressly referenced in section 193 of the Act as a mandatory consideration for the Privacy Commissioner in issuing a Transfer Prohibition Notice.

Chapter 3. Privacy in Electronic Communications

§1. General

96. The IPPs in the Privacy Act 2020 apply to privacy in electronic communications as in other contexts. The IPPs are modified somewhat by a code of practice that applies to certain telecommunications agencies. Additionally, there are several enactments that have some impact upon privacy in relation to electronic communications.

§2. Privacy Act 2020 and Telecommunications Information Privacy Code 2020

97. The IPPs in the Privacy Act 2020 apply to privacy in electronic communications but are not tailored explicitly to the electronic environment. There are, for example, no express statutory obligations in relation to website 'cookies'.

98. Section 32 of the Privacy Act provides for the Privacy Commissioner to issue codes of practice. A code of practice may modify the application of the IPPs by prescribing standards that may vary from those provided by the IPPs or by exempting particular actions from the IPPs. A code may also prescribe how the IPPs are to be applied or complied with.

99. A code of practice may apply to: any specified information or class of information; any agency or class of agency; any activity or class of activity; or any industry, profession or calling or class of industry, profession or calling. It may also regulate information matching in the private sector, set guidelines in respect of charges and make provision for various administrative and mechanical aspects of that code of practice. A code of practice may not limit or restrict the circumstances in which individuals are entitled to exercise their subject access and correction entitlements under IPPs 6 and 7.

100. While the IPPs in the Act regulates most agencies in their handling of personal information in relation to electronic communications, there is a code addressed to agencies in the telecommunications industry. The Telecommunications Information Privacy Code 2020 (TIPC) replaced the Telecommunications Information Privacy Code 2003. The 2003 code had initially been introduced to address compliance difficulties that the industry anticipated having with the 1993 Act and to facilitate privacy protections with the introduction of new data services.

101. The TIPC is particularly focused upon telecommunications network operators and service providers but also has wider application to, for example, directory publishers, ISPs and mobile telephone retailers. Clause 5(2) of the TIPC specifies the class of agencies to which the code applies:

> This code applies to the following classes of agency –
>
> (a) a network operator; or
> (b) a telecommunications service obligation provider or TSO provider; or
> (c) a directory publisher; or
> (d) a directory enquiry agency; or
> (e) an Internet service provider; or
> (f) a call centre which provides call centre services on contract to another agency; or
> (g) a mobile telephone retailer; or
> (h) additionally, for the purposes of Schedule 4 –
> (i) the relevant government agency; or
> (ii) an emergency service provider.

102. The code's rules relax a number of the IPPs to facilitate certain telecommunications industry practices and network requirements, for instance, around the interconnection of networks. It also creates some telecommunications-specific protections, such as requiring directory publishers to include entries only with subscriber authorisation, and to prohibit direct marketing using traffic information obtained as a result of interconnection. Several schedules prescribe how the code must be complied with, including one on caller line information presentation and another on emergency location information.

§3. Other Relevant Enactments

103. There are several other enactments that are relevant to privacy in electronic communications because they constrain non-compliant business practices (e.g., Unsolicited Electronic Messages Act 2007), create consumer remedies for harmful online behaviour (e.g., Harmful Digital Communications Act 2015) or authorise and regulate intrusive state practices (e.g., Search and Surveillance Act 2012).

§4. Unsolicited Electronic Messages Act 2007

104. The Unsolicited Electronic Messages Act 2007 (UEM Act) prohibits the sending of unsolicited commercial electronic messages with an NZ link. It also requires all commercial electronic messages to include information about who authorised the message and to provide a functional unsubscribe facility. Finally, it prohibits address harvesting for the purpose of unsolicited commercial messages.

105. The UEM Act is based on the Australian Spam Act 2003. However, it is simpler than the Australian Act in that it uses general descriptions and definitions and less specific exceptions.

106. The purposes of the UEM Act are set out in section 3 and are, in summary, to:

- prohibit unsolicited commercial electronic messages with a New Zealand link (i.e., messages sent to, from or within New Zealand);
- require commercial electronic messages to include accurate information about the person who authorised the sending of the message and a functional unsubscribe facility to enable the recipient to instruct the sender that no further messages are to be sent to the recipient;
- prohibit address-harvesting software being used to create address lists for sending unsolicited commercial electronic messages;
- deter people from using information and communication technologies inappropriately.

107. Section 4(2) of the UEM Act, provides that an electronic message has a 'New Zealand link' if one or more of the following applies:

(a) the message originates in New Zealand:
(b) the person who sent the message is –
   (i) an individual who is physically present in New Zealand when the message is sent; or
   (ii) an organisation whose central management and control is in New Zealand when the message is sent:
(c) the computer, server, or device that is used to access the message is located in New Zealand:
(d) the recipient is –
   (i) an individual who is physically present in New Zealand when the message is accessed; or
   (ii) an organisation that carries on business or activities in New Zealand when the message is accessed:
(e) if the message cannot be delivered because the relevant electronic address does not exist, assuming that the electronic address existed, it is reasonably likely that the message would have been accessed using a computer, server, or device located in New Zealand:
(f) it is sent to an electronic address that –
   (i) ends with ".nz"; or
   (ii) begins with an international access code directly followed by "64".

108. For the purposes of the UEM Act, an 'electronic message' is a message sent using a telecommunications service to an electronic address. Voice calls, including those using VOIP, are excluded.

109. A message is commercial under section 6(a) if it:

– Markets or promotes good, services, land, interests in land, or business or investment opportunities.
– Assists/enables a person to obtain a financial advantage or gain from another.
– Provides a link/directs a recipient to a message that does either of the above.

110. However, there is an extensive list of exclusions to that general definition in section 6(b).

111. 'Unsolicited commercial electronic message' means a commercial electronic message that the recipient has not consented to receive, although consent may be expressed or inferred and, in certain circumstances, is deemed to have been given.

112. Where a recipient has consented (including inferred or deemed consent) to receiving commercial electronic messages from a sender, the messages must:

– clearly and accurately identifies the person who authorised the sending of the message (section 10); and
– contain a functional unsubscribe facility (section 11).

113. A person must not send, or cause to be sent, an unsolicited commercial electronic message that has a New Zealand link (section 9).

114. A person who sends an unsolicited commercial electronic message or who fails to include accurate sender information of a functional unsubscribe facility. Persons who aid in those actions may also be liable.

115. The UEM Act prohibits the use of 'address-harvesting software' in connection with sending unsolicited commercial electronic messages with a New Zealand link (section 13(1)). 'Address-harvesting software' is defined in section 4 to mean' software that is capable of, or marketed for use for, (a) searching the Internet for electronic addresses; and (b) collecting, compiling, capturing, or otherwise harvesting those electronic addresses'.

116. A breach of the UEM Act is termed a 'civil enforcement event' in section 18 and includes a breach of one or more of the following:

(a) section 9(1) (unsolicited commercial electronic messages must not be sent);
(b) section 10 (commercial electronic messages must include accurate sender information);
(c) section 11(1) (commercial electronic messages must contain functional unsubscribe facility);
(d) section 13(1) (restriction on use of address-harvesting software and harvested-address lists);
(e) section 15 (third-party breaches of the Act).

117. Enforcement of the UEM Act involves a hybrid approach whereby persons affected by an event can take civil action or else the enforcement department may do so. Pecuniary penalties of up to NZD 500,000 are possible. The enforcement department is the Anti-Spam Compliance Unit within the Department of Internal Affairs.

§5. HARMFUL DIGITAL COMMUNICATIONS ACT 2015

118. The Harmful Digital Communications Act 2015 (HDCA) addresses cyberbullying and online harassment. The purpose of the HDCA is stated in section 3 to be to:

(a) deter, prevent, and mitigate harm caused to individuals by digital communications; and
(b) provide victims of harmful digital communications with a quick and efficient means of redress.

119. Section 6 of the HDCA sets out ten communication principles which are:

(1) Principle 1: A digital communication should not disclose sensitive personal facts about an individual.
(2) Principle 2: A digital communication should not be threatening, intimidating, or menacing.
(3) Principle 3: A digital communication should not be grossly offensive to a reasonable person in the position of the affected individual.
(4) Principle 4: A digital communication should not be indecent or obscene.
(5) Principle 5: A digital communication should not be used to harass an individual.
(6) Principle 6: A digital communication should not make a false allegation.
(7) Principle 7: A digital communication should not contain a matter that is published in breach of confidence.
(8) Principle 8: A digital communication should not incite or encourage anyone to send a message to an individual for the purpose of causing harm to the individual.
(9) Principle 9: A digital communication should not incite or encourage an individual to commit suicide.
(10) Principle 10: A digital communication should not denigrate an individual by reason of his or her colour, race, ethnic or national origins, religion, gender, sexual orientation, or disability.

120. The HDCA creates alternative dispute resolution processes through an 'Approved Agency' regarding harm caused to individuals by digital communications. Netsafe Incorporated has been designated as the Approved Agency. In performing functions or exercising powers under this Act, the Approved Agency and courts must take account of the communication principles.

121. Among other matters, the functions of the Approved Agency include receiving and assessing complaints about the harm caused to individuals by digital communications, investigating complaints, and using advice, negotiation, mediation, and persuasion (as appropriate) to resolve complaints.

122. The District Court (DC) will deal with cases of harmful digital communications that the Approved Agency has not been able to resolve. On an application, the court will determine whether the person harassing someone has seriously breached, will seriously breach or has repeatedly breached one or more of the ten communication principles. Applications can be made by the affected individual, their parent or guardian, school leaders, the police or the chief coroner (section 11).

123. The court has the power to order (section 19):

- material to be taken down;
- cease and desist orders;
- someone to publish a correction, an apology or give you a right of reply;
- the release the identity of the person behind an anonymous communication;
- name suppression.

124. Anyone who ignores the DC's orders can be prosecuted and penalised. The penalty is up to six months in prison or a fine up to NZD5,000 for an individual and up to NZD20, 000 for a company. (section. 21).

125. A person commits an offence if they cause harm by posting digital communication (section 22). This might involve posting any information, whether truthful or untruthful, about the victim, and includes the positing of an intimate visual recording (i.e., non-consensual covert recording of a naked person of someone engaged in sexual activity).

126. The HDCA deals explicitly with the issue of liability of online content hosts for content posted by a user. 'Online content host' in relation to digital communication is defined to mean 'the person who has control over the part of the electronic retrieval system, such as a website or an online application, on which the communication is posted and is accessible by the user' (section 4).

127. Section 24 provides protection for an online content host in respect of any specific content of a digital communication posted by a person and hosted by the online content host if the host follows the process in that section. The section creates a detailed 'notice and takedown' process.

§6. Selected Law Enforcement, Intelligence and Security Enactments Affecting Electronic Communications

128. Various statutes authorise and regulate various investigative and surveillance practices of law enforcement and intelligence and security agencies affecting electronic communications. Principal among these enactments are the:

– Telecommunications (Residual Provisions) Act 1987.
– Search and Surveillance Act 2012.
– Telecommunications (Interception Capability and Security) Act 2013.
– Intelligence and Security Act 2017.

§7. Telecommunications (Residual Provisions) Act 1987

129. The Telecommunications Act 1987 has largely been replaced by other statutes but one residual part of the enactment remaining in force governs the issue, effect and operation of the 'call data warrants'.

130. A call data warrant is used in the investigation of offences to obtain information about a suspect's telecommunications in real time or through access to records. On the application by the NZ Police or Customs Service, a judge may issue a call data warrant if satisfied that there is reasonable ground for believing that an offence punishable by imprisonment has been, or is being, or is likely to be committed and that evidence relevant to the investigation of the offence will be obtained by the use of a 'telephone analyser' or from call associated data provided by a network operator: Telecommunications (Residual Provisions) Act 1987 (TRP Act), section 10B. The form of the warrant is set out in the Telecommunications (Call Data Warrant) Regulations 1997.

131. A 'telephone analyser' is any device that can be connected to any part of a network, or to any line, apparatus, or equipment connected to any part of a network and that is designed to record or enable the recording of call associated data, but cannot record or monitor, or enable the recording or monitoring of, the content of any telecommunication (TRP Act, section 2).

132. 'Call associated data' is defined in section 2:

call associated data, in relation to a telecommunication –

(a) means dialling or signalling information –
  (i) that is generated as a result of the making of the telecommunication (whether or not the telecommunication is sent or received successfully); and
  (ii) that identifies the origin, direction, destination, or termination of the telecommunication; and

(b) without limiting the generality of paragraph (a), includes any of the following information:
  (i) the number from which the telecommunication originates:
  (ii) the number to which the telecommunication is sent:
  (iii) if the telecommunication is diverted from one number to another number, those numbers:
  (iv) the time at which the telecommunication is sent:
  (v) the duration of the telecommunication:
  (vi) if the telecommunication is generated from a mobile telephone, the point at which the telecommunication first enters a network; but

(c) does not include the content of the telecommunication.

133. Significantly for privacy purposes, the warrant neither allows interception of the content of communications nor does a call data warrant authorise any person to enter any premises (although a network operator that is subject to a call data warrant must provide assistance to enable any person who is authorised by the warrant to connect a telephone analyser (TRP Act, sections 10C(4) and 10D).

134. The effect of the warrant is that it can be produced by the police or Customs as authority to connect a telephone analyser, or to have a telephone analyser connected to a part of a network and monitor the telephone analyser, or require the relevant network operator to supply call associated data in respect of the person named in the warrant (TRP Act, section 10C).

135. The Act contains various operational and legal requirements to make the call data scheme effective. In terms of safeguards, there is a requirement for the Commissioner of Police and Comptroller of Customs to include statistics relating to the use of the power in their reports to Parliament (TRP Act, section 10R).

§8. Search and Surveillance Act 2012

136. The Act contains five Parts. Part 1 contains general provisions. Parts 2 and 3 of the Act contain various search and surveillance powers that enable police and other enforcement agencies to gather information to assist in the investigation and prosecution of offences and monitoring of compliance with the law. Some of these powers may also be used to prevent offending. Part 4 of the Act sets out general provisions in relation to the exercise of search, surveillance and inspection powers by any enforcement officer. Part 5 contains amendments, repeals and miscellaneous provisions.

137. While various aspects of Parts 2 and 3 may impact the privacy of electronic communications, it is the provisions in Part 3 concerning 'surveillance device warrants' that have the most relevance. A surveillance device warrant empowers an enforcement officer to use an interception, tracking or visual surveillance device.

Where warrants would authorise visual surveillance involving trespass or interception, they can only be applied for by constables and a higher threshold must be met.

138. The Act does not define surveillance. Instead, it refers to the use of a 'surveillance device'.

139. 'Surveillance device' is defined as an interception device, tracking device or visual surveillance device. Unless an exception applies, enforcement officers must obtain a surveillance device warrant in order to use:

- an interception device to intercept a private communication;
- a tracking device (unless no trespass is involved and the purpose is solely to detect whether a thing has been opened, tampered with or otherwise dealt with);
- a surveillance device in a manner involving trespass to land or goods; or
- a visual surveillance device to:
  - (i) observe and/or record private activity in private premises; or
  - (ii) observe and/or record private activity in the curtilage of private premises if the observation exceeds three hours in a twenty-four-hour period or eight hours in total (for the purposes of a single investigation or connected series of investigations).

140. The use of a surveillance device to 'intercept a private communication' is most directly relevant to the privacy of electronic communications.

141. Surveillance device warrants can only be issued by judges. A judge may issue a surveillance device warrant if they are satisfied there are reasonable grounds to suspect that a relevant offence has been, is being or will be committed and to believe that the use of the device will obtain evidential material in respect of the offence. Two additional restrictions apply if the warrant would permit the use of an interception device:

- The warrant must relate to an offence that is punishable by at least seven years' imprisonment or certain other specified offences.
- The warrant can only be applied for by the police.

142. The Act contains many provisions regulating the use of the devices and of the evidence gained as a result of their use.

§9. Telecommunications (Interception Capability and Security) Act 2013

143. The Telecommunications (Interception Capability and Security) Act 2013 (TICSA) establishes obligations for New Zealand's telecommunications network operators in two key areas: interception capability and network security.

144. Sections 5 and 7 of TICSA sets out its twin purposes as:

Purpose of this Act relating to interception capability

The purpose of this Act in relation to interception capability is to –

(a) ensure that surveillance agencies are able to effectively carry out the lawful interception of telecommunications under an interception warrant or any other lawful interception authority; and
(b) ensure that surveillance agencies, in obtaining assistance for the interception of telecommunications, do not create barriers to the introduction of new or innovative telecommunications technologies; and
(c) ensure that network operators and service providers have the freedom to choose system design features and specifications that are appropriate for their own purposes.

Purpose of this Act relating to network security

The purpose of this Act in relation to network security is to prevent, sufficiently mitigate, or remove security risks arising from –

(a) the design, build, or operation of public telecommunications networks; and
(b) interconnections to or between public telecommunications networks in New Zealand or with networks overseas.

145. Section 6 of the Act sets out some principles relating to interception capability which bear on the protection of privacy in electronic communications:

Principles relating to interception capability

The following principles must be applied by persons who exercise powers and carry out duties under this Act in relation to interception capability, if those principles are relevant to those powers or duties:

(a) the principle that the privacy of telecommunications that are not subject to an interception warrant or any other lawful interception authority must be maintained to the extent provided for in law:
(b) the principle that the interception of telecommunications, when authorised under an interception warrant or any other lawful interception authority, must be carried out without unduly interfering with any telecommunications.

146. NZ Police have the responsibility for maintaining a register of network operators that holds information, on behalf of all of the surveillance agencies, about network operators and their compliance with the obligations set out in the Act. Police also assess whether a network operator should be exempt from some of their obligations, and enforce non-compliance with the interception capability requirements in the Act. The Government Communications Security Bureau (GCSB) is responsible for administering the network security provisions of the TICSA.

147. Part 3 of the TICSA, which relates to network security, establishes a framework under which network operators are required to engage with the GCSB about changes and developments with their networks where these intersect with national security.

148. The legislation sets out a path to identify and address, prevent, mitigate, or remove network security risks which may arise. To assist in applying TICSA, the Director-General of the GCSB has issued guidelines for network operators, and has granted a number of exemptions from the duty to notify which are in place.

149. The GCSB works with network operators so that risks to New Zealand's national security arising from the design, build or operation of public telecommunications networks and their interconnection to other networks both domestically and overseas are identified and addressed as early as possible.

§10. Intelligence and Security Act 2017

150. This legislation governs New Zealand's two intelligence and security agencies, the New Zealand Security Intelligence Service (NZSIS) and GSCB and well as providing various safeguards such as the Inspector-General of Intelligence and Security.

151. Among other things, Part 4 of the Intelligence and Security Act (ISA) enables the issue of intelligence warrants that authorise the carrying out of activities that would otherwise be unlawful, including in the context of electronic communications, intercepting any private communications or classes of private communications (ISA, section 67(1)(b)).

152. Additionally, Part 5 of ISA creates a scheme for accessing information held by other agencies. Part of this involves statutory approval for accessing 'business records.' One class of 'business agencies' that hold 'business records' are telecommunications network operators (ISA, section 144).

153. In relation to a business agency that is a telecommunications network operator, the definition of 'business records' in section 144 includes all information in the possession or under the control of the telecommunications network operator that is generated or received in the course of the operator's business, including:

A. customer information (for example, names and contact details);
B. subscriber information (for example, names and contact details);
C. bank account number details;
D. credit card number details;
E. IP addresses;
F. billing information and records;
G. call associated data (within the meaning of s. 3 of the Telecommunications (Interception Capability and Security) Act 2013);

H. device-related information;
I. details of mobile data usage;
J. information on linked accounts;
K. details of any persons communicating with the network operator.

154. The definition excludes:

A. personal information about the network operator's employees and directors;
B. the content of telecommunications;
C. any information relating to the business operations of the network operator (including finances, budgets, plans, and strategies);
D. the content of any other communications or files held by the network operator in providing any service to a customer (for example, cloud storage servers or insurance);
E. web browsing history.

Chapter 4. Other Relevant Provisions on the Protection of Privacy

§1. Introduction

155. There are many enactments (both Acts and regulations made thereunder) that deal in part with the protection of privacy. Such legislation covers, for example, the areas of freedom of information;[49] criminal law sanctions for certain breaches of privacy; spent criminal convictions; and surveillance. There are also a great number of individual statutory provisions scattered over many pieces of legislation that directly or indirectly protect privacy interests in one way or another. For example, the secrecy provisions in the Electoral Act 1993 not only protect the integrity of the voting system, but the privacy of the voter. There are a number of legal regulatory frameworks in New Zealand for dealing with privacy issues.

I. Regulation of Broadcasters

156. In line with the rights to freedom of expression and freedom of the press, news entities are exempt from the provisions of the Privacy Act to the extent that are engaged in news activities.[50] The Broadcasting Act 1989, however, requires all broadcasters to observe standards that are consistent with the privacy of the individual. If these standards are breached, individuals may complain to the Broadcasting Standards Authority (BSA).[51] This body, which was established under the Broadcasting Act, has formulated a number of privacy principles that it enforces. The authority has the power to impose sanctions, including damages for privacy breaches. There is extensive BSA case law on privacy issues.[52]

II. Health and Disability Commissioner Act 1994

157. In addition to the Health Information Privacy Code 2020, a code of practice made under the Privacy Act, the Health and Disability Commissioner Act 1994 is relevant to aspects of privacy in the provision of health and disability services. The Code of Health and Disability Services Consumers' Rights made under the Act provides for the right of consumers to have their privacy rights respected. Where there is a breach of the code, individuals may lodge a complaint with either the Health and Disability Commissioner or to a health and disability services consumer advocate. Unresolved complaints may be taken to the Human Rights Review Tribunal (HRRT), and on appeal to the courts of general jurisdiction.

49. Official Information Act 1982, Local Government Official Information and Meetings Act 1987: *see* Part I, Ch. 1.2.5 above, and Part IX, Ch. 2 below.
50. Privacy Act, s. 8(b)(x); *see also* Part IX, Ch. 1.1.
51. *See* bsa.govt.nz.
52. *See* bsa.govt.nz/decisions/search?search=searchdecision&task=no, and Michael Stace, *Privacy: Interpreting the Broadcasting Authority's Decisions January 1990 to June 1998* (Dunmore Press, Palmerston North, 1998).

III. Freedom of Information Legislation

158. New Zealand's freedom of information legislation, consisting of the Official Information Act 1982 and the LGOIM Act, protects individuals' privacy in relation to the disclosure of public sector information to third parties.[53] Thus, one of the purposes of the Official Information Act is 'to protect official information to the extent consistent with the public interest and the preservation of personal privacy'.[54] In particular, one of the exceptions to the presumption of availability of official information is where withholding the information is necessary to 'Protect the privacy of natural persons, including that of deceased natural persons',[55] where there is no countervailing public interest in disclosure.

159. The Ombudsmen, appointed under the Ombudsman Act 1975, oversee the freedom of information regime. There are a number of areas where the Ombudsmen and the Privacy Commissioner under the Privacy Act have overlapping roles and duties of mutual consultation. Jurisdictional issues can arise where personal information requested under the Privacy Act also deals with official information about another individual. Such issues arise where there is a relationship or interaction between two or more people, one of whom is the individual making the access request.

§2. Privacy Protections under the Criminal Law

160. There are a number of criminal offences that arise from intrusions into people's privacy, such as peering into someone's home;[56] taking photographs or video recordings without permission;[57] criminal trespass;[58] electronic eavesdropping;[59] computer hacking;[60] and opening someone else's mail without reasonable excuse.[61]

161. There are also a number of offences that apply to the unauthorised use or disclosure of personal information, such as information relating to voting;[62] information obtained from the national cervical screening programme;[63] information

53. *See* below, Part IX, Ch. 2.
54. Long title to the Official Information Act 1982; *see also* s. 4(c). The Local Government Official Information and Meetings Act 1987 contains parallel provisions.
55. Official Information Act 1982, s. 9(2)(a); Local Government Official Information and Meetings Act 1987, s. 7(2)(a).
56. Summary Offences Act 1981, s. 30.
57. Private Security Personnel and Private Investigators (Code of Conduct – Surveillance of Individuals) Regulations 2011, reg. 6; and Crimes Act 1961, ss 216G–216N, which deal with intimate visual recording where an individual has a reasonable expectation of privacy.
58. Trespass Act 1980.
59. Crimes Act 1961, Part 9A.
60. *Ibid.*, Part 10.
61. Postal Services Act 1998, s. 23.
62. Electoral Act 1993, ss 203.
63. Health Act 1956, Part 4A.

given to a Mortality Review Committee;[64] information about a radio communication by someone who is not the intended recipient;[65] information about the contents of a postal article;[66] unlawful access to or disclosure of information stored on a DNA profile databank;[67] wrongful use or disclosure of information obtained by the intelligence service;[68] wrongful disclosure of information about a person's criminal record;[69] breach of a court suppression order;[70] breaching the confidentiality of tax information;[71] breaching the confidentiality of government statistics information;[72] information relating to the setting of certain public sector salaries;[73] information relating to proceedings before the Judicial Conduct Panel;[74] corrupt use or disclosure of public sector ('official') information;[75] unlawful publication of information of the identifying details of suspects ordered to provide a DNA sample;[76] unlawful access to or disclosure of information stored on a DNA profile databank;[77] and information provided by the Parole Board to an offender that identifies or enables the identification of the victim.[78]

§3. SEARCH AND SURVEILLANCE ACT 2012

162. The Search and Surveillance Act 2012 was introduced to consolidate, rationalise, and update police and non-police powers that had developed over time and were scattered in various statutes.[79] It builds on the New Zealand Bill of Rights Act 1990 right to be free from unreasonable search and seizure by specifying police powers in this area more closely so as to be consistent with human rights values, including the rights and entitlements contained in the Privacy Act. The legislation sets out in considerable detail the rules relating to search and seizure powers, including the circumstances where warrants are required and what may or may not be searched. The Act contains a new regime for production and examination orders, computer searches, the use of surveillance devices, and other surveillance and interception activities.

163. There are two further laws that are devoted to the regulation of surveillance and interception by surveillance and intelligence agencies, though they do not

64. New Zealand Health and Disability Act 2000, s. 187(7).
65. Radiocommunications Act 1989, s. 133A.
66. Postal Services Act 1998, s. 20(2).
67. Criminal Investigations (Bodily Samples) Act 1995, s. 27.
68. New Zealand Security Intelligence Service Act 1969, s. 12A.
69. Criminal records (Clean Slate) Act 2004, s. 17.
70. Criminal Justice Act 1985, ss 138–140.
71. Tax Administration Act 1994, ss 143C and 143D.
72. Statistics Act 1975, s. 21.
73. Remuneration Authority Act 1977, s. 9.
74. Judicial Conduct Commissioner and Judicial Conduct Panel Act 2004, s. 30.
75. Crimes Act 1961, ss 105A and 105B.
76. Criminal Investigations (Bodily Samples) Act 1995, ss 4 and 19.
77. Criminal Investigations (Bodily Samples) Act 1995, s. 27.
78. Parole Act 2002, s. 13(8).
79. Relevant non-police enforcement officers include customs, fishery, dog control, and immigration officers in certain circumstances.

have any particular privacy protection function other than putting certain types of surveillance and interception on a legal basis: the Telecommunications (Interception Capability and Security) Act 2013, and the GCSB Act 2013. This legislation allows of the possibility of mass surveillance.

§4. Privacy and Data Protection at Common Law and Equity

164. New Zealand case law based on common law and equity deals with a number of aspects of privacy. This body of law falls into three categories for present purposes: tort, equity, and miscellaneous common law actions that can relate to privacy.

I. The Privacy Tort

165. New Zealand is one of the few common law countries that have come to recognise a common law tort for invasion of privacy.[80] In *Hosking v. Runting*,[81] the CA held that the cause of action is made out if publicity is given to private facts about someone where there is a reasonable expectation of privacy, and that publicity is highly offensive to an objective reasonable person.[82] In a subsequent 2012 case,[83] the HC went on to recognise a related privacy tort of intrusion upon seclusion. The elements of this tort require an intentional and unauthorised intrusion into seclusion (an intimate personal activity, space or affairs) that infringes a reasonable expectation of privacy and which is highly offensive to a reasonable person.

166. The New Zealand Law Commission (NZLC) had considered whether the tort ought to be put on a statutory basis rather than left to be developed by the common law.[84] The Law Commission found the tort to be somewhat open-ended, with a number of key elements still requiring judicial elucidation. In the result, it concluded that the tort should be retained and allowed to develop through case law.

80. Early cases in the development of the tort in New Zealand include: *Tucker v. News Media Ownership Ltd* [1986] 2 NZLR 716, 733; *T v. A-G* (1988) 5 NZFLR 357; *Morgan v. TVNZ Ltd* (High Court, Christchurch, 1 Mar. 1990, CP 67/90); *Marris v. TV3* (High Court, Wellington, 14 Oct. 1991 CP 754/91); *X v. A-G* [1994] NZFLR 433; *Bradley v. Wingnut Films Ltd* [1993] 1 NZLR 415; *P v. D* [2000] 2 NZLR 591; and *L v. G* [2002] DCR 234.

81. [2003] 3 NZLR 385 (High Court) and [2005] 1 NZLR 1 (Court of Appeal).

82. Other cases on the privacy tort include: *Brash v. Doe* (High Court, Wellington, 16 Nov. 2006, CIV 2006-485-2605); *Brown v. Attorney-General* [2006] NZAR 552 (DC); *Andrews v. Television NZ Ltd* [2006] NZHC 1586, [2009] NZLR 220; and *Television New Zealand Ltd v. Rogers* [2008] 2 NZLR 277 (Supreme Court).

83. *C v. Holland* [2012] 3 NZLR 672.

84. *Invasion of Privacy: Penalties and Remedies*, Review of the Law of Privacy, Stage 3, Issues Paper 14 (Wellington, March 2009).

II. Breach of Confidence

167. Breach of confidence is an equitable cause of action and protects values that are partly rooted in privacy concerns. The three elements of the action are that the information concerned must have the necessary quality of confidence about it; the information must have been communicated in circumstances importing an obligation of confidence; and there was, or is going to be, an unauthorised use of that information to the detriment of the person who communicated it.[85] This cause of action has formed a basis for the protection of privacy in Great Britain, but New Zealand law has preferred to develop a separate common law tort rather than strain existing equitable doctrine. The main obstacle to the use of this cause of action to protect privacy is the second element that must be proved: communication of the information in circumstances importing an obligation of confidence, which normally requires a confidential relationship, such as doctor/patient, banker/customer. British courts have found that an obligation of confidence can arise in circumstances where it is obvious that information is confidential, even if it is not communicated in the course of a confidential relationship.[86]

III. Incidental Protection under Other Common Law Causes of Action

168. There have long been other civil remedies under the common law where a person can seek damages or an injunction if a privacy interest has been breached. These causes of action are not directed primarily at protecting privacy *per se*, but other principles or closely related interests that have the effect of protecting one's privacy. The main causes of action are briefly described below.

A. Defamation

169. A cause of action in defamation is available where there is a disclosure or publication of false information about an individual that may bring the person into hatred, contempt, or ridicule.[87] The aim of such a legal action is to vindicate the individual's reputation and provide compensation for the damage to reputation, distress, and hurt feelings. This cause of action can be viewed as supporting data quality and data correction principles. An important difference, however, is that defamation deals only with information that is false, whereas true privacy protections should cover personal information that is true as well as false. Other respects in which defamation provides relatively weak protection for privacy interests include the fact that there are qualified privilege defences, which do not require fair

85. *Coco v. A N Clark (Engineers) Ltd* [1969] RPC 41.
86. *See*, for example, *Attorney-General v. Guardian Newspapers (No 2)* [1990] 1 AC 109 (House of Lords), *Campbell v. MGN* [2004] 2 AC 457 (House of Lords), *Douglas and others v. Hello! Ltd* [2005] EWCA Civ 595, [2006] QB 125, and *Murray v. Big Pictures (UK) Ltd* [2008] EWCA Civ 446.
87. The tort of defamation was put on a statutory footing in New Zealand by the Defamation Act 1992.

information practices; there is no access mechanism for individuals to discover when defamation has occurred in non-media contexts; and defamation litigation tends to be very time consuming and costly. As with the privacy tort, a defamation claim may not be brought in respect of a deceased individual, because the dead cannot suffer the sort of harm with which this cause of action is concerned. Similarly, the New Zealand Privacy Act only applies to living individuals except in regard to health information.

B. Nuisance

170. An unreasonable interference with a person's right to the use or enjoyment of an interest in land constitutes a private nuisance. This tort action can be used to protect privacy interests.[88]

C. Harassment

171. Where an individual is subjected to a pattern of harassment that causes anxiety or distress, this can amount also to an interference with the individual's privacy. The Harassment Act 1997 provides for both civil and criminal penalties for various types of harassment. The legislation is aimed against such behaviour as watching, loitering near, or preventing or hindering access to or from, an individual's residence, business, workplace, or any other place that a person frequents; following, stopping, or accosting an individual; entering or interfering with property in an individual's possession; making contact with an individual in any way; and acting in any other way that causes an individual to reasonably fear for his or her safety.[89]

D. Malicious Falsehood

172. The tort of malicious falsehood is available for a written or oral falsehood, published maliciously, which is intended to, and does, cause damage to an individual.

E. Negligence

173. There are two New Zealand cases where the negligent disclosure of personal information caused emotional harm, giving rise to a sustainable cause of action.[90]

---

88. *Lyons v. Wilkins* [1899] 1 Ch. 255.
89. Harassment Act 1997, s. 4.
90. *Furniss v. Fitchett* [1958] NZLR 396; *Balfour v. Attorney-General* [1991] 1 NZLR 519; *G v. Attorney-General* [1994] 1 NZLR 714.

F. Conversion

174. The tort of conversion may occur where someone takes and converts to one's own use someone else's property without consent, such as correspondence.[91]

91. *Thurston v. Charles* (1905) 21 TLR 659.

Part II. National Data Protection Law

Chapter 1. Background: Description of the Privacy Act 2020

§1. Introduction

175. The Privacy Act 2020 updates and replaces the Privacy Act 1993, largely in line with the 2011 recommendations of the NZLC.[92]

176. The legislative purpose of the Privacy Act 2020 is to promote and protect individual privacy by:

(a) providing a framework for protecting an individual's right to privacy of personal information, including the right of an individual to access their personal information, while recognising that other rights and interests may at times also need to be taken into account; and
(b) giving effect to internationally recognised privacy obligations and standards in relation to the privacy of personal information, including the OECD Guidelines and the International Covenant on Civil and Political Rights.[93]

177. The Privacy Act focuses on information privacy in both the public and private sectors. It covers all 'personal information' in whatever shape or form, even if it is held only in a person's memory.[94] 'Personal information' is defined as any information about an identifiable individual;[95] and an 'individual' is a living natural person,[96] except where a sector-specific code of practice made under the Act applies to information about deceased individual.[97] The Privacy Act applies to personal information collected, held, or used by a New Zealand agency (which includes individuals); an overseas agency carrying on business in New Zealand; and individuals who, while not ordinarily resident in New Zealand, collect information or hold it while present in New Zealand.[98] There are a few specific exceptions from the scope of the Act, but for all practical purposes, nearly every person and organisation (with the

92. *Review of the Privacy Act 1993: Review of the Law of Privacy*, Stage 4, Report 123, June 2011.
93. Privacy Act, s. 3.
94. *Re Application by L* [1997] NZCRT 11 (14 Apr. 1997); (1997) 3 HRNZ 716.
95. Privacy Act, s. 7(1).
96. *Ibid.*
97. Privacy Act, s. 32(6). *See*, for example, the Health Information Privacy Code 2020, rr 11 and 12.
98. Privacy Act, s. 4(1).

notable exception of the news media) falls under the Act.[99] The Privacy Act contains three main groups of provisions, as discussed below.

§2. The Information Privacy Principles

178. The IPPs set out in section 22 of the Act deal with the collection of personal information; security safeguards; access to and correction of personal information; use and disclosure of personal information; and unique identifiers.

179. The IPPs themselves do not give rise to legally enforceable rights outside the Privacy Act, with the one exception of the right to access one's personal information when it is held by a public sector agency.[100] The IPPs give rise only to a right of process, whereby enforcement is subject to the mechanisms and limitations that are set out in the Act. Legally enforceable rights only crystallise when there has been an 'interference with the privacy of an individual', which generally requires a breach of an IPP and some harm or loss to the individual concerned.[101] Where the principles relating to access to and correction of personal information are concerned (IPPs 6 and 7), however, no harm or loss is required to be proved.[102] All complaints must be processed through the investigation and conciliation procedure of the Privacy Commissioner before a case can be heard in the HRRT. The Privacy Commissioner may only legally determine complaints at first instances about charges for access to or correction of personal information under the Act,[103] and access requests.[104] Only the latter may be appealed to the Tribunal; decisions by the Commissioner concerning charges are final and binding. The majority of complaints under the Act are concluded or settled by the Privacy Commissioner and are not decided by the Tribunal.

180. The IPPs are largely in line with the OECD principles.

I. Collection Limitation

181. The IPPs set limits to the collection of personal information. Information must be collected by lawful and fair means, usually with the knowledge or consent of the individual (the OECD collection limitation principle).[105]

99. *Ibid.*, ss 8(b) and 9(b)–(d).
100. Privacy Act, s. 31. This right is enforceable directly in a Court of law if the individual concerned chooses to pursue this avenue of enforcement. In practice, however, this route is rarely taken, because the Privacy Commissioner's complaint resolution process is free of charge.
101. Privacy Act, s. 69(1).
102. *Winter v. Jans and Jans* [2004] NZHC 236 (6 Apr. 2004).
103. Privacy Act, s. 93.
104. Privacy Act, s. 92. This involves the making of an access direction.
105. IPPs 1, 2, 3, and 4.

II. Data Quality

182. Agencies that hold personal information must ensure that it is relevant to their intended use; it should be accurate, complete, and up-to-date; and it should not be retained for longer than it may be lawfully used (the OECD data quality principle).[106]

III. Purpose Specification

183. The purpose for which personal information is collected should normally be specified at the time of its collection, and subsequent use should be limited to that purpose or a directly related purpose (the OECD purpose specification principle).[107]

IV. Use Limitation

184. Personal information should not be used or disclosed for purposes other than those specified earlier unless the individual consents or if there is legal justification (the OECD use limitation principle).[108]

V. Security Safeguards

185. Personal information must be protected by reasonable security safeguards (the OECD security safeguards principle).[109]

VI. Openness

186. There should be readily available means of establishing the existence and nature of personal information, the main purposes of its use, and the identity and address of who holds it (the OECD openness principle).[110]

VII. Individual Participation

187. Individuals have the right to obtain confirmation of whether or not information is held about them, and to obtain access to it within a reasonable time at a reasonable charge and in an intelligible form. Where access is denied, individuals

106. IPP 8 and 9.
107. IPP 3.
108. IPPs 10 and 11.
109. IPP 5.
110. IPPs 3 and 6.

must be given the reasons and have the right to challenge the decision. Individuals also have the right to challenge information about them, and have a remedy of correction or erasure (the OECD individual participation principle).[111]

188. Part 4 of the Act relates specifically to access to and correction of personal information. Subpart 1 of Part 4 of the Act deals with the mechanical aspects of making access requests, the various reasons which agencies may (but are not required to) rely upon to refuse access to personal information, and the mechanics of making personal information available. Subpart 2 sets out the mechanical aspects relating to the correction of personal information by the individual concerned. Subpart 3 deals with charges for access to and correction of personal information. As was the position under freedom of information legislation prior to the enactment of the Privacy Act 1993, personal information held by public sector agencies is available free of charge. Private sector agencies are permitted to impose a reasonable charge for making information available, and for correction.[112] Where access to or correction of information is refused, the agency must give its reasons and inform the requester of the right to seek an investigation and review of the refusal by the Privacy Commissioner.[113]

VIII. Unique Identifiers

189. In addition to the principles that track those in the OECD Guidelines, there is also a principle that limits the assignment and use of unique identifiers.[114]

IX. Privacy Commissioner's Power to Grant One-Off Exceptions

190. The Privacy Commissioner may, upon application, grant one-off exceptions in special circumstances to authorise the collection, use, storage, or disclosure of personal information that would otherwise breach IPP 2 and IPPs 9 to 12.[115]

X. Codes of Practice Under the Privacy Act

191. The Privacy Commissioner has the power to issue codes of practice that modify the application of one or more of the IPPs in order to take into account the special characteristics of specific industries, professions, activities, or classes of personal information.[116] At present, there are three sectoral codes: the Health Information Privacy Code 2020,[117] the Telecommunications Information Privacy Code

111. IPPs 6 and 7, and Parts 5 and 8 of the Act.
112. Privacy Act, s. 66(1) (access) and s. 66(2) (correction), and s. 66(4) (charge must be reasonable).
113. Privacy Act, ss 55(2) (denied access) and s. 63(3) (denied correction).
114. IPP 13.
115. Privacy Act, s. 30.
116. Privacy Act, s. 32.
117. This replaces the 1994 code.

2020,[118] and the Credit Reporting Privacy Code 2020.[119] In addition, there is a code that supplements the authority of agencies to collect, use, and disclose personal information for certain purposes in response to declared national emergencies, the Civil Defence National Emergencies (Information Sharing) Code 2020.[120] There are also two codes that deal with unique identifiers in particular sectors: the Superannuation Schemes Unique Identifier Code 2020,[121] and the Justice Sector Unique Identifiers Code 2020.[122]

§3. Special Categories of Personal Information Held by Public Sector Agencies

192. A number of provisions in the Privacy Act relate to specific types of personal information held by public sector agencies. These are contained in Part 7 of the Act, which deals with sharing, accessing, and matching personal information.

I. Information Sharing

193. Subpart 1 of Part 7 deals with information sharing. The purpose of this subpart of the Act is to enable agencies to be authorised to share personal information with other agencies, or within parts of the same agency, in accordance with an approved information sharing agreement.[123] Such agreements must be approved by an order in Council, a form of delegated legislation made under the Act. The aim of these agreements is to facilitate the provision of public services.

II. Identity Information

194. Subpart 2 of Part 7 deals with identity information. The purpose of this subpart of the Act is to authorise specified accessing agencies, when carrying out specified functions, to verify an individual's identity by accessing identity information held about that individual by a specified agency that holds it.[124] Identity information includes biometric information, which is defined as including a photograph of all or any part of the individual's head and shoulders; fingerprint impressions; iris scans; and an electronic record of the personal information that is capable of being used for biometric matching.[125]

118. This replaces the 2003 code.
119. This replaces the 2004 code.
120. This replaces the 2013 code.
121. This replaces the 1995 code.
122. This replaces the 1998 code.
123. Privacy Act, s. 136.
124. 'Accessing' and 'holding' agencies are specified in the Third Schedule to the Privacy Act.
125. Privacy Act, s. 164.

III. Law Enforcement Information

195. Subpart 3 of Part 7 deals with law enforcement information. The purpose of this subpart of the Act is to authorise specified public sector agencies to obtain access to specified law enforcement information that is held by other specified agencies about identifiable individuals.[126]

IV. Information Matching Programmes

196. Subpart 4 of Part 7 deals with authorised information matching programmes. The purpose of this subpart of the Act is to authorise agencies to compare personal information in accordance with an authorised information matching programme.[127] These programmes involve the comparison (electronic or otherwise) of any document that contains personal information of ten or more individuals with one or more other documents containing personal information about ten or more individuals. The purpose of these matching programmes is to produce or verify information that may be used for the purpose of taking adverse action against an identifiable individual.[128] Such matching programmes must be legislatively authorised by an information matching provision.[129]

§4. Operational Aspects of the Privacy Act

I. The Privacy Commissioner and Complaints under the Act

197. The provisions dealing with the operational aspects of the Privacy Act include those that establish the office and set out the functions of the Privacy Commissioner,[130] and those that describe the mechanisms and procedures for the making and handling of complaints under the Act, as well as the remedies for breaches. The latter provisions both satisfy the OECD accountability principle.[131]

II. Notifiable Privacy Breaches

198. Subpart 1 of Part 6 of the Act deals with notifiable privacy breaches, which are defined as breaches where it is reasonable to believe that serious harm has been or is likely to be caused.[132] Such privacy breaches do not include those where the personal information in question is held by an agency who is an individual and the

126. The specified accessing and holding agencies, as well as the specified law enforcement information, are set out in Schedule 4 to the Privacy Act.
127. Privacy Act, s. 174.
128. Privacy Act, s. 177.
129. Such provisions are specified in Schedule 5 to the Privacy Act.
130. Privacy Act, Part 2.
131. Privacy Act, Part 5.
132. The criteria for assessing 'serious harm' in this context are set out in s. 113.

information is held solely for the purposes of, or in connection with, the individual's personal or domestic affairs.[133] A privacy breach in this context means an unauthorised or accidental access to, or disclosure, alteration, loss, or destruction of the personal information, or an action that prevents the agency from accessing the information, whether on a temporary or permanent basis.[134] Agencies are required to notify the Privacy Commissioner of a notifiable privacy breach as soon as practicable,[135] and, subject to some exceptions, must also notify the affected individual or give public notice of the notifiable breach.[136]

III. Compliance Notices

199. Subpart 2 of Part 6 of the Act deals with the issuing of compliance notices to an agency by the Privacy Commissioner. The Commissioner may issue such a notice when there has occurred a breach of the Act,[137] an action that is to be treated as a breach of an IPP or an interference with the privacy of an individual under another Act,[138] or breach of a code of practice under the Act or a relevant code of conduct issued under another Act.[139] When an agency receives a compliance notice, it must take steps to comply with the notice. The Commissioner may vary or cancel the notice if it has been complied with or it is no longer needed.[140] If there is no compliance with the notice, or the agency has failed to lodge an appeal against it, the Commissioner may take enforcement proceedings in the Tribunal.[141]

IV. Transfer Prohibition Notices

200. Part 8 of the Act deals with the Privacy Commissioner's power to issue transfer prohibition notices, which prohibit the onward transfer of personal information received in New Zealand from overseas.

V. Appointment of Privacy Officers

201. Also noteworthy is the requirement for agencies to appoint one or more privacy officers (from within or outside the agency) in order to encourage the agency

133. Privacy Act, s. 112.
134. Privacy Act, s. 112.
135. Privacy Act, s. 114.
136. Privacy Act, ss 115 and 116.
137. Privacy Act, s. 123(1)(a)
138. Privacy Act, s. 123(1)(b).
139. Privacy Act, s. 123(1)(c).
140. Privacy Act, s. 127.
141. Privacy Act, s. 130.

to comply with the IPPs, deal with requests made to the agency under Act, work with the Privacy Commissioner in relation to investigations under the Act, and ensure that the agency complies with the Act.[142]

142. Privacy Act, s. 201.

Chapter 2. Scope of the National Law

§1. Material Scope

I. General Application

202. The Privacy Act applies to both automated and non-automated processing of personal information, in any form.[143] The exceptions are set out below. The concept of a 'filing system' is irrelevant to the application of the Act.

II. Constitutional, Political, Judicial, and Investigative Exclusions

203. There are a number of specified exclusions from the Act's application on the grounds of constitutional, political, judicial, and accountability functions:[144] the Sovereign of New Zealand and the Governor-General; the House of Representatives; Members of Parliament in their official capacity; the Parliamentary Service Commission; the Parliamentary Service, except in relation to employment matters; courts and tribunals in relation to their judicial functions; and the ombudsmen and other official investigative or inquisitorial bodies.

III. News Media

204. The Act does not apply to news entities to the extent that they are engaged in news activities.[145] This exception recognises the importance of journalistic freedom and free expression in a democratic society.

IV. Personal and Domestic Affairs

205. The IPPs in the Act do not apply to information collected or held for personal or domestic affairs,[146] except if the collection, use, or disclosure of the personal information would be highly offensive to a reasonable person.[147]

V. Intelligence and Security Agencies

206. Most of the IPPs that apply to the collection of personal information do not apply to personal information collected by an intelligence and security agency.[148] These are IPP 2 (subject to exceptions, personal information must be collected from

143. *See* on the meaning of 'personal information', *see* below at Part II, Ch. 3.1.
144. Privacy Act, s. 8(b).
145. Privacy Act, s. 8(b)(x); *see* further at Part IX, Ch. 1.1.
146. Privacy Act, s. 27(1).
147. Privacy Act, s. 27(2).
148. Defined in s. 7(1) as the New Zealand Security Intelligence Service and the Government Communications Security Bureau.

the individual concerned); 3 (requirements where an agency collects personal information from the individual concerned), and 4(b) (information may only be collected by means that are fair and do not unreasonably intrude upon an individual's personal affairs). Moreover, provisions in the Act that deal with the Privacy Commissioner's investigative procedure[149] for dealing with complaints of breach of the IPPs do not apply to an intelligence and security agency. There is instead a special procedure that involves the Privacy Commissioner investigating the action complained of and providing a report that sets out the Commissioner's opinion on the matter if an interference with the privacy of an individual has been found.[150] If the agency takes no steps in response to the report, the Commissioner may send a copy of the report to the Prime Minister, who may present the report to the House of Representatives.

VI. IPPs on Access and Correction Do Not Apply to Certain Information

207. IPPs 6 and 7, which deal with access to and correction of personal information, respectively, do not apply to certain miscellaneous forms of personal information: information during transmission by post, personal delivery, electronic, or electronic means; information contained in any communication that relates to an investigation between an agency and an Ombudsman or officer appointed under the Ombudsman, the Privacy Commissioner, or an employee of the Commissioner (not being information that was in existence before the commencement of the investigation); information held by the Auditor-General or others in connection with the Auditor-General's functions, duties, or powers; or information contained in evidence given or submissions made to a government or public inquiry until the final report is presented, or where there is some other official inquiry into a specific matter.[151] IPP 7 on the correction of personal information does not apply to personal information collected by Statistics New Zealand under the Statistics Act 1975.[152]

VII. Relationship of Act to Other New Zealand Law

208. Nothing in IPPs 6 ('Access to personal information'), 11 ('limits on disclosure of personal information') and 12 ('Disclosure of personal information outside New Zealand') limits or affects anything in a New Zealand enactment that authorises or requires personal information to be made available; or a provision contained in any other New Zealand Act that imposes a prohibition or restriction concerning the availability of personal information; or regulates the manner in which personal information may be obtained or made available.[153]

149. As set out in the Privacy Act, ss 85, 91, 93, 94, and subpart 3 of Part 3.
150. Privacy Act, s. 95.
151. Privacy Act, s. 29(1).
152. Privacy Act, s. 29(2).
153. Privacy Act, s. 24(1).

209. An action taken by an agency does not breach any of the other IPPs (1 to 5, 7 to 10, or 13) if the action is authorised or required by or under New Zealand law.[154]

§2. Personal Scope

I. 'Personal Information'

210. The Privacy Act covers 'personal information', which is defined as 'information about an identifiable individual'.[155] The term 'individual' is in turn defined as 'a natural person, other than a deceased natural person'. The Act therefore is largely concerned with living natural persons.

II. Coverage of Deceased Persons

211. There are provisions in the Act that extend coverage to deceased individuals. First, the definition of 'personal information' also includes information relating to a death on the official register of deaths.[156] Second, The Privacy Commissioner may issue a sector-specific code of practice that applies one or more of the IPPs to information about deceased persons,[157] as in the case of the Health Information Privacy Code 2020.[158] Third, an agency may refuse access to information if its disclosure 'would involve the unwarranted disclosure of the affairs of … a deceased person'.[159] Fourth, a deceased person can be an 'affected person' for the purposes of the provisions relating to notifiable privacy breaches under Part 6, subpart 1 of the Act. In that case, an 'affected person' includes a deceased person if there is a sector-specific code of practice issued under section 32 that applies to personal information about deceased persons, and to the extent that the code applies one or more IPPs to that information.[160]

154. Privacy Act, s. 24(2).
155. Privacy Act, s. 7(1), para. (a); *see* further below, at Part II, Ch. 3.1.
156. Privacy Act, s. 7(1), para. (b). The death register is currently established under the Births, Deaths, Marriages, and Relationships Registration Act 1995.
157. Privacy Act, s. 32(6)(a). *See also* s. 112(1)(c) in relation to notifiable privacy breaches, where 'affected individual' includes a deceased person covered by a sector-specific code of practice that applies to information about deceased persons.
158. Rules 11(6) and (7) ('Limits on disclosure of health information'); Sch. 3(1)(a) ('permitted secondary purpose' of Use and Disclosure of Information Derived from Newborn Babies' Blood Spot Samples) and Sch. 3(2)(b) ('Use and disclosure of derived information')
159. Privacy Act, s. 53(b)(ii).
160. Privacy Act, s. 112(1) ('Interpretation').

III. Coverage of Children and Mentally Disordered Persons

212. There is no minimum age for coverage by the Act: children are covered by the Act from any age, though they may have representatives act for them.[161] Likewise, mentally disordered persons are also covered by the Act and can also be represented in relation to their rights under the Act. Complaints may be lodged in the Tribunal by a representative on behalf of an aggrieved individual.[162] Where there has been or is likely to be a serious privacy breach under Part 6 of the Act, representatives are entitled to notification.[163]

IV. Application of the Concept of 'Personal Information' to Two or More Individuals

213. The expression 'individuation' can refer to the extent to which personal information must relate to one individual as opposed to a collection or aggregate of individuals.[164] Although 'personal information' by definition is information about an identifiable individual, it is possible for some information to be about two or more identifiable individuals at once, in which case the issue arises as to whether a jurisdiction has a strict or more relaxed 'individuation' approach to what qualifies as 'personal information.'

214. In one Tribunal case, adopted on appeal by the HC,[165] the only reference to the individual concerned was her surname, which she shared with her husband. Both the Tribunal and HC accepted that the surname alone was sufficient to qualify as 'personal information' about the wife so that she was entitled to access to a lawyer's letter under IPP 6. Her then husband was not involved in the IPP 6 request or the eventual complaint to the Privacy Commissioner and Tribunal. The HC found that the letter referred to two individuals who were able to be identified, the plaintiff and her husband, even though the surname alone was used, and did not denote one particular individual. The implication of this decision is that if there are two (or more) individuals who are referred to by a collective reference that does not identify one specific individual in particular, then an individual falling under that collective reference may have entitlements under the Act, even though the information concerned is not clearly 'about' just that one individual alone.

161. *See* Privacy Act, ss 40 and 59, which provide that an IPP 6 access or IPP 7 correction request 'may be made only by the individual concerned or that individual's representative'; cf. s. 57(c)(ii) ('Responsibilities of agency before giving access to personal information').
162. Privacy Act, s. 98(1). *See*, for example, *Marshall v. IDEA Services Ltd (Privacy Act)* NZHRRT 13.
163. Privacy Act, s. 116(3), (6), and s. 117(2).
164. *See*, for example, Lee Bygrave, *Data Protection Law: Approaching its Rationale, Logic and Limits* (Kluwer Law International, The Hague, 2002), at 47–48.
165. *Sievwrights v. Apostolakis* HC, Wellington CIV-2005-485-527, 17 Dec. 2007.

§3. Territorial Scope

I. Territorial Application of the Act

215. The Privacy Act applies to 'New Zealand agencies' in relation to personal information they collect or hold, and to 'overseas agencies' in relation to personal information they collect or hold in the course of carrying on business in New Zealand.[166] In respect of both types of agencies, it is immaterial where the personal information is, or was collected by the agency where the personal information is held by the agency; or where the individual concerned is, or was, located.[167] The expression 'carrying on business in New Zealand' can apply to an overseas agency without it necessarily being a commercial operation, having a place of business in New Zealand, receiving any monetary payment for the supply of goods or services, or intending to make a profit from its business in New Zealand.[168]

216. A 'New Zealand agency' is defined as an individual who is ordinarily resident in New Zealand, a public sector agency, a New Zealand private sector agency, and a court or tribunal, except in relation to its judicial functions.[169] An 'overseas agency' is defined as an overseas person, body corporate, or unincorporated body that is not a New Zealand agency, the government of an overseas country, an overseas government entity to the extent that it performs any public functions on behalf of the overseas government, or a news entity, to the extent that it carries out news activities.[170]

217. The Act also applies to an individual who is not ordinarily resident in New Zealand in relation to any action relating to personal information collected while present in New Zealand, regardless of where the information is subsequently held by the individual or where the individual to whom the information relates is, or was, located; and also in relation to personal information held while present in New Zealand (but not collected while present in New Zealand), regardless of where the individual to whom the information relates is, or was, located.[171] The expression 'ordinarily resident in New Zealand' is defined as meaning that the person's home is in New Zealand; or the person is residing in New Zealand with the intention of residing in New Zealand indefinitely; or having resided in New Zealand with the intention of establishing their home in New Zealand, or with the intention of residing in New Zealand indefinitely, the person is outside New Zealand but intends to return to establish their home in New Zealand or to reside in New Zealand indefinitely.[172]

166. Privacy Act, s. 4(1)(a) and (b).
167. Privacy Act, s. 4(2).
168. Privacy Act, s. 4(3).
169. Privacy Act, s. 8(a). For exclusions from the definition, *see* above, Ch. 2.1.2.
170. Privacy Act, s. 9.
171. Privacy Act, s. 4(1)(c).
172. Privacy Act, s. 7(2).

218. The offences provision of the Act applies to a New Zealand agency, an overseas agency, an individual who is present in New Zealand, and a person who is outside New Zealand if any act or omission forming part of any offence occurs in New Zealand, or if any event necessary to the completion of any offence occurs in New Zealand.[173]

219. Where an agency takes an action in relation to information held overseas, the IPPs are not breached if the action is required by or under the law of any country other than New Zealand.[174]

II. Application of the Act to Disclosures of Personal Information Outside New Zealand

220. IPP 12 ('Disclosure of personal information outside New Zealand') deals with the disclosure of personal information outside New Zealand to foreign persons and entities. A 'foreign person or entity' is an individual who is neither present nor ordinarily resident in New Zealand,[175] or is an incorporated or unincorporated body that is not established under New Zealand law, and does not have its central control and management in New Zealand.[176] The purpose of IPP 12 is to ensure that when personal information is disclosed to overseas agencies, it must be subject to comparable privacy safeguards as exist in New Zealand.

221. IPP 12 provides that an agency may only disclose personal information to a foreign person or entity if it is subject to privacy safeguards that are comparable to those in New Zealand. IPP 12 does not apply to IPP 11(1)(b) (disclosure to individual concerned), (d) (source of information is a publicly available publication) and (g) (disclosure necessary for functioning of intelligence and security agencies), which means that those IPP 11 exceptions apply to the personal information concerned. With regard to the other IPP 11 exceptions, the foreign person or entity must be reasonably believed to be subject to the Privacy Act; subject to privacy safeguards comparable to those in the Privacy Act; the recipient is a participant in a prescribed binding scheme; or the recipient is subject to privacy laws of a prescribed country.

222. The wording of IPP 12 was intended to affirm the importance of enabling the free flow of data. This was one of the purposes behind the 1980 OECD Guidelines. The guidelines, contained in the OECD Council recommendation 'Concerning the Protection of Privacy and Transborder Flows of Personal Data', states in its

173. Privacy Act, s. 4(5). The Act's offences provision is s. 212, discussed at Part VIII, Ch. 6.5.
174. Privacy Act, s. 23.
175. Privacy Act, s. 7(1) provides that a person is 'ordinarily resident in New Zealand' if the person's home is in New Zealand; or the person resides in New Zealand with the intention of residing in New Zealand indefinitely; or if the person has resided in New Zealand with the intention of establishing their home there or intending to reside there indefinitely, is outside New Zealand but intends to return to establish their home or reside there indefinitely.
176. Privacy Act, s. 7(1).

third recital: 'Recognising that Member countries have a common interest in promoting and protecting the fundamental values of privacy, individual liberties and the global free flow of information'. IPP 12 is therefore expressed in enabling language in order to support the free flow of data subject to safeguards.[177]

III. Two Categories of Disclosures and Associated Exceptions in IPP 12

223. There are two categories of disclosures of personal information to a foreign person or entity outside New Zealand under IPP 12, and associated exceptions. First, here are disclosures where three exceptions to IPP 11 apply. This is where disclosure is to the individual concerned;[178] the source of the information is a publicly available publication (and in the circumstances, it would not be unfair or unreasonable to disclose the information);[179] or the disclosure is necessary to enable an intelligence and security agency to perform any of its functions.[180]

224. Second, there are disclosures made in reliance to other exceptions in IPP 11,[181] in which case the requirements for disclosure under IPP 12(1) apply. These exceptions provide that: the individual authorises the disclosure to the overseas agency after being expressly informed by the disclosing agency that the overseas agency may not be required to protect the information with comparable safeguards overall to those in the Privacy Act;[182] the disclosing agency reasonably believes that the overseas agency carries on business in New Zealand and is subject to the Privacy Act;[183] the disclosing agency reasonably believes that the overseas agency is subject to privacy laws that provide comparable safeguards overall to those in the Privacy Act;[184] the disclosing agency reasonably believes that the overseas agency is a participant in a prescribed binding scheme;[185] the disclosing agency reasonably believes that the overseas agency is subject to privacy laws of a prescribed country;[186] or the disclosing agency reasonably believes that the overseas agency is required to protect the information that provides comparative safeguards overall to those in the Privacy Act.[187] IPP 12(2), however, provides that IPP 12(1) does not apply to the disclosing agency if the information is to be disclosed to the overseas agency in reliance on IPP 11(1)(e) or (f) 'and it is not reasonably practicable in the

177. Ministry of Justice *Departmental Report Part Two, Privacy Bill* (2019), at para. 142.
178. IPP 11(1)(b).
179. IPP 11(1)(d).
180. IPP 11(1)(g).
181. IPP 11(1)(a), (c), (e), (f), (h) and (i).
182. IPP 12(1)(a). This exception is correlative to IPP 11(1)(c), which simply provides that 'the disclosure is authorised by the individual'.
183. IPP 12(1)(b). For the meaning of the expression 'carrying on business in New Zealand', *see* above at Part II, Ch. 2.3.1.
184. IPP 12(1)(c).
185. IPP 12(1)(d). A 'prescribed binding scheme' is defined in s. 22(3) as a scheme specified by regulations made under s. 213 of the Act.
186. IPP 12(1)(e). A 'prescribed country' is one that is specified by regulations made under s. 214 of the Act.
187. IPP 12(1)(f). For example, where the parties have entered into an agreement to that effect.

circumstances' for it to comply with the requirements of IPP 12(1). IPPs 11(1)(e) and (f) deal with maintenance or enforcement of the law and the conduct of legal proceedings; and the prevention or mitigation of a serious threat to public health or safety, or the life or health of an individual, respectively.

225. The Privacy Commissioner may in particular circumstances authorise an agency (upon application) to 'disclose personal information even if the disclosure of that information would otherwise be in breach of IPP 11 or 12'.[188]

IV. Application of IPP 12 to Agents and Service Providers

226. The Act does not apply to agents or service providers that are merely holding or processing personal information for another agency. Accordingly, the transfer of such information does not amount to a disclosure or use of the information by the agent or service provider for the purposes of IPP 11 or IPP 12.[189] This is the case whether or not the agent or service provider is located outside New Zealand, or holds the information outside New Zealand.[190] Thus, for example, IPP 12 does not apply to cloud services.[191]

V. Prohibition of Onward Transfers of Personal Information Overseas

227. Part 8 of the Act ('Prohibiting onward transfer of personal information received in New Zealand from overseas') deals with the Privacy Commissioner's power to issue transfer prohibition notices. These prohibit the onward transfer of personal information received in New Zealand from overseas.

188. Privacy Act, s. 30(1)(d).
189. Privacy Act, s. 11(2) and (5).
190. Privacy Act, s. 11(4).
191. Ministry of Justice, *Departmental Report, Part One, Privacy Bill* (2019), at para. 145.

Chapter 3. Concepts and Definitions

§1. 'PERSONAL INFORMATION'

I. Definition

228. The concept of 'personal information' lies at the heart of the Privacy Act, since the IPPs set out in section 22 deal with these.[192] The Act defines 'personal information' as 'information about an identifiable individual'. An 'individual' denotes a natural living person.[193]

II. Deceased Persons

229. The expression 'personal information' includes information relating to a death on the official register of deaths,[194] and it can also relate to deceased persons in a sector-specific code of practice made under the Act.[195]

230. While the definition of 'personal information' suggests that deceased persons otherwise do not have privacy rights, this is not necessarily the case. An access request for personal information under IPP 6 ('Access to personal information') may be refused on the ground that 'disclosure of the information would involve the unwarranted disclosure of the affairs … of a deceased individual'.[196] The privacy of deceased persons therefore receives limited protection under IPP 6, but because information about deceased people is generally not 'personal information', it is not protected under the other IPPs.

III. 'Information'

231. The term 'information' is not defined in the Act, which appears to have been deliberate, as to define a word is to limit it. In one freedom of information case,[197] the HC observed that the word 'information' is 'not confined to the written

192. *See* discussion of the concept at Paul Roth 'What is Personal Information?' (2002) 29 NZULR 40; Katrine Evans 'Personal Information in New Zealand: Between a Rock and a Hard Place' (paper presented to Interpreting Privacy Principles: Chaos or Consistency? Symposium, Sydney, 2006), available at: www.privacy.org.nz/news-and-publications/speeches-and-presentations/personal-information-in-new-zealand-between-a-rock-and-a-hard-place/; New Zealand Law Commission, *Review of the Privacy Act 1993* (NZLC IP17, 2010) at paras 3.2–3.31; New Zealand Law Commission, *Review of the Privacy Act 1993* (NZLC R123, 2011) at paras 2.38–2.53; Paul Roth, *Privacy Law and Practice*, Wellington, LexisNexis, 1995–2020, at para. PA7.20.
193. Privacy Act, s. 7(1).
194. Privacy Act, s. 7(1)(b).
195. Privacy Act, s. 32(6). Currently, the only code that contains such an extended scope is the Health Information Privacy Code 2020, rr 11 and 12.
196. Privacy Act, s. 53(b)(ii).
197. *Commissioner of Police v. Ombudsman* [1985] 1 NZLR 578, at p. 586, Jeffries J.

word but embraces any knowledge, however gained or held'. The term 'information' includes information that has not been committed to document form, but is merely held in a person's memory (individual or institutional).[198] Had the legislation been limited to documents, holders of information would be able to evade their obligations through the destruction of documents before they were requested, or else it would have encouraged avoidance of recording certain information in documentary form.

232. The term 'document' is separately defined,[199] and its relevance in this context is directed at the various forms in which information may be made available in response to an access request under IPP 6.[200] The term is defined as including:[201]

- any writing on any material;
- any information recorded or stored by means of any computer or other device, and any material subsequently derived from information so recorded or stored;
- any label, marking, or other writing that identifies or describes anything of which it forms part, or to which it is attached by any means;
- any book, map, plan, graph, or drawing;
- any photograph, film, negative, tape, or any device in which one or more visual images are embodied so as to be capable (with or without the aid of some other equipment) of being reproduced.

IV. Identifiability

233. The individual to whom personal information relates does not have to be identifiable from the information on its own, or to the world at large. It is sufficient that identification can be made on the basis of an extrinsic link leading to the individual's identification, and if only one other person can make that connection. The Tribunal has held that so long as information 'had the capacity to identify (the individual) to some members of the public', it was personal information for the purposes of the Act.[202]

198. *Re Application by L [information stored in person's memory]* [1997] NZCRT 1 (30 Jan. 1997), (1997) 3 HRNZ 716, 719–720; *L v. J* [1999] NZCRT 9, (1999) 5 HRNZ 616 (26 Apr. 1999); *Case Note 37930* [2002] NZPrivCmr 10 (June 2002); *Case Note 210106* [2010] NZPrivCmr 14 (June 2010); *Case Note 211497* [2010] NZPrivCmr 22 (16 Dec. 2010); *Case Note 292270* [2019] NZPrivCmr 6 (11 May 2019).
199. Privacy Act, s. 7(1).
200. Privacy Act, ss 55 and 56.
201. Privacy Act, s. 7(1).
202. *Proceedings Commissioner v. Commissioner of Police* [1999] NZCRT 37 (16 Dec. 1999); [2000] NZAR 277.

V. Wide Ambit of the Concept of 'Personal Information'

234. The meaning of the concept of 'personal information' can be deceptively complex because of its potentially wide ambit. The Act adopts a wide approach to what constitutes 'personal information'. Ultimately what renders information 'personal' (i.e., *about* an identified or an identifiable individual) can depend on the context in which the issue arises. In one frequently cited Tribunal decision on denied access to personal information,[203] the HRRT observed that:

> there is no 'bright line' test which separates that which is obviously personal information about an identifiable individual from that which is not. Much will depend in any given case on the context in which the information is found. There may be particular factors in different settings that compel a conclusion that, although the requesting individual is not named in the information, nonetheless there is a sufficient connection between the information and the requester to justify a conclusion that the information is personal information 'about' the requester.

235. In another case, the HC noted that the issue is to be resolved by 'a fact-based analysis', and that context was 'all important'.[204]

236. By way of illustration, labels and return addresses on envelopes have been found to be 'personal information' about the recipient;[205] likewise, information about informers and complainants in relation to the person being informed upon or complained about;[206] information about one's assailants;[207] a record of people having access to an individual's personal file;[208] and details held by a local authority in relation to property owned by an individual.[209]

203. *CBN v. McKenzie Associates* [2004] NZHRRT 48 (30 Sep. 2004), at para. 41.

204. *Sievwrights v. Apostolakis* HC Wellington CIV-2005-485-527, 17 Dec. 2007, paras 10 and 15; *see also Geary v. New Zealand Psychologists Board* [2012] NZHC 384, [2012] 2 NZLR 414; *Grupen v. Director of Human Rights Proceedings* [2012] NZHC 580, (2012) 9 HRNZ 635 at para. 32; and *Siemer v. Privacy Commissioner* [2013] NZHC 1483 at para. 35.

205. *Case Note 35433* [2003] NZPrivCmr 17 (from 'Community Probation Service, Department of Corrections'); *Case Note 23067* [2003] NZPrivCmr 23 (envelope contained mammogram x-rays); *Case Note 87729* [2006] NZPrivCmr 8 (package containing incontinence pads); *Case Note 203014* [2009] NZPrivCmr 8 (from 'Mental Health Inpatient Unit').

206. *Hadfield v. Police* (1996) 3 HRNZ 115 *Adams v. New Zealand Police* [1997] NZCRT 16 (12 Jun. 1997); *Director of Human Rights Proceedings v. Commissioner of Police* [2007] NZHRRT 22 (6 Nov. 2007).

207. *Proceedings Commissioner v. Commissioner of Police* [2000] NZCRT 18 (10 Jul. 2000).

208. *Case Note 208123* [2010] NZPrivCmr 12 (names of police employees who accessed complainant's file).

209. *Case Note 103185* [2008] NZPrivCmr 8 (1 Aug. 2008); *Case Note 103185* [2008] NZPrivCmr 8; *Case Note 209742* [2010] NZPrivCmr 21.

§2. 'Health Information'

237. 'Health information' is treated differently than 'personal information' under the Privacy Act regime.[210] The term 'health information' is specified in the Health Information Privacy Code 2020 as applying to the following information about an identifiable individual:[211]

- information about the health of that individual, including his or her medical history; or
- information about any disabilities that individual has, or has had; or
- information about any health services or disability services that are being provided, or have been provided, to that individual; or
- information provided by that individual in connection with the donation, by that individual, of any body part or any bodily substance of that individual or derived from the testing or examination of any body part, or any bodily substance of that individual; or
- information about that individual which is collected before or in the course of, and incidental to, the provision of any health service or disability service to that individual.

238. Subclause 4(2) goes on to provide that the code applies only to specific agencies or classes of agency, such as health and disability service providers; agencies involved in the training, registration, and discipline of health professionals; agencies concerned with the provision of health insurance; and other agencies involved in dealing with or handling health information.[212]

§3. Concepts Relating to Processing

239. The comprehensive term 'processing' is not employed in the Privacy Act to denote operations performed in respect of personal information. Instead, the IPPs are structured around specific terms that deal with particular aspects of processing. These are discussed below.

I. Collect

240. The term 'collect' is relevant to the interpretation of IPPs 1–4, which deal with the collection of personal information. The term 'collect' means 'in relation to

210. As noted above at 3.1.2, the ambit of 'personal information' extends to deceased as well living persons for the purposes of Rules 11 and 12 of the Health Information Privacy Code ('Limits on disclosure of health information'), and potentially to other codes of practice made under the Act.
211. Health Information Privacy Code, cl 4(1) ('Application of code').
212. *Ibid.*, cl. 4(2) ('Application of code'), and Sch. 1 to the Code.

personal information … to take any step to seek or obtain the personal information, but does not include receipt of unsolicited information'.[213] The term 'collect' thus implies an active, as opposed to a passive, activity. There had been some doubt under earlier legislation whether or not 'collect' included information obtained through surveillance,[214] but the definition was altered in the Act to make it clear that any attempt to seek or obtain personal information would fall under the concept of 'collect'.

241. While 'collect' excludes the receipt of unsolicited information, unsolicited information is still covered under the Act's other IPPs on the basis that it will be 'held' by an agency. Thus, an agency must protect the information by reasonable security safeguards (IPP 5); individuals enjoy access and correction entitlements in respect of the information (IPPs 6 and 7); the information must be checked for accuracy before it is used (IPP 8); an agency must not retain the information for longer than is required for the purposes for which it may lawfully be used (IPP 9); and the agency must not disclose it unless an exception to IPP 11 or IPP 12 applies. IPP 10 provides that an agency that holds personal information that was 'obtained' in connection with one purpose may not use it for any other purpose unless an exception applies. The term 'obtain' is not defined in the Act, but it is undoubtedly wider than 'collect', as it would include 'unsolicited information'.

A. *Collection of Information That Is Already Held*

242. There is a potential issue as to whether it is possible to 'collect' information that one already (perhaps technically) 'holds'. It is arguable that information that is already 'held' by an agency (IPPs 5, 6, 7, 8, 9, 10, 11, and 12), or new information that is created from information already held by an agency, cannot, by definition, be 'collected' in terms of the Act. This issue has particularly important implications in the employment context, for it apparently renders it permissible (under the Act at least) for employers to collect and read an employee's work emails because they already 'hold' it in their computer system. The same reasoning could apply to files and other information held in an employee's desk, though probably not in relation to the examination of personal items stored in facilities supplied by the employer for that purpose because the employee has a property right (and corresponding expectation of privacy) in relation to such items. This is in contrast to the use of the employer's computers and other items that are associated with the employer's business. It should be noted, however, that an agency's authority to use personal information does not turn on the definition of 'collect'. Whether or not an agency 'collects' an employee's work emails does not answer the question as to how the agency might be allowed to use any personal information contained in them.

213. Privacy Act, s. 7(1).

214. *See*, for example, New Zealand Law Commission, *Review of the Privacy Act 1993: Review of the Law of Privacy Stage 4* (NZLC R123, 2011), at paras 2.77–2.81, 2.85, and R7.

243. The issue whether one can collect information one already holds arose in *Boyle v. Manurewa RSA Incorporated*,[215] where the Tribunal found that there had been no collection of information about a club member (name, address, and club number) where the information was already held. The plaintiff had been suspended for a year for misconduct. The club's secretary wrote to seven associated clubs in the vicinity advising them of the plaintiff's suspension, which was common practice for the clubs. Furthermore, the Tribunal noted that the club held the information of the plaintiff's suspension not because it had 'collected' it, but because the information concerned was the particular outcome of a disciplinary process against the plaintiff that had run its course.

II. Access

244. The Act sets out the ways in which personal information contained in a document may be made available to a requestor in response to an IPP 6 access request.[216] These are by providing the requestor a reasonable opportunity to inspect the document; providing the requestor with a hard or electronic copy; where sound or visual images are involved, by arranging for the requestor to hear or view the sounds or visual images; by providing the requestor with a written transcript of the words recorded or contained in the document, where words are recorded in a manner in which they are capable of being reproduced in the form of sound or in which words are contained in the form of shorthand writing or in codified form; by providing an excerpt or summary of the document's contents; or by giving oral information about the document's contents.

245. Unless there are good reasons for providing the information in another form, the information must be made available in the way preferred by the requestor.[217] An agency may provide information in another form if the efficient administration of the agency would otherwise be impaired; it would be contrary to a legal duty regarding the document; or it would prejudice an interest protected under the Act's grounds for withholding personal information. If the agency does not provide information in the way preferred by the requestor, it must provide its reasons for not doing so. The requestor may request the grounds in support of the reason for not providing the information in a way preferred, unless disclosure of the grounds would prejudice an interest protected under the Act.[218]

215. [2003] NZHRRT 16 (12 Jun. 2003).
216. Privacy Act, s. 56(1).
217. Privacy Act, s. 56(2).
218. Privacy Act, s. 56(3)–(4).

III. Correct

246. IPP 7 deals with an individual's entitlement to seek correct of personal information. The term 'correct' is defined as 'to alter that information by way of correction, deletion, or addition', and the noun 'correction' has a corresponding meaning.[219] IPP 7 does not oblige an agency to correct information, but if it does not, then the requestor is entitled to provide a statement of correction sought but not made by the agency concerned, and requests the agency to attach the statement of correction to the information, so that the statement will always be read with the information.[220]

IV. Use

247. The term 'use' appears in IPP 8 ('Accuracy, etc., of personal information to be checked before use or disclosure'), IPP 9 ('Agency not to keep personal information for longer than necessary'), and it is the subject of IPP 10 ('Limits on use of personal information') of the Act. IPP 10 provides that an agency that holds personal information obtained in connection with one purpose may not use it for any other purpose unless the agency reasonably believes that one of the specified exceptions applies.

248. The Act treats 'use' and 'disclosure' separately, in that 'use' is covered by IPP 10, and 'disclosure' is dealt with by IPPs 11 and 12. The distinction, however, is largely artificial, as disclosure can be viewed as a form of use. The only differences between IPPs 10 and 11 is that IPP 11 contains two additional exceptions to compliance that are not covered under IPP 10 because they would be inapplicable: Principle 11(1)(c) exempts disclosures made to the individual concerned, and Principle 11(1)(i) exempts disclosures that are 'necessary to facilitate the sale or other disposition of a business as a going concern'. Moreover, IPP 10 would be inapplicable to the subject matter of IPP 12, in that the latter deals with disclosures of personal information outside New Zealand.

A. Transfer of Information to an Agent Not a 'Use' of Personal Information

249. Transfer of personal information to an agent is not treated as a 'use' or 'disclosure' if the information is held on behalf of the other agency, for example, for safe custody or processing.[221] In such circumstances, the information is treated as being held by the principal for the purposes of the Act, so long as the agent does not use or disclose the information for its own purposes. It is immaterial whether or not the agent is outside New Zealand or holds the information outside New Zealand.

219. Privacy Act, s. 7(1).
220. Privacy Act, s. 22, IPP 7(3)–(4).
221. Privacy Act, s. 11.

B. Electronic Retrieval of Information and 'Use'

250. There is an issue whether merely consulting information that has been electronically retrieved (or 'browsing') is, without anything more, a 'use' of that information. The leading case on the matter is a British House of Lords decision that dealt with a case arising under the Data Protection Act 1984 (UK).[222] The defendant, a police officer, had used a computer to check the registration numbers of vehicles owned by debtors being investigated by a friend of his, who was a debt collector. Under the Data Protection Act, it was an offence to use personal data for a purpose other than the purpose for which it was held, which in this case, was that of policing. There was no evidence, however, that the police officer concerned actually passed on the information he had retrieved.

251. The trial judge accepted that the offence was committed once the information was retrieved from the computer with the intent of using the information for an unregistered purpose (whether or not it was put to any actual use). The defendant appealed his conviction, and the CA allowed the appeal on the basis that, applying the ordinary meaning of 'use', it was necessary to do something to or with the data. The mere actions of accessing the data, causing it to be displayed on a screen, and reading it, did not amount to 'using' the data in terms of the Data Protection Act. A majority of the House of Lords accepted this approach and dismissed the Crown's appeal. Lord Goff noted that since the term 'use' was not defined in the Act, it had to be given its natural and ordinary meaning, 'to make use of' or 'to employ for a purpose.[223] Accordingly, he held that 'the retrieval is not the use; it is simply a prerequisite of the use'.[224] Similarly, Lord Hoffmann stated: 'Retrieving data from a computer seems to me a use of the computer rather than a use of the data'.[225] He added, however, that the term 'use' is not necessarily limited to positive conduct. He commented:

> There has been no consideration of what might amount to use; for example, whether not taking steps one might otherwise have taken is using the information. For my part, I think it can. A person who refrains from entering a field with a notice saying 'Beware of the Bull' is using the information obtained from the notice.[226]

252. This decision was distinguished by the Tribunal in a New Zealand case on Rule 8 of the Health Information Privacy Code,[227] where the plaintiff complained about a hospital employee's search of the National Health Index (NHI) database

---

222. *R v. Brown* [1996] 1 All ER 545.
223. *Ibid.*, at 548.
224. *Ibid.*, at 549.
225. *Ibid.*, at 560.
226. *Ibid.*, at 561.
227. *C D v. Hawkes Bay District Health Board* [2002] NZHRRT 15 (19 Dec. 2002). Rule 8 is analogous to IPP 8 of the Act.

connected with a hospital visit by the plaintiff. There was no evidence that information extracted from the database was used in the patient's treatment by the hospital, but information from the database was recorded in writing. The plaintiff argued, on the basis of *R v. Brown*, that the information had been used 'simply by writing the information down from the NHI database'.[228] The Privacy Commissioner supported this submission, and commented that if information is retrieved from a database and then written down, then 'the step of writing it down would have been a use of the information for the purpose of recording it'.[229] The defendant, however, submitted that the mere recording of information cannot be regarded as a 'use', which in the circumstances of the case 'carries with it some connection to diagnosis or treatment'. The Tribunal agreed, and stated:

> We are inclined to agree … that in the circumstances of a case such as the present the act of writing down information that has been retrieved from a computer does not take one very far beyond the act of retrieval. But we do not exclude the possibility that in another case the mere fact of writing some information that has been retrieved from a computer might involve a 'use' of that information which brings the obligations of Rule 8 into play.[230]

253. Whether the electronic retrieval of information about an individual constituted a 'use' of personal information was considered by the Privacy Commissioner in a case where the complainant had been interviewed by the New Zealand Employment Service and was asked whether she was receiving counselling.[231] When the complainant queried why this question had been asked, she was told that her file indicated that she had a problem with drug and alcohol abuse. She stated that this was incorrect, and at her request the comment was deleted from her file. The complainant subsequently complained that the agency breached IPP 8 ('Accuracy, etc., of personal information to be checked before use'). This necessarily raised the issue whether her personal information had been 'used'. The Privacy Commissioner considered that:

> 'use', for the purposes of Principle 8, requires something more than this. It implies that in order to show that usage has occurred, the retrieval has to be followed by some act. This had not occurred before the information was deleted.

254. It is arguable, however, that the information in question had in fact been used, as it formed the basis for the interviewer's question. A way of getting around such an objection would be to interpret the term 'use', in IPP 8 in such a way that

228. *Ibid.*, at para. 45.
229. *Ibid.*, at para. 48.
230. *Ibid.*, at para. 49.
231. *Case Note 9257* [1997] NZPrivCmr 4 (1 Jul. 1997).

it does not apply to uses under IPP 8 itself. Since IPP 8 is aimed at the use of personal information without verification, where personal information is disclosed in order to verify its accuracy in compliance with IPP 8, such a 'reflexive' use ought not to be caught by it.

V. Disclose

255. IPPs 8 ('Accuracy, etc., of personal information to be checked before use or disclosure'), IPP 11 ('Limits on disclosure of personal information'), and 12 ('Disclosure of personal information overseas') deal with the 'disclosure' of personal information. As noted above,[232] the Act treats 'use' and 'disclosure' separately, in that 'use' is covered by IPP 10, and 'disclosure' is dealt with in IPPs 11 and 12. The distinction, however, is largely artificial, as disclosure can be viewed as a form of use. The only differences between IPPs 10 and 11 is that IPP 11 contains two additional exceptions to compliance that are not covered under IPP 10 because they would be inapplicable: Principle 11(1)(c) exempts disclosures made to the individual concerned, and Principle 11(1)(i) exempts disclosures that are 'necessary to facilitate the sale or other disposition of a business as a going concern'. Moreover, IPP 10 would be inapplicable to the subject matter of IPP 12, in that the latter deals with disclosures of personal information outside New Zealand.

256. The term 'disclose' is not defined in the Act, but the concept of disclosure has been treated under the Act and case law under it, as discussed below.

A. Transfer of Information to an Agent Not a 'Disclosure'

257. Transfer of information to an agent is not treated as a 'use' or 'disclosure' of personal information if the information is held on behalf of a principal, for example, for safe custody or processing.[233] In such circumstances, the personal information is treated under the Act as being held by the principal, so long as the agent does not use or disclose the information for its own purposes. It is immaterial whether or not the agent is outside New Zealand or holds the information outside New Zealand.

B. Position Where Disclosure Made by a Third Party

258. Where an agency has disclosed personal information, but it is used or disclosed by another to cause harm or loss to an individual, the agency that originally disclosed the information can carry full liability for the disclosure if the complainant chooses not to proceed against the third party. In one case,[234] the police made

232. At Part II, Ch. 3.3.5.
233. Privacy Act, s. 11.
234. *K v. The Police Commissioner* [1999] NZCRT 33 (26 Nov. 1999).

the original disclosure (that the complainant was a disqualified driver) to the complainant's parents, and the mother subsequently disclosed this information to a friend of the complainant, causing her to feel humiliated. The Tribunal did not accept an argument that the harm was caused by the mother, and stated:

> We are simply required to be satisfied that the harm specified resulted from the breach. We think it is immaterial that the disclosure which resulted in the harm alleged was mediated through a third person. In this case, but for the disclosure to the mother, the friend would not have obtained the information at issue.[235]

259. The disclosure by a third party in a subsequent case was similarly sheeted back to the party who made the original disclosure.[236] The defendant in that case was the state accident insurance agency, which had inadvertently disclosed the plaintiff's accident payment entitlements to a third party, who in turn informed the complainant's son, who then informed the complainant's wife. As a result, the plaintiff's wife became outraged after considering the small allowance she had been given by her husband over the years. This decision, like the earlier one noted above, was undoubtedly influenced by the fact that the defendant in each case had 'deep pockets'. Moreover, it would have been awkward to proceed against a friend or relative.

C. 'Disclosure' Where Information Already Disclosed by Someone Else or Already Known

260. The Privacy Commissioner has long adopted the approach that personal information is not 'disclosed' by an agency in terms of the legislation if it has already been disclosed by someone else,[237] and that for there to be a disclosure under IPP 11, 'it is necessary to show that a third party received information of which it was previously unaware'.[238] The Tribunal accepted this approach,[239] and noted, after examining high overseas case authority in various contexts,[240] that 'implicit in the term "disclose" as it appears in IPP 11 is the requirement that the information at issue has not already been disclosed by someone else'.

---

235. *Ibid.*, at 7.
236. *Feather v. Accident Compensation Corporation* [2003] NZHRRT 29 (4 Sep. 2003).
237. *Case No 8649* [1997] NZPrivCmr 3.
238. *Case No 13518* [1999] NZPrivCmr 11; *see also Case Note 51765* [2003] NZPrivCmr 13 (June 2003).
239. *A v. G* [1999] NZCRT 18, (1999) 5 HRNZ 598; *see also J v. Police* [2000] NZCRT 2 (3 Mar. 2000); *K E H v. Chief Executive Department of Work and Income* [2000] NZCRT 40 (19 Dec. 2000); *Williams v. Department of Corrections* [2004] NZHRRT 4 (9 Mar. 2004); *Clearwater v. Accident Compensation Corporation* [2004] NZHRRT 2 (23 Feb. 2004).
240. *Bank of Credit and Commerce International (Overseas) Ltd (in liq) v. Price Waterhouse* [1997] 4 ALL ER 781 (Chancery Division); *A-G v. Associated Newspapers Ltd* [1994] 1 All ER 556, at para. 561; [1994] 2 AC 238, at 255 (House of Lords); *see also* the South Australian Supreme Court decision in *King v. South Australian Psychological Board* [1998] SASC 6621; [1998] EOC 92-929 (Digest).

261. In a subsequent case,[241] however, the Tribunal departed from the weight of previous authority on the point without even considering it. In that case, the Tribunal found that the defendant 'disclosed' personal information to a person who already knew it. The Tribunal explained that:

> the exceptions in principle 11 do not include the circumstance where the information disclosed is already known to the recipient. The focus of principle 11 is on the disclosure by the agency, not on what may or may not already be known by the recipient. It is difficult to see how principle 11 could provide effective protection against the disclosure of personal information if that protection is made dependent on the state of knowledge (or absence of knowledge) on the part of the receiving agency or person, a state of knowledge which may be of uncertain degree and in any event, difficult to establish. It is unlikely that Parliament intended that the operation of principle 11 turn on the subjective state of mind of the recipient of the information.[242]

262. In light of this decision, the Privacy Commissioner altered his position on the meaning of 'disclose',[243] and noted that a 'disclosure' occurs simply whenever information is disclosed, and does not turn on whether or not the recipient already knows the information concerned.

D. Confirmation of Known Facts Can Constitute Disclosure

263. A distinction can be made between mere repetition of known information, and where a subsequent statement amounts to confirmation of a previous disclosure. In a case investigated by the Privacy Commissioner,[244] the police were found to have disclosed personal information about an individual to a social worker. The police contended that the officer concerned simply confirmed matters that the social worker already knew. The social worker's identification of the individual concerned, however, was found to be mere conjecture rather than actual knowledge. It hardened into knowledge on receiving the police officer's confirmation. The Privacy Commissioner commented that 'confirming facts could constitute a disclosure if that confirmation provided information not previously known to the recipient'.

264. In another case, the Tribunal noted that while it is implicit in the concept of 'disclosure' that 'the information at issue has not already been disclosed by someone else', it conceded that 'There may well be circumstances in which confirmation of information constitutes a disclosure because there is fresh information included in the confirmation.'[245]

---

241. *Hammond v. NZCU Baywide* [2015] NZHRRT 6 (2 Mar. 2015).
242. *Ibid.*, at para. 141.
243. *Case Note 276280* [2018] NZPrivCmr 2 (Feb. 2018).
244. *Case Note 20545* [2003] NZPrivCmr 15 (July 2003).
245. *J v. New Zealand Police* [2000] NZCRT 2 (3 Mar. 2000), at 6–7, reiterating its earlier view in *A v. G* [1999] NZCRT 18, (1999) 5 HRNZ 598.

E. Confirmation of Suspicion Can Constitute Disclosure

265. A disclosure can be made not only by directly answering a question concerning the identity of an individual, but also by acknowledging that someone's suspicions about the identity of an individual (in that case, the complainant) was correct.[246] The case concerned the disclosure of a complainant's identity to the third party against whom she had made an animal welfare complaint.

F. Disclosure by Action or Implication

266. A disclosure can be made non-verbally. In one case,[247] the Tribunal found that a police officer disclosed information as to the complainant's identity and address by his actions in conspicuously uplifting a protection order at the Family Court and allowing himself to be followed by television journalists when serving it. The Tribunal commented that:

> the act of disclosing information is not limited to the use of words or language, it includes behaviour which results in information being disclosed. We think this means that the focus, in the determination whether there has been a disclosure, is on the result of a transfer of information and not the means by which that result was achieved. It follows that it will matter not whether a disclosure was intended by the person responsible for the transfer of information

267. In a case investigated by the Privacy Commissioner,[248] a debt collection agency was found to have disclosed information about a woman to other people in her place of work. The agency had been attempting to contact her at her workplace, but when it was unable to speak to her, it left a message with a co-worker asking for the woman to contact it and provided its name and contact number for this purpose. This information was then put on a note and placed on a notice board where other staff members could read it. The agency maintained that it had not disclosed any personal information about the woman: it neither discussed the nature of the call, any financial details, nor any previous history during the conversation with the workmate. However, the Privacy Commissioner considered that 'even disclosing the name of the agency in relation to its dealings with the woman constituted personal information about her. This was on the basis that the name of the agency could easily be associated with debt collection services'. Moreover, the complainant in this case reported that her co-workers had made this association. In the result, the agency accepted that it had disclosed personal information about the complainant, and it was willing to accept the modest settlement proposal put forward by her.

---

246. *Parker v. Ministry of Agriculture and Forestry* [2002] NZHRRT 9 (23 Sep. 2002).
247. *Proceedings Commissioner v. Commissioner of Police* [1999] NZCRT 37 (16 Dec. 1999), [2000] NZAR 277.
248. *Case Note 215508* [2011] NZPrivCmr 5 (20 Jul. 2011).

G. No 'Disclosure' If No Receipt of Disclosure

268. It should be obvious that there will be no 'disclosure' under IPP 11 if no one actually receives it. The corollary of this is that if a disclosure is made, the fact that it has been received may need to be proved. If evidence of receipt of a disclosure is required, this will be impossible where the identity of a witness is unknown.[249] The HC has commented on this point:

> we do not think it would necessarily be a bar to a finding of disclosure merely because the member of the public to whom it was disclosed did not give evidence. There may be situations where someone is considerably humiliated by the release of their previous convictions, to unknown members of the public, and who are shown to suffer humiliation and the necessary matters required by the Privacy Act, irrespective of how it was perceived by the person to whom it was disclosed.[250]

269. In several Privacy Commissioner case notes, it was found that generic words on envelopes or return addresses amounted to a disclosure of the addressee's personal information. This indicates the importance of context in determining whether or not particular information is 'personal'. However, such 'disclosures' will not amount to a breach of IPP 11 if it cannot be shown that anyone actually reads the relevant words, and that the disclosure caused some harm or loss to the addressee. In one case, a return address that included the words 'Community Probation Service, Department of Corrections' was found by implication to constitute a disclosure of personal information about the person to whom the letter was addressed.[251] The Privacy Commissioner, however, did not uphold the IPP 11 complaint because the complainant did not adduce evidence to show that anyone, other than the postal service worker, saw the envelope that was addressed to him. The Commissioner noted that 'There was no evidence ... to suggest that anyone, other than he, had noticed the return address, or drew any inference from it'.

§4. 'AUTHORISATION'

270. The term 'consent' is neither used in the Privacy Act, nor is consent a requirement for processing to be legitimate. Instead, IPP 2 requires that information must be collected from the individual concerned unless an exception to this principle applies; and IPP 3 provides that the agency must take reasonable steps to ensure that the individual is aware of the fact that information is being collected, the purpose for the collection, the intended recipients of the information, whether the collection is legally authorised or required, and the consequences (if any) if the

249. *J v. New Zealand Police* [2000] NZCRT 2 (3 Mar. 2000).
250. *J v. The Commissioner of Police*, Wellington, AP 64/00 (14 Mar. 2001), at para. 23. This appeal upheld the Tribunal's decision in *J v. New Zealand Police* [2000] NZCRT 2 (3 Mar. 2000).
251. *Case Note 35433* [2003] NZPrivCmr 17.

requested information is not provided.[252] Consent to the collection of personal information neither needs to be express and unambiguous, nor is it required to be recorded in any way. At a minimum the individual is normally required to be made aware that personal information is being collected. Consent to the collection of personal information can be implicit; it can be sought as soon as practicable after the collection of information;[253] it can be taken as given where the agency has carried out the required notification on a recent previous occasion in relation to the collection of the same sort of information;[254] or, where an exception is reasonably believed to apply, in which case it may be dispensed with altogether.[255]

271. The closest concept to 'consent' in the Act is that of 'authorisation', which is not defined in the Act, but it has been interpreted in the case law. The term is used in four exceptions to the IPPs: where the individual authorises the collection of personal information from a third party;[256] and where the individual authorises the use[257] or disclosure[258] of personal information for a purpose other than that for which it was collected; and where an individual authorises the disclosure of personal information to a foreign person or entity after being expressly informed that the latter may not be required to protect the information in a way that, overall, provides comparable safeguards to those in the Privacy Act.[259]

272. The concept of authorisation is arguably stronger than that of consent. The term 'consent' is sometimes used in the expressions 'implied consent' and 'informed consent', suggesting that consent need not be either express or informed. The term 'authorise', on its own, more clearly denotes a positive and conscious act by the individual, and that is the way it has been approached in case law under the Act. Thus, in a case where a bank merely informed a couple who were applying to open a joint savings account that it would get the application 'checked', and then went on to carry out a credit check without their knowledge, the Privacy Commissioner found that the bank had not obtained authorisation for the credit check.[260] The Commissioner commented that 'authorisation requires a positive act'.

I. Implied Authorisation

273. In an employment-related case,[261] the Privacy Commissioner did not accept that the sending of a copy of a former employer's reference was implied authorisation to contact him. The application form asked for nominated referees, but the

252. Privacy Act, s. 22, IPP 3(1).
253. Privacy Act, s. 22, IPP 3(2).
254. Privacy Act, s. 22, IPP 3(3).
255. Privacy Act, s. 22, IPP 3(4).
256. Privacy Act, s. 22, IPP 2(2)(c).
257. Privacy Act, s. 22, IPP 10(1)(c).
258. Privacy Act, s. 22, IPP 11(1)(c).
259. Privacy Act, s. 22, IPP 12(1)(c).
260. *Case No 2976* [1996] NZPrivCmr 1 (1 Nov. 1996).
261. *Case No 19740* [2002] NZPrivCmr 5 (1 May 2002).

former employer was not on the list. The applicant did not expect the employer to contact a non-nominated person as a referee. The prospective employer was found to have breached IPP 3 on the basis that there was a departure from the procedure it had advised applicants it would follow in respect of contacting referees. Elsewhere, the Privacy Commissioner noted that a job applicant who supplies a list of referees in a curriculum vitae could be taken to have impliedly authorised contact with the referees concerned, but cautiously advised that 'it is still safer to check with the applicant beforehand'.[262] In a case where a job applicant had authorised the employer to carry out a pre-employment police background check,[263] the employer was found to have breached IPP 2 when it carried out the check over a year later and dismissed the employee in the course of an employment dispute. The Commissioner considered that the employee's authorisation for the police check was no longer valid because of the passage of time. Moreover, under police guidelines, vetting requests were required to be made within three months of the date the applicant consents to the background check. In another case involving an employment dispute,[264] a co-worker of the complainant made unauthorised use of an earlier authorisation given by the complainant in connection with receiving advice from the employer law centre. The authorisation was limited to obtaining her personal information from a social service agency so that she could obtain budgetary advice from the law centre. The employee, however, had neither known about nor authorised the later uses of her authorisation to obtain her personal information, which was instead sought in connection with employment issues.

274. The concept of implied authorisation appears to be more accepted in cases arising in the medical context. In *L v. J*,[265] the plaintiff complained that a general practitioner breached Rule 11 of the Health Information Privacy Code by disclosing information in the plaintiff's medical notes, without her specific consent, to a psychiatrist to whom the plaintiff had been referred. The Tribunal, however, found that the general practitioner had implied consent to disclose the information as the plaintiff had provided the psychiatrist with the name of her general practitioner, and 'There must have been the clear implication that by asking for this information the psychiatrist would access her medical file, or those parts of it which were relevant to his treatment of her'.[266] In *L v. L*,[267] another complaint concerning the disclosure of health information in breach of Rule 11, the Tribunal found that there was implied authorisation to disclose information to the patient's husband after a surgical procedure. This was on the basis of the previous conduct of the parties on a number of occasions and no specific instruction on this occasion that the complainant's husband was not to be contacted.

262. Office of the Privacy Commissioner, 'Hints on job references', *Private Word*, No 10, Oct. 1996, at 2.
263. *Case Note 312002* [2021] NZPrivCmr 2 (16 Mar. 2021).
264. *Cook v. Manawatu Community Law Centre* [2021] NZHRRT 10 (15 Feb. 2021).
265. [1999] NZCRT 9 (26 Apr. 1999), (1999) 5 HRNZ 616.
266. *Ibid.*, at 623.
267. [2001] NZCRT 15 (26 Jul. 2001), affirmed on appeal in affirmed on appeal in *L v. L*, High Court, Auckland, AP95-SW01 (31 May 2002).

275. In a case where a dissatisfied client complained to the Privacy Commissioner about a law firm's disclosure of information to the Law Society, the Commissioner considered that the client had impliedly authorised the disclosure.[268] The client had lodged a complaint against the firm with the Law Society, and to defend itself, the firm provided the Law Society with a copy of a file note that the woman had provided to the firm containing her account of a telephone conversation relating to a legal dispute. The file note illustrated the complex nature of the dispute and the woman's attitude to it. The client complained that the firm's disclosure of the file note breached her privacy. The Commissioner considered that while 'Normally, a positive act of authorisation is required', here there had been an implied authorisation of the disclosure. By lodging a complaint against the firm with the Law Society, the woman accepted that the firm would have to defend itself. In order to do so, it would have to provide relevant information to Law Society to determine the dispute.

268. *Case Note 94042* [2007] NZPrivCmr 5 (Mar. 2007).

Part III. General Principles

Chapter 1. Data Quality Principles

§1. Lawfulness, Fairness, and Transparency

I. Lawfulness

276. IPPs 1 ('Purpose of collection of personal information') and 4 ('Manner of collection of personal information') are the main regulators of the lawful collection of personal information in the Privacy Act. IPP 1(1)(a) provides that an agency must not collect personal information unless 'the information is collected for a lawful purpose', and IPP 4(a) requires than an agency may collect personal information only 'by a lawful means'.

II. Fairness

277. The main provision relating to the fairness of processing in the Act is IPP 4(b) ('Manner of collection of personal information'), which provides that an agency may only collect personal information:

> (b) by a means that, in the circumstances of the case (particularly in circumstances where personal information is being collected from children or young persons), --
> (i) is fair; and
> (ii) does not intrude to an unreasonable extent upon the personal affairs of the individual concerned.

278. Fairness is also relevant to the application of an exception to IPPs 10 ('Limits on use of personal information') and 11 ('Limits on disclosure of personal information'), which provide that an agency may use or disclose personal information if the agency reasonably believes that 'the source of the information is a publicly available publication and that, in the circumstances of the case, it would not be unfair or unreasonable'.[269]

---

269. Privacy Act, s. 22, IPPs 10(1)(d) and 11(1)(d). A 'publicly available publication' is defined in s. 7(1) of the Act as 'a publication (including a register, list, or roll of data) in printed or electronic form that is, or will be, generally available to members of the public free of charge or on payment of a fee'.

III. Transparency

279. One aspect of fairness is transparency,[270] which involves agencies informing individuals concerning the purpose of the processing of their personal information, the identity of the agencies involved, and other relevant information to ensure fairness. The Act provides for the basic requirements of transparency in IPP 3 ('Collection of information from subject'). There are also a number of other provisions scattered throughout the Act that relate to transparency. These concern decisions and actions taken by agencies under the Act.[271]

§2. Purpose Limitation

I. The Concept of 'Purpose' in the Act

280. IPP 1 ('Purpose of collection of personal information') establishes the purpose limitation principle, which runs as a thread through several of the other IPPs in the Act. This is a key principle, as the purpose of collecting personal information will determine in what circumstances it may be used or disclosed. IPP 1 provides that the purpose for the collection of personal information must be lawful; the collection must be connected with a function or activity of the agency; and the collection must be necessary for that purpose.

281. The concept of 'purpose' is key for governing the use and disclosure of personal information in IPP 10 ('Limits on use of personal information') and IPP 11 ('Limits on disclosure of personal information'). IPP 10 provides that personal information obtained for one purpose may not be used for any other purpose unless the agency reasonably believes than one of the specified exceptions applies. IPP 11 provides that personal information must not be disclosed unless the agency reasonably believes that disclosure is one of the purposes for its collection, or another exception applies.[272] Other IPPs refer back to the purpose for the collection of personal information as well. IPP 2 ('Source of personal information') provides that personal information need not be collected from the individual concerned if that would prejudice the purposes of the collection.[273] IPP 3 ('Collection of information from subject') requires that the individual concerned must be notified of the purpose for the collection of the information,[274] unless an exception applies.[275] IPP 7 ('Correction of personal information') requires that an agency that holds personal information must take reasonable steps to ensure that the information is accurate, up-to-date, complete, and not misleading, having regard to the purposes for which

270. OECD Guidelines, para. 7.
271. For discussion of transparency, *see* further at Part III, Ch. 1.
272. Privacy Act, s. 22, IPP 11(1)(a).
273. Privacy Act, s. 22, IPP 2(b).
274. Privacy Act, s. 22, IPP 3(1)(b).
275. In particular in this context, the exception at IPP 3(1)(4)(c), 'that compliance would prejudice the purposes of the collection'.

the information may lawfully be used.[276] IPP 9 ('Agency not to keep personal information for longer than necessary') requires agencies not to keep personal information 'for longer than is required for the purposes for which the information may lawfully be used.'

282. The concept of 'purpose' in the Act is something that is implicitly 'specific'. The Act, however, contains no requirement for recording or other means of definitively 'fixing' purpose, though doing so would be wise in case an issue arises concerning purpose.

II. Secondary Purposes

283. IPP 10(1)(a) provides that an agency may not use personal information for a purpose other than the one for which it was obtained unless it reasonably believes that it is 'directly related' to the purpose for which it was obtained. IPP11(1)(a) similarly provides that an agency must not disclose personal information unless the agency reasonably believes that disclosure of one of the purposes or is 'directly related' to the purposes for which it was obtained. The issue of what constitutes a permissible secondary purpose has been considered in many Privacy Commissioner case notes and Tribunal cases. The issue always falls to be determined on a case-by-case basis, and no rules or tests of general application have emerged.

III. Other Exceptions to the Purpose Limitation Principle

284. Exceptions to the Act's purpose limitation principle in relation to collection, use, and disclosure may be invoked where the agency concerned reasonably believes that: the information is to be used in a form in which the individual is not identified, or is to be used for statistical or research purposes and will not be published in a form that could reasonably identify the individual;[277] the individual has authorised the collection, use, or disclosure of the information;[278] the source of the information is a publicly available information, and in the case of use or disclosure, it would not be unfair or unreasonable to use or disclose it in the circumstances;[279] disclosure is to facilitate the sale or other disposition of a business as a going concern;[280] collection, use, or disclosure is necessary for the protection of various public interests (avoiding prejudice to maintenance of the law, enforcement of a law imposing a pecuniary penalty, protection of public revenue, the conduct of legal proceedings);[281] collection, use, or disclosure is necessary to prevent or lessen threats to public health, public safety, or the life or health of an individual;[282] use or

276. Privacy Act, s. 22, IPP 7(2).
277. Privacy Act, s. 22, IPP 2(2)(g), IPP 3(4)(e), IPP 10(1)(b) and IPP 11(1)(h).
278. Privacy Act, s. 22, IPP 2(2)(c), IPP 10(1)(c) and IPP 11(1)(c).
279. Privacy Act, s. 22, IPP 2(d), IPP 10(1)(d) and IPP 11(1)(d).
280. Privacy Act, s. 22, IPP 11(1)(h)(i).
281. Privacy Act, s. 22, IPP 2(2)(e), IPP 3(4)(b), IPP 10(1)(e) and IPP 11(1)(e).
282. Privacy Act, s. 22, IPP 2(2)(e)(v), IPP 10(1)(f) and IPP 11(1)(f).

disclosure is necessary for enabling an intelligence and security agency to perform any of its functions;[283] collection would not prejudice the individual's interests;[284] or disclosure is to the individual concerned.[285]

§3. Data Minimisation

I. IPP 1 Overview

285. IPP 1 ('Purpose of collection of personal information') deals with the data minimisation principle, and incorporates the principle of proportionality. IPP1(1) provides that an agency (a) must not collect personal information unless it is collected for a lawful purpose connected with a function or activity of the agency, and (b) the collection of the information is necessary for that purpose. IPP 1(2) ensures further data minimisation by providing that if the lawful purpose does not require the collection of an individual's identifying information, then the agency may not require it. IPP 1 neither contains any exceptions, nor does it provide for individuals to be able to contract out of it.[286] However, liability under the Privacy Act will still depend on the causation of some harm or loss in terms of the Act,[287] except in the case where a compliance notice is sought.[288]

286. Relevancy of personal information is provided for by the requirement that the information that is collected must be collected for a 'purpose connected with a function or activity of the agency'. Proportionality for the collection of personal information is provided for by the requirement that the information collected must not be excessive in relation to the purposes for its collection: it must be 'necessary' for the purpose (and any subsequent use or disclosure must be 'directly related'),[289] and the individual's identifying information must not be collected if the purpose for its collection does not require it.

II. The Standard of 'Necessity' in IPP 1

287. Although the standard of non-excessiveness of information collected is expressed in the Privacy Act in terms of a standard of 'necessity', in practice the limitation is not interpreted in a literally strict manner. It nevertheless operates to ensure that personal information that is collected or otherwise processed is not 'excessive'. In *Lehmann v. Canwest Radioworks Ltd*,[290] the Tribunal found that the term 'necessary' carried the sense of 'reasonably necessary'. This was on the basis

283. Privacy Act, s. 22, IPP 10(2), 11(1)(g).
284. Privacy Act, s. 22, IPP 2(2)(a), IPP 3(4)(a).
285. Privacy Act, s. 22, IPP 11(1)(b).
286. *Case 298263* [2019] NZPrivCmr 8 (14 Aug. 2019).
287. Privacy Act, s. 69(2).
288. Privacy Act, Part 6, subpart 2.
289. Privacy Act, s. 22, IPP 10(1)(a) and IPP 11(1)(a).
290. *Lehmann v. Canwest Radioworks Ltd* [2006] NZHRRT 35 (26 Sep. 2006).

that IPP 1 was 'intended to set a standard that is workable and achievable, having regard to the circumstances of each case.'[291] The *Lehmann* case concerned repeated 'missing person' radio broadcasts to locate the plaintiff, who owed a debt to the radio station. The Tribunal found that the broadcasts were not, strictly speaking, 'necessary' for locating the plaintiff, but from a practical point of view it was a reasonable way of locating him in the circumstances. In the subsequent decision in *Tan v. New Zealand Police*,[292] however, the Tribunal noted that a number of the IPPs draw a distinction between an agency's belief, which must be based on 'reasonable grounds', and the reasonable belief in the 'necessity' for non-compliance with the relevant IPP. The Tribunal commented:

> Because 'reasonableness' and 'necessity' are uniformly contrasted throughout the information privacy principles the terms cannot be conflated. This points to a conclusion that 'necessity' has a higher threshold than 'reasonableness'.[293]

288. The Tribunal, however, did not refer at all to its treatment of the concept of 'necessary' in its earlier *Lehmann* decision, or other decisions.

289. There are many Privacy Commissioner case notes where the amount or type of personal information has been investigated by the Commissioner. Normally, the agency collecting the information is given the benefit of the doubt: for example, where collection of personal information involved a personality test administered to a job applicant;[294] surreptitious tape-recording of an employee interview concerning missing stock;[295] the use of biometric finger-scanning technology for an agency's timekeeping and payroll system;[296] employer bag and vehicle inspections against a background of specific security concerns;[297] employer surveillance of a locker room after reported thefts;[298] and the videotaping of a protest against a local property developer which reasonably feared for the security of its property.[299] The Tribunal has found collections of personal information to be 'necessary' in cases where an employer inquired into the background and habits of an employee accused of sexual harassment;[300] and where an insurance company collected information relating to previous convictions from applicants for insurance cover.[301]

---

291. *Ibid.*, para. 50.
292. *Tan v. New Zealand Police* [2016] NZHRRT 32 (18 Oct. 2016).
293. *Ibid.*, at para. 74.3.
294. *Case Note 2418* [1999] NZPrivCmr 6.
295. *Case Note 16479* [2001] NZPrivCmr 6.
296. *Case Note 33623* [2003] NZPrivCmr 5.
297. *Case Note 38463* [2002] NZPrivCmr 11.
298. *Case Note 32277* [2003] NZPrivCmr 25.
299. *Case Note 71808* [2006] NZPrivCmr 14.
300. *Clydesdale v. Christchurch Polytechnic* [2001] NZCRT 8 (19 Apr. 2001).
301. *Cassidy v. NZI Insurance*, [2000] NZCRT 14 (30 Jun. 2000).

§4. ACCURACY

I. IPP 8: Obligation to Check Personal Information Before Use or Disclosure

290. IPP 8 ('Accuracy, etc., of personal information to be checked before use or disclosure') requires an agency that proposes to use or disclose personal information to take reasonable steps in the circumstances to ensure that the information is 'accurate, up-to-date, complete, relevant, and not misleading'.[302]

291. The successful cases tend to be those where the particular circumstances call for personal information to be accurate. In a case involving health information under the Health Information Privacy Code,[303] the complainant's attendant care and home help was cancelled by a public health insurance agency on the basis of inaccurate information contained in an assessor's report. The Privacy Commissioner considered that in the circumstances, the complainant ought to have been given an opportunity to respond given the seriousness of the decision and need for the assessor's opinion to be verified. In a case involving a credit reporting agency that mistakenly ascribed debts to the complainant, causing him difficulties in purchasing a house,[304] the Commissioner considered that while errors do occur, the importance of credit information was such that the agency ought to have carried out basic checks that the correct information was loaded into the database. This was particularly required in this case because the individual concerned had a common name. The Tribunal has commented that 'The language of principle 8 makes it clear that the more serious the potential consequences of using the personal information held by the agency, the greater the degree of care which must be exercised *before* the information is used.'[305]

292. IPP 9, which requires agencies not to keep personal information for longer than necessary, is relevant to the obligation in IPP 8 in that the longer data are kept, the more likely they will become out of date, incomplete, or misleading.

II. Accuracy of Fact of Received Content Versus Accuracy of Content

293. The Tribunal has drawn a distinction between the accuracy of reporting the fact that second-hand information has been received, versus the accuracy of its

302. IPP 8 draws on para. 8 of the *OECD Guidelines*, the data quality principle. As in the *Guidelines*, IPP 8 of the Act links data quality to the purposes for which personal information is proposed to be used.
303. *Case Note 17749* [1999] NZPrivCmr 13.
304. *Case Note 13039* [2001] NZPrivCmr 3. *See also Case Note 312145* [2021] NZPrivCmr 1 (3 Feb. 2021), which dealt with a situation of mistaken identity by a debt management company. In *Taylor v. Orcon Ltd* [2015] NZHRRT 15 (14 May 2015), the defendant telecommunications company breached IPP 8 by mistakenly claiming a debt was owed to it, and instructed a debt collection agency to recover it, which had a damaging effect on the plaintiff's credit rating.
305. *Taylor v. Orcon Ltd* [2015] NZHRRT 15 (14 May 2015), at para. 46.

content. Such a distinction is analogous to the treatment of hearsay, which distinguishes between evidence that a statement was made, which amounts to original evidence and so is admissible, versus the introduction of a statement made to a witness as proof of the truth of its contents, which is inadmissible. In *L v. J*,[306] the defendant, a general medical practitioner, had received unsolicited information from a relative of the plaintiff that there was a history of psychiatric difficulties in the plaintiff's family. This information was included in the plaintiff's medical file, which in due course was disclosed to others who were treating the plaintiff. The plaintiff claimed that the defendant breached Rule 8 of the Health Information Privacy Code (analogous to IPP 8) on the basis that the defendant had failed to verify the accuracy of this information before disclosing it to others. The Tribunal, however, found that Rule 8 had not been breached, as the information disclosed by the defendant was accurate. The Tribunal noted that the issue was not whether or not the plaintiff disagreed with his relative about the extent of the family history of psychiatric illness, but whether the information provided to others by the defendant was accurate. Since the defendant disclosed that the family history information had been provided by the relative, Rule 8 had not been breached. The fact that the relative had provided the information was accurate, whether or not the actual content of that information was accurate.

III. Accuracy of Fact Versus Accuracy of Opinion

294. The Tribunal has drawn a distinction between the accuracy of fact, versus opinion. In a case investigated by the Privacy Commissioner,[307] the complainant claimed that when undergoing a police check in connection with a job application, the police did not properly check his information. The complainant had authorised the police to release information about him to his potential employer, and the police returned the man's application to his potential employer with an indication that he was not recommended to have unsupervised access to children or other vulnerable people. The complainant complained that the police were using inaccurate or misleading information about him when he had been acquitted twice on serious violence-related charges. The Privacy Commissioner, however, formed the view that police had taken reasonable steps to check the man's information before using it. Accordingly, IPP 8 had not been breached. The Commissioner considered that the complaint was really about the police's opinion, and he commented that 'Whether an opinion is justified is not something we can consider under principle 8.' The Commissioner noted that the complainant had agreed to the police vetting process, which included the police providing their view about him to his prospective employer. Even if an individual does not have convictions on his criminal record, the police can still find that an individual's record indicates behaviour of a violent or sexual nature, leading the police to form the opinion that the individual should not have unsupervised access to vulnerable people. The Commissioner remarked

306. [1999] NZCRT 9 (26 Apr. 1999), (1999) 5 HRNZ 616.
307. *Case Note 225627* [2012] NZPrivCmr 2 (June 2012).

that 'Under principle 8, we may only look at the use of the information and its accuracy. We are not able to examine the reasons for arriving at an opinion based on that information'.

IV. IPP 7 and Accuracy

295. IPP 7 ('Correction of personal information') relates to maintaining the accuracy of personal information in two ways. First, IPP 7, together with IPP 6 ('access to personal information'), establish an accountability mechanism whereby individuals can seek access to their personal information, and then request correction of it if they find that it is inaccurate, out of date, incomplete, or misleading.[308] Second, IPP 7(2) requires that agencies 'must, on request or on its own initiative, take such steps (if any) that are reasonable in the circumstances to ensure that, having regard to the purposes for which the information may lawfully be used, the information is accurate, up-to-date, complete, and not misleading'.

296. If an agency is not willing to correct personal information, the data subject may request that a statement of correction sought but not made be attached to the information, so that it will always be read together with the information.[309] The agency will be required to 'take such steps (if any) as are reasonable in the circumstances' to comply with such a request. If an agency corrects personal information or attaches a statement of correction to it, the agency 'must, so far as is reasonably practicable, inform every other person to whom the agency has disclosed the information'.[310] This obligation, however, neither extends to verifying that the other agency has taken note of that correction, nor is there any obligation to pass on the correction further to other agencies.[311]

§5. Storage Limitation

I. Retention of Personal Information

297. IPP 9 of the Privacy Act ('Agency not to keep personal information for longer than necessary') provides that 'An agency that holds personal information must not keep that information for longer than is required for the purposes for which the information may lawfully be used.' IPP 9 of the Act therefore comes into play when the purposes for the use of personal information are 'spent', but it does not actually require the erasure or destruction of information. Given that information may be used or disclosed for the purpose for which it was obtained or for a 'directly related' purpose,[312] it would ordinarily be difficult to predict in advance when its

308. On the right of rectification, *see* further at Part IV, Ch. 3.
309. Privacy Act, s. 22, IPP 7(3).
310. Privacy Act, s. 22, IPP 7(4).
311. *Case Note 7327* [2002] NZPrivCmr 7.
312. Privacy Act, s. 22, IPP 10(1)(a) (use) and IPP 11(1)(a) (disclosure).

lawful purposes are spent. Moreover, the use of information for archival, historical or statistical purposes could run indefinitely.

298. There are not many cases that deal with IPP 9, and the majority are unsuccessful. Most cases have arisen in the employment sphere. It is acceptable to retain information if it may be relevant to any future legal action that could be brought by an employee or the tax authorities. In one case investigated by the Privacy Commissioner, for example, a former employee who settled an employment dispute with his employer complained that the employer continued to hold his file that contained damaging allegations against him.[313] The Commissioner found that this did not breach IPP 9, as it was the employer's practice to retain such files for five years in case an employee decided to take further legal action. Another case indicated that information about an existing employee can be retained if it relates to the employee's suitability, even if the information was relevant to a past suspension and the employee was reinstated with a promise to remove the information from the employee's file (but not to destroy it).[314] IPP 9 was successfully invoked, however, in a case where an unsuccessful job applicant for a position in a government department complained that another company used for pre-employment screening retained his personal information.[315] The Commissioner found that the company was in breach of IPP 9. The form that it used to collect information about potential employees stated that all of the information collected would be retained by it indefinitely, and would form part of its own database for the purpose of determining that person's suitability for any future position for which they might apply. The Commissioner commented that 'principle 9 is incompatible with indefinite retention.' The police, however, 'have an ongoing lawful purpose for retaining the information on their database' to support their work of detecting, preventing, investigating, and prosecuting crime.[316] Accordingly, they may retain information indefinitely, though they are still subject to other IPPs, such as the need to check the accuracy of personal information before using it, and to provide for access and correction requests.

299. Under section 30(1)(b) of the Act, an agency can apply to the Privacy Commissioner for authorisation to 'keep personal information even if the keeping of that information would otherwise be in breach of IPP 9'. The Commissioner may only grant such an authorisation if satisfied of a number of matters in the specific circumstances of the case.

II. Specific Exemptions Concerning Retained Information

300. IPPs 10 and 11 on use and disclosure contain identical exemptions that permit the use or disclosure of personal information where the information:

313. *Case Note 5532* [1996] NZPrivCmr 3.
314. *Case Note 13066* [1998] NZPrivCmr 10.
315. *Case Note 218236* [2011] NZPrivCmr 4.
316. *Case Note 204195* [2009] NZPrivCmr 5 (Mar. 2009); *see also E F G v. Commissioner of Police* [2006] NZHRRT 48 (21 Dec. 2006), which also dealt with the retention of personal information on the national police database.

(i) is to be used in a form in which the individual concerned is not identified; or
(ii) is to be used for statistical or research purposes and will not be published in a form that could reasonably be expected to identify the individual concerned.[317]

301. IPP 9, like most of the other IPPs, is subject to other New Zealand laws where an action is authorised or required.[318] There are a number of statutes that are relevant to the retention of personal information. For example, the Public Records Act 2005 requires all government organisations to create and maintain full and accurate records of their affairs in accordance with normal, prudent business practice (including records of matters contracted out to independent contractors), and these records must be accessible over time; government organisations must not dispose of public records without the authority of the Chief Archivist.[319] The Chief Archivist is empowered under the Act to issue mandatory record-keeping standards, which include standards for appraising records for disposal.[320] Information that has been collected, analysed or archived under the Statistics Act 1975 may also be retained. Particular rules govern the retention of health information. The Health (Retention of Health Information) Regulations 1996 require health records to be retained by all health agencies for a minimum of ten years. The Medicines Regulations 1984 require records on a Sale of Medicines register to be kept for at least three years.[321] Information retention rules also apply to certain tax records and employment records.[322]

§6. Integrity and Confidentiality

I. IPP 5

302. The security of personal information is dealt with under IPP 5 ('Storage and security of personal information'). It provides that an agency that holds personal information must ensure that the information is protected by reasonable security in the circumstances to safeguard it against loss and unauthorised access, use, modification, disclosure, and other misuse.

303. IPP 5 is binding on both agencies and agents or contractors who process the agency's data. IPP 5(b) provides that where it is necessary that the information be given to a person in connection with the provision of a service to the agency 'everything reasonably within the power of the agency' must be done 'to prevent unauthorised use or unauthorised disclosure of the information'.[323] In one case,[324]

317. Privacy Act, s. 22, IPPs 10(1)(b) and 11(1)(h).
318. Privacy Act, s. 24(2).
319. Public Records Act 2005, s. 18.
320. Public Records Act 2005, s. 27(1)(a)(ii).
321. Medicines Regulations 1984, cl. 58(1).
322. *See*, for example, s. 130(2) of the Employment Relations Act 2000.
323. Privacy Act, s. 22, IPP 5(b).
324. *Case No 2663* [1998] NZPrivCmr 6 (April 1998).

for example, IPP 5(b) was found to have been breached by a debt collecting agency that used process servers to recover debts. Moreover, the Act elsewhere provides that both the agency and the processor are legally liable in cases of breaches of the Act by the processor as an agent of the agency, unless the act is done or omitted without the agency's express or implied authority.[325] This reflects the ordinary New Zealand law on agency.

304. The standard of reasonableness 'in the circumstances' for the taking of security safeguards is consistent with the proportionality principle set out in Principle 6 ('Security measures') of the OECD *Recommendation on Digital Security Risk Management for Economic and Social Prosperity*,[326] which provides that 'Security measures should be appropriate to and commensurate with the risk'. Particularly sensitive or private information, such as bank information,[327] information about legal bills,[328] and mental health information,[329] is required to be protected by stringent security safeguards. The onus of proving that the security safeguards in question are or were reasonable in the circumstances lies on the defendant.[330]

II. Accidental Breaches of Security Where Safeguards Are Adequate

305. IPP 5 is not necessarily breached in case of a one-off human error or accident. IPP 5 is directed to the *quality* of the particular security measures in place, not to whether a breach of these measures has occurred (though of course the occurrence of breaches may reflect on the quality of the security measures taken by an agency). Security measures do not have to be absolutely foolproof, so long as they are 'reasonable in the circumstances'. Thus, there is no absolute liability for a mistake and the like where the security safeguards are reasonable in the circumstances.[331] The Privacy Commissioner has noted that:

> Principle 5 is not primarily concerned with individual instances of unauthorised access. Rather it focuses upon the overall systems in place to prevent such occurrences and whether these are reasonable in the circumstances. This is

325. Privacy Act, s. 211(1)(b) ('Liability of employers, principals, and agencies').
326. OECD (2015), *Digital Security Risk Management for Economic and Social Prosperity: OECD Recommendation and Companion Document*, OECD Publishing, Paris, s. 1. Principles.
327. *Case Note 2448* [1998] NZPrivCmr 2 (Jan. 1998).
328. *Case Note 13518* [1999] NZPrivCmr 11 (Aug. 1999).
329. *Case Note 203014* [2009] NZPrivCmr 8 (Mar. 2009).
330. *W v. Director-General of Social Welfare* [1998] NZCRT 11 and 12 (11 Jun. 1998 and 21 Aug. 1998); *K v. Police Commissioner* [1999] NZCRT 33 (26 Nov. 1999); and *Proceedings Commissioner v. Commissioner of Police* [1999] NZCRT 37 (16 Dec. 1999), [2000] NZAR 277.
331. *See*, for example, *Case Note 14982* [1998] NZPrivCmr 15 (October 1998); *Case Note 26280* [2002] NZPrivCmr 2 (Jan. 2002); *Case Note 26781* [2003] NZPrivCmr 21 (Sept. 2003); *Case Note 28351* [2003] NZPrivCmr 22 (Sept. 2003); *Case Note 100962* [2008] NZPrivCmr 5 (Aug. 2008); and *Case Note 83994* [2008] NZPrivCmr 6 (Aug. 2008).

because no system can be foolproof. Agencies can put in place significant safeguards but one-off incidents can and do still occur, whether due to human error or deliberate intent.[332]

306. For example, in a case where a piece of tax department correspondence was incorrectly addressed and delivered to the complainant's neighbours, who opened it, the Privacy Commissioner considered that the sending agency had not failed to take reasonable steps to protect the information.[333] As the agency had policies and training in place to impress upon staff the importance of care in handling information, the Commissioner considered that 'one mistake by an employee did not necessarily mean the Department's security measures were inadequate'. Similarly, in another case,[334] the Commissioner found that there had been no breach of IPP 5 where a life assurance company developed a 'sample plan' for marketing purposes that was based on an actual financial plan. The individuals whose personal information formed the basis for the sample plan were able to be identified from it, and they lodged a complaint with the Privacy Commissioner. The Commissioner, however, formed the view that although there had been a breach of IPP 11 ('Limits on disclosure of personal information'), IPP 5 had not been breached, as IPP 5 'does not require that safeguards are failsafe but that they are "reasonable" in the circumstances'. In the circumstances, they were found to be reasonable, and there was merely a one-off error of judgment.[335] Such errors did not fall under IPP 5 unless there was some form of systemic failure in relation to security safeguards.[336] In such cases, when considering whether security safeguards are reasonable the Commissioner takes into account such matters as the steps or policies in place to guard against a breach of IPP 5; whether those steps and or policies have been followed; the training provided to staff; and the sensitivity of the information.[337]

III. The Significance of Privacy Policies and Training

307. While agencies that have privacy policies and training are well on the road to compliance with IPP 5, this is not necessarily sufficient. In a case where an agency had privacy procedures that were not followed,[338] the Privacy Commissioner commented:

> I considered that Principle 5 requires more than the existence of a procedure and a training programme, because they do not guarantee the procedure will

332. *Case Note 202115* [2009] NZPrivCmr 18 (Oct. 2009).
333. *Case Note 14982* [1998] NZPrivCmr 15 (Oct. 1998).
334. *Case Note 26280* [2002] NZPrivCmr 2 (Jan. 2002).
335. *See also Case Note 83994* [2008] NZPrivCmr 6 (Aug. 2008), which involved a breach of IPP 11, but not IPP 5, due to accidental misfiling of a client's sensitive documents by a law firm.
336. *See Gallagher v. Dispute Resolution Services Limited* [2009] NZHRRT 7 (23 Apr. 2009) where the Tribunal found that IPP 5 had been breached on the basis that the agency was unable to explain what processes had been put in place to prevent a letter being misaddressed.
337. *Ibid.*
338. *Case Note 10668* [1997] NZPrivCmr 12.

be followed. To implement a procedure effectively, some steps need to be taken to ensure it is followed. Steps might include retraining on procedures following a particular problem and giving regular training and refresher courses. It might be appropriate to include a disciplinary provision so staff know there will be consequences for failing to follow the procedure. This is particularly important where a procedure has been developed to ensure that customers' needs are met in an area where there is a potential for them to suffer harm.

308. In *W v. Director-General of Social Welfare*,[339] the plaintiff claimed that the defendant agency breached IPP 5 by failing to ensure that personal information about her was protected from unauthorised disclosure to a third person. The Tribunal accepted the Privacy Commissioner's submission that the issue would turn on the policies and procedures that were in place to assist staff to decide when a person was acting as the agent of another person, and so when it was appropriate to disclose information about a social welfare benefit to the other person. The issue therefore focused on what security safeguards it was reasonable to have in place to ensure that such personal information was not disclosed. The Tribunal phrased this question in the alternative as 'was this a mistake which was preventable?'[340] In the Tribunal's subsequent decision in this matter, it amplified this by stating that the correct approach to determining whether there has been compliance with IPP 5 'is to first define the problem and work back to determine whether there were sufficient security safeguards which in the circumstances it was reasonable for the agency to take to address or account for that problem'.[341] The Tribunal accepted that even where safeguards are reasonable in the circumstances, mistakes may occur. Nevertheless, when a defendant wishes to give evidence of its security safeguards in a case such as this, those measures should be relevant to the matter about which there was complaint. Something more than mere evidence of training was therefore required. The Tribunal considered that the issue of unauthorised disclosure was not adequately addressed by the defendant in its training or manual. What was reasonable in the circumstances was a training programme for all front-line staff that included specific training on what information could be disclosed to whom, and what the consequences would be for failure to observe internal protocols on the issue. The Tribunal found that the defendant did not meet this standard and so breached IPP 5.

339. [1998] NZCRT 11 and 12 (11 Jun. and 21 Aug. 1998). The latter decision was reported at (1998) 5 HRNZ 580.
340. [1998] NZCRT 11 (11 Jun. 1998), at 4.
341. [1998] NZCRT 12 (21 Aug. 1998), (1998) 5 HRNZ 580, at 583.

Chapter 2. Legal Grounds for Processing Personal Data

309. The Privacy Act is largely harm-based, which involves focusing on consequences, and not on whether processing is legitimate or not *ab initio*. Moreover, the term 'processing' is neither widely used in the Act nor is it defined. The expression is only relevantly used twice in the narrow sense of one agency processing personal data that it holds on behalf of another agency.[342] The Act does not set out particular requirements that render the processing of data lawful on their own. Instead, the legislation sets out a set of principles which, when breached and result in some harm or loss to the individual, gives rise to legal liability that retrospectively render processing illegitimate. The only exceptions to this harm-based approach are in relation to the principles and associated procedural rules that deal with access to and correction of personal information, which do not require any harm or loss to be proved.

310. Analysis of Act in terms of the European concept of 'legitimate processing' is therefore directly inapplicable, though the GDPR definition of 'processing' does encompass operations or actions that are broadly covered under the Privacy Act's IPPs, namely, collection, storage, use, disclosure, and erasure. Permitted exceptions to the Act's IPPs on collection, use, and disclosure may be invoked where the agency concerned reasonably believes that: the information is to be used in a form in which the individual is not identified, or is to be used for statistical or research purposes and will not be published in a form that could reasonably identify the individual;[343] the individual has authorised the collection, use, or disclosure of the information;[344] the source of the information is a publicly available information, and in the case of use or disclosure, it would not be unfair or unreasonable to use or disclose it in the circumstances;[345] disclosure is to facilitate the sale or other disposition of a business as a going concern;[346] collection, use, or disclosure is necessary for the protection of various public interests (avoiding prejudice to maintenance of the law, enforcement of a law imposing a pecuniary penalty, protection of public revenue, the conduct of legal proceedings);[347] collection, use, or disclosure is necessary to prevent or lessen threats to public health, public safety, or the life or health of an individual;[348] use or disclosure is necessary for enabling an intelligence and security agency to perform any of its functions;[349] and disclosure is to the individual concerned.[350] Additional exceptions to the collection principles are that: compliance would prejudice the purposes of the collection;[351] non-compliance

342. Privacy Act, s. 22, IPP 11(1) and (5)(b).
343. Privacy Act, s. 22, IPP 2(2)(g), IPP 3(4)(e), IPP 10(1)(b) and IPP 11(1)h).
344. Privacy Act, s. 22, IPP 2(2)(c), IPP 10(1)(c) and IPP 11(1)(c).
345. Privacy Act, s. 22, IPP 2(d), IPP 10(1)(d) and IPP 11(1)(d).
346. Privacy Act, s. 22, IPP 11(1)(h)(i).
347. Privacy Act, s. 22, IPP 2(2)(e), IPP 3(4)(b), IPP 10(1)(e) and IPP 11 (1)(e).
348. Privacy Act, s. 22, IPP 2(2)(e)(v), IPP 10(1)(f) and IPP 11(1)(f).
349. Privacy Act, s. 22, IPP 10(2), 11(1)(g).
350. Privacy Act, s. 22, IPP 11(1)(b).
351. Privacy Act, s. 22, IPP 2(2)(b), IPP 3(4)(c).

would not prejudice the individual's interests;[352] and compliance is not reasonably practicable in the particular circumstances.[353]

311. It is important to note that the various exceptions to the IPPs come into play not when the conditions for their application actually exist, but when the agency concerned reasonably believes that they exist (when the agency 'believes, on reasonable grounds'). There is therefore a mixed subjective/objective test for their application, rather than simply an objective test. An agency cannot 'reasonably believe' that a relevant exception applies unless there is some objective factual basis for that belief to render that belief 'reasonable' in the circumstances. The importance of the objective element in the test, therefore, should not be underestimated. While the mixed subjective/objective test is not as strict as one based on actual objective fact, the test has the advantage of making allowances for genuine misunderstandings by an agency (so long as there is a reasonable basis for this), and for ambiguous situations, rather than providing for absolute liability in all circumstances.

352. Privacy Act, s. 22, IPP 2(2)(a), IPP 3(4)(a).
353. Privacy Act, s. 22, IPP 2(2)(f), IPP 3(4)(d).

Chapter 3. Special Categories of Personal Data

§1. General Approach of New Zealand Law

312. An understanding of the additional safeguards applicable to special categories of personal information requires a consideration of a number of enactments in addition to the Privacy Act 2020.

313. New Zealand privacy law does not follow the approach favoured in the European data protection instruments in respect of specified categories of information. The European instruments (notably GDPR, Article 9, and Council of Europe Modernised Data Protection Convention (COE), Article 6) allow use of certain specified categories of information only with additional prescribed safeguards. By contrast, New Zealand privacy law identifies no special categories. However, the Privacy Act does enable the issue of codes of practice to provide additional safeguards to types of information that would in Europe be considered 'special categories.'

314. However, while New Zealand privacy law identifies no special categories, New Zealand anti-discrimination laws do. Operation of those other laws does to some degree restrict the circumstances in which information related to the 'prohibited grounds of discrimination' may lawfully be used. Privacy law can work in tandem with these anti-discrimination law categories as the collection and use of information for purposes that are unlawful under those other laws will likely be a breach of IPPs.

§2. Privacy Law

315. The Privacy Act 1993 did not follow the approach favoured in European data protection instruments to prescribe additional safeguards in respect of specified categories of information. The Privacy Act 2020 maintained the approach of the 1993 Act.

316. The New Zealand law has followed the approach recommended in the OECD Privacy Guidelines of 1980. The Experts Group that developed the 1980 Guidelines considered whether the guidelines should be structured to deal with different types of data but decided against doing so concluding that 'it is probably not possible to identify a set of data which are universally regarded as being sensitive' (OECD Group of Experts on Data Barriers and Privacy Protection, *Explanatory Memorandum to the OECD Guidelines on the Protection of Privacy and Transborder Flows of Personal Data*, 1980, paragraph 19).

317. However, the Privacy Act 1993 contained provision for codes of practice and this was continued in Part 3 Subpart 2 of the Privacy Act 2020. Section 32 of the 2020 Act provides that codes can, among other things, prescribe more stringent standards in respect of any specified class or classes of information.

318. Accordingly, a code of practice has been issued that requires additional safeguards with respect to health information – a class of information that would constitute a 'special category of personal data' under the GDPR or COE. The Health Information Privacy Code 2020 (which continued a 1994 code) imposes several safeguards in relation to health information such as:

- Requiring the use of ethics committees in relation to health research using health records (refer Health Information Privacy Code 2020, rules 2(2)(g)(iii) and 11(2)(c)(iii)).
- Requiring that recourse to certain exceptions to the disclosure rule be had only if 'it is either not desirable or not practicable to obtain authorisation from the individual concerned' (Health Information Privacy Code 2020, rule 11(2)).

319. Although not treated as a special category of personal data or processing in the European instruments, the Credit Reporting Privacy Code 2020 (which continues a 2004 code) essentially treats credit information and credit reporting as a special category and imposes a series of special safeguards such as, access control, account freezing, audit, and enhanced subject access rights.

320. A final example of a category of personal information that is essentially treated as a special category of personal data, although not considered as such in the European instruments, concerns 'unique identifiers' which are defined in section 7 of the Privacy Act 2020 as:

> *unique identifier*, in relation to an individual, means an identifier other than the individual's name that uniquely identifies the individual

321. IPPs 13 imposes special controls on the processing and display of unique identifiers and provides:

> **Information privacy principle 13**
>
> *Unique identifiers*
>
> (1) An agency (A) may assign a unique identifier to an individual for use in its operations only if that identifier is necessary to enable A to carry out 1 or more of its functions efficiently.
> (2) A may not assign to an individual a unique identifier that, to A's knowledge, is the same unique identifier as has been assigned to that individual by another agency (B), unless:
> (a) A and B are associated persons within the meaning of subpart YB of the Income Tax Act 2007; or
> (b) the unique identifier is to be used by A for statistical or research purposes and no other purpose.
> (3) To avoid doubt, A does not assign a unique identifier to an individual under subclause (1) by simply recording a unique identifier assigned to the individual by B for the sole purpose of communicating with B about the individual.

(4) A must take any steps that are, in the circumstances, reasonable to ensure that:
   (a) a unique identifier is assigned only to an individual whose identity is clearly established; and
   (b) the risk of misuse of a unique identifier by any person is minimised (for example, by showing truncated account numbers on receipts or in correspondence).

(5) An agency may not require an individual to disclose any unique identifier assigned to that individual unless the disclosure is for one of the purposes in connection with which that unique identifier was assigned or is for a purpose that is directly related to one of those purposes.

322. As can be seen, IPP 13 prohibits the assignment of unique identifiers in certain circumstances (IPP13(1)-3)) or their display or disclosure (IPP13(4)-(5)).

§3. Anti-discrimination Law: Sex, Marital Status, Religious Belief, Ethical Belief, Colour, Race, Ethnic or National Origins, Disability, Age, Political Opinion, Employment Status, Family Status and Sexual Orientation

323. There are two main New Zealand laws that specifically promote and protect human rights. One is the HR Act. The other is the Bill of Rights Act 1990.

324. The HR Act protects people in New Zealand from discrimination in a number of areas of life. It does this by specifying a series of 'prohibited grounds of discrimination' and applying these in particular ways in certain specified areas of unlawful discrimination.

325. The prohibited grounds of discrimination listed in section 21 of the HR Act are:

(a) sex;
(b) marital status;
(c) religious belief:
(d) ethical belief;
(e) colour;
(f) race;
(g) ethnic or national origins;
(h) disability;
(i) age;
(j) political opinion;
(k) employment status;
(l) family status;
(m) sexual orientation.

326. These are all characteristics that an individual may possess. The meaning of marital status, disability, age, employment status, and sexual orientation are elaborated on within s. 21.

327. The HR Act outlaws discrimination on the prohibited grounds of discrimination in the following areas (among other forms of unlawful discrimination):

- employment matters;
- partnerships;
- industrial and professional associations, qualifying bodies, and vocational training bodies;
- access to places, vehicles, and facilities;
- provision of goods and services;
- provision of land, housing, and other accommodation;
- access to educational establishments.

328. As this is an anti-discrimination rather than a privacy law it is not generally couched in data processing terminology but rather in phrases such as 'to refuse or omit to employ', 'afford less favourable terms', 'subject to any detriment' or 'treat differently from other persons'. However, the implication of treating a person in a discriminatory manner by reason of a characteristic falling within the prohibited grounds is not dissimilar to data protection language of using or processing personal information about a person in a way that is unfair or prohibited.

329. In addition to the HR Act itself, there are two other enactments that use the categories set out in s. 21 of the Human Rights Act as 'prohibited grounds of discrimination': the New Zealand Bill of Rights Act 1990 and the Employment Relations Act 2000 (ER Act).

330. Section 19 of the New Zealand Bill of Rights Act 1990 provides:

> **19 Freedom from discrimination**
>
> (1) Everyone has the right to freedom from discrimination on the grounds of discrimination in the HR Act.
>
> (2) Measures taken in good faith for the purpose of assisting or advancing persons or groups of persons disadvantaged because of discrimination that is unlawful by virtue of Part 2 of the HR Act do not constitute discrimination.

331. Section 103 of the ER Act enables an employee to take a legal claim (referred to as a 'personal grievance') that the employee has been discriminated against in the employee's employment. Discrimination is defined in section 104 and section 105 makes it clear that the meaning of 'prohibited grounds of discrimination' is as set out in section 21(1) of the HR Act.

§4. Anti-discrimination Law: Involvement in Union Activities or Union Membership Status

332. In addition to a right to take a personal grievance under section 103 of the Employment Relations Act for discrimination on the prohibited grounds of discrimination as defined in the HR Act, an employee may take a claim on the basis of discrimination in relation to an individual's 'involvement in union activities' or 'union membership status.'

333. Section 104 of the ER Act defines discrimination for the purposes of section 103 as:

104 Discrimination

(1) For the purposes of section 103(1)(c), an employee is **discriminated against in that employee's employment** if the employee's employer or a representative of that employer, by reason directly or indirectly of any of the prohibited grounds of discrimination specified in section 105, or the employee's union membership status or involvement in union activities in terms of section 107, –
  (a) refuses or omits to offer or afford to that employee the same terms of employment, conditions of work, fringe benefits, or opportunities for training, promotion, and transfer as are made available for other employees of the same or substantially similar qualifications, experience, or skills employed in the same or substantially similar circumstances; or
  (b) dismisses that employee or subjects that employee to any detriment, in circumstances in which other employees employed by that employer on work of that description are not or would not be dismissed or subjected to such detriment; or
  (c) retires that employee, or requires or causes that employee to retire or resign.

(2) For the purposes of this section, *detriment* includes anything that has a detrimental effect on the employee's employment, job performance, or job satisfaction.

(3) This section is subject to the exceptions set out in section 106.

334. Section 107 defines 'involvement in union activities' for the purposes of s. 104 to mean that, within the 18 months before the action complained of, the employee:

- was an officer of a union or part of a union, or was a member of the committee of management of a union or part of a union, or was otherwise an official or representative of a union or part of a union;
- had acted as a negotiator or representative of employees in collective bargaining; or
- had participated in a strike lawfully;

- was involved in the formation or the proposed formation of a union;
- had made or caused to be made a claim for some benefit of an employment agreement either for that employee or any other employee, or had supported any such claim, whether by giving evidence or otherwise;
- had submitted another personal grievance to that employee's employer;
- had been allocated, had applied to take, or had taken any employment relations education leave under this Act; or
- was a delegate of other employees in dealing with the employer on matters relating to the employment of those employees.

335. The section further defines 'union membership status' to mean that, within the previous eighteen months the employee was a member of a union or intended to join a union.

§5. Human Rights Act, Section 23: Particulars of Applicants for Employment

336. IPP 1 of the Privacy Act only permits the collection of personal information if it is collected for a lawful purpose, connected with a function or activity of the agency, and if it is necessary for that purpose. Accordingly, a job applicant should not be asked to provide personal information that is irrelevant to the position to be filled. IPP 1 supplements pre-employment anti-discrimination law found in Part II of the HR Act which deals with acting on the basis of particular prohibited grounds of discrimination.

337. The Human Rights Act does not generally focus directly upon the collection and use of personal information in those terms. However, one section in which the HR Act is explicit in relation to collection of personal information is s. 23, which provides:

> **Particulars of applicants for employment**
>
> It shall be unlawful for any person to use or circulate any form of application for employment or to make any inquiry of or about any applicant for employment which indicates, or could reasonably be understood as indicating, an intention to commit a breach of section 22.

338. Section 23 of the HR Act is a good example of where the Privacy Act overlaps with the HR Act, to the extent that both are concerned with the appropriateness of the information that goes into a decision whether or not to employ an individual.

339. Section 23 covers both forms of application for employment and inquiries of, or about, job applicants. Application forms themselves will in most cases 'inquire of' the applicant, in the sense of asking questions for the applicant to answer. As well as prohibiting material or inquiries that indicate an intention to commit a breach of section 22 (which outlaws discrimination on the prohibited grounds in employment), the material or inquiries covered by section 23 include those that 'could reasonably be understood' as indicating such an intention.

340. In a case relating to religious belief, *Human Rights Commission v. Eric Sides Motors Co Ltd* (1981) 2 New Zealand Administrative Reports 447, an advertisement for a 'keen Christian girl' to work as a forecourt attendant was held to provide clear evidence of a breach what is now section 23 of the HR Act.

341. A case example concerning health information is *Imperial Enterprises Ltd v. Attwood* [2002] 2 Employment Reports of New Zealand 740. The defendant had been asked to detail 'any medical problems of any kind' on a pre-employment form. She had listed only conditions that she believed to be relevant to the job but, following disagreement over her contractual duties and a period of sick leave for an undisclosed condition, she was dismissed for misrepresentation. In upholding the Employment Relations Authority finding that the defendant had been unjustifiably dismissed, the court held that the employer could not rely, for disciplinary purposes, on an incomplete answer to a question that breached section 23. No obligation to answer such a question arose.

342. In the same case, the judge noted that there was no indication on the pre-employment form about the purpose that the employer had in collecting the information, as required by IPPs 1 of the Privacy Act 1993, which again rendered the question about 'any medical conditions' inappropriate and established no obligation to answer it.

343. The HR Act section 23 prohibition includes acts that 'could reasonably be understood as indicating' an intention to discriminate. In *McCready v. Hawkins and Hawkins Associates*, unreported, Dec No 10/97, CRT 30/96, the Complaints Review Tribunal (now known as the HRRT) found that the defendant recruitment agency had indicated an intention to discriminate in terms of section 23 of the HR Act against the plaintiff because it had obtained details of the years during which he had attended high school. This was construed as an inquiry about the plaintiff's age which is one of the prohibited grounds of discrimination under the HR Act. The plaintiff was 52 years old with computer, accounting and other business qualifications and experience. The defendant stated that its purpose for collecting the information was 'to obtain information like the period of time an applicant remained at secondary school or the time which elapsed between secondary schooling and tertiary education' (p. 6). The Tribunal noted that while the collection of such information did not breach the HR Act, it could be obtained more directly by simply asking the job applicant the relevant questions. On the test for a breach of section 23, which renders it unlawful to seek information about a job applicant which could reasonably indicate an intention to breach the anti-discrimination provisions of the Act, the Tribunal stated:

> The test is an objective one. It matters not, therefore, whether the first defendant intended to discriminate by making the inquiry, although that intention

> may well be relevant to the issue of whether a remedy is appropriate. The question then becomes: could this inquiry indicate an intention to commit a breach of s 22? In our view it could because attendance at secondary school is something that almost all the New Zealand population does at a particular age i.e., between the ages of 12 and 18. The information about what years a person attended secondary school yields almost instantly the probable age of a person within 12 to 18 months. (p. 6)

§6. Other Relevant Enactments: Conviction Information

344. New Zealand's core anti-discrimination laws do not directly cover discrimination on the basis of criminal conviction. However, several other laws provide safeguards which guard against the risks that the use of conviction information may present for the interests of the individuals concerned, notably the risk of discrimination.

345. The principal law of relevance is the Criminal Records (Clean Slate) Act 2004 ('Clean Slate Act'). This Act establishes a clean slate scheme to limit the effect of an individual's convictions in most circumstances (subject to certain exceptions) if the individual satisfies the relevant eligibility criteria.

346. If an individual satisfies the relevant eligibility criteria:

(a) he or she is deemed to have no criminal record for the purposes of any question asked of him or her about his or her criminal record; and
(b) he or she has the right to have his or her criminal record concealed by government departments and law enforcement agencies that hold or have access to his or her criminal record. (Clean Slate Act, s. 14)

347. An individual is said to have no criminal record if of the following are true. The individual has:

- had no convictions within the last seven years;
- never been sentenced to a custodial sentence (such as prison, corrective training or borstal);
- never been convicted of a sexual offence ('specified offence');
- fully paid any fine, compensation, reparation or costs ordered by the court in a criminal case;
- never been banned from driving until further notice (indefinite disqualification); and
- never been held in hospital by the court in a criminal case instead of being sentenced, due to a mental condition.

348. Another law relevant both to criminal convictions and one of the prohibited grounds of discrimination under the HR Act is the Criminal Records (Expungement of Convictions for Historical Homosexual Offences) Act 2018. While consensual sex between men aged 16 and over has been legal in New Zealand since 1986, the Act addresses the fact that men with historical homosexual convictions can face ongoing stigma and prejudice.

349. The purpose of the Criminal Records (Expungement of Convictions for Historical Homosexual Offences) Act is to reduce prejudice, stigma, and all other negative effects, arising from a conviction for a historical homosexual offence by:

(a) enabling an application for expungement of the conviction to be made under this Act by an eligible person (before that person's death) or a representative (after the eligible person's death); and
(b) expunging the conviction if the secretary's decision on the application is that, on the balance of probabilities, the conviction meets the test for expungement.

§7. Comparison with European Special Categories of Personal Data

350. The two principal European data protection instruments that establish 'special categories of personal data' and apply rules to them are the EU GDPR, Article 9, and COE, Article 6.

351. The categories under the two instruments overlap substantially with each other but are not identical. Those European categories substantially overlap with New Zealand's categories within the 'prohibited grounds of discrimination' (together with the additional enactments mentioned above) but are not identical with the New Zealand categories falling short in some areas and being more extensive in others.

352. The rules applied to special categories under the EU GDPR and COE are not identical. The EU approach is prescriptive being a prohibition followed by a limited set of exceptions. This is not the approach followed in New Zealand except, perhaps, with respect to pre-employment collection of personal information (HR Act, section 23 refers). The Council of Europe approach, by contrast, is less prescriptive merely calling for 'appropriate safeguards are enshrined in law' and further providing that such safeguards must 'guard against the risks that the processing of sensitive data may present for the interests, rights and fundamental freedoms of the data subject, notably a risk of discrimination.' The New Zealand approach of embedding anti-discrimination protections in law does not follow the GDPR model but is quite closely aligned to the approach of the COE.

353. The following summary record the special categories in the European data protection instruments against applicable New Zealand enactments:

- Racial or ethnic origin: NZ Bill of Rights Act 1990, HR Act, ER Act.
- Political opinions: NZ Bill of Rights Act 1990, HR Act, ER Act.
- Religious or philosophical beliefs: NZ Bill of Rights Act 1990, HR Act, ER Act.
- Trade union membership: ER Act.

- Genetic data: No corresponding enactment.
- Biometric data: No corresponding enactment.
- Data concerning health: In relation to disability only – NZ Bill of Rights Act 1990, HR Act, ER Act. In relation to health information; Health Information Privacy Code 2020.
- Data concerning a natural person's sex life: No corresponding enactment.
- Sexual orientation: NZ Bill of Rights Act 1990, HR Act, ER Act.
- Personal data relating to offences, criminal proceedings and convictions, and related security measures (a Council of Europe category): In relation to convictions only – Criminal Records (Clean Slate) Act 2004.

Part IV. Data Subject Rights

Chapter 1. Right to Be Informed

§1. Information to be Provided When Personal Information is Collected

354. IPP 2(1) ('Source of personal information') provides that where an agency collects personal information, it must do so from the individual concerned, subject to a number of exceptions. When personal information is collected from a source other than the individual concerned pursuant to one of these exceptions,[354] there is no obligation to inform the individual of its collection. The individual would only find out about its collection if a request for access to personal information is made to the agency concerned under IPP 6 ('Access to personal information'), or if the individual found out through informal sources.

355. IPP 3(1) goes on to provide that when an agency collects personal information from the individual concerned, the agency must take reasonable steps in the circumstances to ensure that the individual is aware of:

(a) the fact that the information is being collected; and
(b) the purpose for which the information is being collected; and
(c) the intended recipients of the information; and
(d) the name and address of:
    (i) the agency that is collecting the information; and
    (ii) the agency that will hold the information; and
(e) if the collection of the information is authorised or required by or under law:
    (i) the particular law by or under which the collection of the information is authorised or required; and
    (ii) whether the supply of the information by that individual is voluntary or mandatory; and
(f) the consequences (if any) for that individual if all or any part of the requested information is not provided; and
(g) the rights of access to, and correction of, personal information provided by the IPPs.

354. Privacy Act, s. 22, IPP 2(2).

356. The individual is required to be informed of the above matters before personal information is being collected. If that is not 'practicable', then the individual must be informed 'as soon as practicable' after the information has been collected.[355]

§2. Exceptions to the IPP 3 Notification Requirements

357. An agency is not required to notify the individual concerned of the matters set out in IPP 3(1) if the agency has already done so on a recent previous occasion, and the information or information of the same kind has been collected.[356] Non-compliance with the notification requirement of IPP 3 is also permitted where an agency reasonably believes that: non-compliance would not prejudice the individual's interests;[357] non-compliance is necessary for the protection of various public interests (avoiding prejudice to maintenance of the law, enforcement of a law imposing a pecuniary penalty, protection of public revenue, the conduct of legal proceedings);[358] compliance would prejudice the purposes of the collection;[359] compliance is not reasonably practicable in the particular circumstances;[360] or the information is to be used in a form in which the individual is not identified, or is to be used for statistical or research purposes and will not be published in a form that could reasonably identify the individual.[361]

§3. No Right to Be Informed When Personal Information Collected from Another Source

358. The Privacy Act does not provide for notification of the individual concerned when information is collected from a source other than the individual in terms of IPP 2. However, the other IPPs relating to the holding, use, and disclosure of their personal information, as well as entitlements to access and correction, will still apply. Likewise, the Act also does not provide for notification of the data subject when an agency receives unsolicited information, which falls outside the definition of 'collect' in section 7(1) of the Act. But the individual is similarly protected by all of the IPPs other than those that relate to collection in respect of the agency that has received the information. Moreover, the individual would have rights and remedies in relation to the person or agency that provided the unsolicited information if the information was not disclosed with the individual's authorisation, and no exception to the disclosure principle applies.

355. Privacy Act, s. 22, IPP 3(2).
356. Privacy Act, s. 22, IPP 3(3).
357. Privacy Act, s. 22, IPP 3(4)(a).
358. Privacy Act, s. 22, IPP 3(4)(b).
359. Privacy Act, s. 22, IPP 3(4)(c).
360. Privacy Act, s. 22, IPP 3(4)(d).
361. Privacy Act, s. 22, IPP 3(4)(e).

§4. Notifications Required to Be Given in Respect of Access and Correction Requests

359. The Act systematically provides for an individual to be informed of decisions or reasons for decisions made by an agency relating to the entitlements under IPP 6 and IPP 7. The individual has the right to be informed of:

- the transfer to another agency of a request for access to or correction of personal information;[362]
- the identity of the agency to which an access or correction request could be transferred if the agency that received the request, but does not hold the information, does not transfer the request because it has good cause to believe that the requestor does not want the request transferred to another agency;[363]
- an agency's decision to extend the twenty-day time limit to decide on an access or correction request. Notice of the extension must be given within twenty days specifying the period of the extension, the reason for the extension, and the requestor must be informed of the right to complain to the Privacy Commissioner;[364]
- whether, in response to an access request, an agency does not hold personal information in a way that is readily retrievable; or does not hold any personal information about the individual concerned; or access to the personal information is granted or refused; or the agency neither confirms nor denies that it holds personal information about the individual concerned;[365]
- the right to complain to the Privacy Commissioner where an agency neither confirms nor denies that it holds the requestor's personal information;[366]
- the way personal information is to be made available; the charge (if any) in respect of the access request; and the requestor's right to complain to the Privacy Commissioner about the charge, when the agency has decided that access to personal information will been granted;[367]
- the reason for the refusal, and the requestor's right to complain to the Privacy Commissioner about the refusal, when access to personal information has been refused.[368] The notice must also state the grounds in support of the reason for the refusal if the information concerned is evaluative material under section 50, and if it is not evaluative material, then the grounds in support must be provided if the requestor has requested these, so long as their disclosure does not prejudice any interests protected under the Act;[369]
- the reason for the deletion, and the requestor's right to complain to the Privacy Commissioner, when information is deleted from a document made available to

362. Privacy Act, s. 43(2) (access request) and s. 62(2) (correction request).
363. Privacy Act, s. 43(3)–(4) (access request) and s. 62(3)–(4) (correction request).
364. Privacy Act, s. 48 (access request) and s. 65 (correction request).
365. Privacy Act, s. 44(2).
366. Privacy Act, s. 47(2).
367. Privacy Act, s. 45(1).
368. Privacy Act, s. 46(2).
369. Privacy Act, s. 46(3).

the individual.[370] The notice must also state the grounds in support of the reason for the deletion if the information concerned is evaluative material under section 50(1),[371] and if it is not evaluative material, then the grounds in support must be provided if the requestor has requested these,[372] so long as their disclosure does not prejudice any interests protected under the Act;[373]

- the right to request correction of information under IPP 7 after being given access to personal information under IPP 6;[374]
- an agency's decision whether or not it will grant a correction request under IPP 7. If the agency refuses to correct the information, the agency must inform the requestor of the reason for its refusal; the requestor's entitlement to provide a statement of the correction sought but not made, for attachment to the information; and the requestor's right to complain to the Privacy Commissioner about the refusal to correct the information;[375]
- an agency's decision whether or not to grant a correction request under IPP 7(3)(b) to attach a statement of correction sought but not made. If the request is granted, the notice must inform the requestor of the action the agency has taken to attach the statement of correction to the information. If the request is not granted, the notice must inform the requestor of the right to complain to the Privacy Commissioner.[376]

§5. Notifiable Privacy Breaches

360. The Act deals with data breach notification,[377] which requires that the Privacy Commissioner as well as affected individuals are notified of a 'notifiable privacy breach'. Agencies must notify an affected individual as soon as practicable after becoming aware of the occurrence of a notifiable privacy breach unless an exception applies.[378] If it is not reasonably practicable to notify an affected individual or each member of a group of affected individuals, the agency must give public notice of the breach, unless an exception applies or a delay is permitted.[379]

361. An agency is not required to notify an affected individual if the agency believes that it would be likely to: prejudice the security or defence of New Zealand or its international relations; prejudice the maintenance of the law by a public sector agency, including the prevention, investigation, and detection of offences, and the right to a fair trial; endanger any person's safety; or reveal a trade secret.[380] An

370. Privacy Act, s. 55(2).
371. Privacy Act, s. 55(3).
372. Privacy Act, s. 55(3).
373. Privacy Act, s. 55(4).
374. Privacy Act, s. 22, IPP 6(2).
375. Privacy Act, s. 63.
376. Privacy Act, s. 64.
377. Privacy Act, Part 6, Subpart 1 ('Notifiable privacy breaches').
378. Privacy Act, s. 115(1).
379. Privacy Act, s. 115(2).
380. Privacy Act, s. 116(1).

agency is also not required to notify an affected individual if the individual is under 16 and the agency believes notification would be contrary to that individual's interests, or if, after consultation with an individual's health practitioner, where practicable, the agency believes that notification would be likely to prejudice the individual's health.[381] In either case, the agency must consider whether it would be appropriate to notify the individual's representative.[382]

362. If it is not reasonably practicable to notify an affected individual or individuals, the agency must notify them at a later time if circumstances change, so that it is practicable or notify them or the exception or reason for delay no longer applies, and there remains a risk that the privacy breach will cause serious harm.[383] A delay is permitted if it is necessary because notification may have risks for the security of personal information held by the agency, and the risks outweigh the benefits for the relevant period.[384]

§6. Proposed Adverse Action after Information Sharing and Matching

363. Where personal information has been shared under an approved information sharing agreement between agencies under Part 7, subpart 1 of the Act, a party to the agreement must give written notice to an individual before it takes any adverse action against the individual.[385] The notice must provide details of the proposed adverse to be taken, and the personal information on which the action is based. The notice must state that the individual has ten working days from the giving of the notice to dispute the correctness of the personal information.[386] An information sharing agreement may provide for the giving of a shorter period of notice, or dispense with the giving of notice. If the agreement does not include provision for a shorter period of notice, or no notice, the Privacy Commissioner may, upon the application of a party to the agreement, allow the party, in the circumstances of the particular case, to give a shorter period of notice than ten days, or dispense with the giving of notice.[387]

364. Where personal information has been matched under an authorised information matching programme under Part 7, subpart 4 of the Act, a specified agency must not take adverse action against an individual on the basis of a discrepancy produced by a match unless the agency has given written notice to the individual that

381. Privacy Act, s. 116(2).
382. Privacy Act, s. 116(3).
383. Privacy Act, s. 115(4)
384. Privacy Act, s. 116(4).
385. Privacy Act, s. 152(1). An 'adverse action' is defined in s. 177 of the Act as 'any lawful action of an agency that may adversely affect the rights, benefits, privileges, obligations, or interests of any specific individual'.
386. Privacy Act, s. 152(2).
387. Privacy Act, s. 153.

specifies particulars of the discrepancy of the proposed adverse action, and states that the individual has five days from receipt of the notice to show cause why the action should not be taken.[388]

388. Privacy Act, s. 181(1).

Chapter 2. Right of Access

§1. The Right of Access

365. The right of access under IPP 6 ('Access to personal information') is the most commonly exercised right under the Privacy Act, and there are extensive Privacy Commissioner case notes and case law on the subject. IPP 6 provides that an individual is entitled to obtain confirmation of whether or not an agency holds personal information about the individual, and to request access to that information.

366. Thus, even if there is a good reason in terms of the Act to refuse disclosure of personal information, the individual still has a right to confirmation of whether or not the agency holds personal information, subject to the limited exception whereby in narrowly defined circumstances, an agency is entitled to give notice that it neither confirms nor denies the existence or non-existence of personal information.[389] In *Proceedings Commissioner v. Health Waikato*,[390] for example, where information was withheld from the requestor without informing him of its existence (later claimed to be justified on the grounds of legal professional privilege), the Tribunal held that at least the existence of the information should have been disclosed to the complainant in response to his access request.

367. Where access is given, the individual must be advised that correction of that information may be requested pursuant to IPP 7. IPP 6 is subject to the provisions of Part 4 of the Act,[391] which deal with the procedural aspects of seeking access to personal information, including the reasons for which access to personal information may be refused[392] or limited.[393]

368. The entitlement to confirmation and access in IPP 6(1) is a 'legal right' in relation to personal information held by a public sector agency,[394] which means that the individual may go directly to a Court of law to enforce the entitlement rather than work through the processes of the Act, if the data subject wishes to do so. Requestors tend to use the processes provided for under the Act, however, as it is free of charge.

369. Although agencies may impose conditions on the use, communication or publication of information made available if the request could otherwise be refused,[395] they may not impose conditions on making information available pursuant to an IPP 6 access request if there is no ground for withholding the information. In *Case No 22968*,[396] a hospital and health service attempted to impose such

389. Privacy Act, s. 47.
390. [2000] NZCRT 3 (14 Mar. 2000).
391. Subpart 1 ('Access to personal information').
392. Privacy Act, ss 49–53.
393. Privacy Act, ss 54–56.
394. Privacy Act, s. 31(2).
395. Privacy Act, s. 54.
396. [1999] NZPrivCmr 5 (1 May 1999).

a condition. The requestor, acting as a duly authorised agent for his son, requested a report commissioned by the agency into the son's care while he was a patient of the agency. The report contained information about the son's condition, treatment, upbringing, and parents. Before releasing the report, the agency required the father to sign a form waiving any privacy rights and indemnifying the agency against future claims arising from the release of the report. The Privacy Commissioner considered that the requirement imposed by the agency amounted to a refusal to make the information available in response to the IPP 6 request. The Commissioner stated that the agency 'was not entitled to impose the condition that a waiver be signed before the information would be released'.

370. When an agency that holds personal information (whether or not in the form of a document) is owed money, it may be tempted not to make it available to the requestor until the debt is paid. Such a situation may arise where the requestor is the debtor. This would be a variation of the common law 'artisan's' or 'workman's' lien. In such a situation, however, the individual to whom the information relates would be entitled to access to the information under IPP 6, subject to any relevant exception in Part 4 of the Act.[397] To similar effect, the Health Act 1956 provides that a person who holds health information does not have a 'lawful excuse' for withholding it on the basis that 'any payment due to the holder of any information or to any other person has not been made.'[398]

371. IPP 6 is problematic in applying to cases of mistaken identity cases because strictly speaking, IPP 6 applies only to the requestor's personal information. If the information is possibly about someone else, then there is no right of access to it. In such cases, the proper approach seems to be that the Privacy Commissioner will determine whether there is an access entitlement after assessing whether the information is about the requestor. In *Case Note 225347*,[399] the complainant requested information in order to clear up a credit agency's mistake. The agency had sent final demand letters to the complainant about a tenancy debt that he did not owe. In order to clear his name, the complainant requested information from the agency about the debt, but the request was declined on the basis that if the complainant was not the debtor, the disclosure of the true debtor's details would breach the Act since it would not be his personal information and would involve the unwarranted disclosure of another individual's affairs. The Privacy Commissioner examined the information at issue, and found that the details of the complainant and the debtor were similar. However, there were discrepancies that raised questions about the accuracy of the information that the credit agency was relying on to pursue the man. After an investigation, the Commissioner confirmed to the credit agency that the complainant was not the debtor. The credit agency apologised to the complainant and assured him

397. *Case Note 7837* [1997] NZPrivCmr 2 (Apr. 1997); *Case Note 16579* [2001] NZPrivCmr 23 (Nov. 2001); *C B N v. McKenzie Associates*, [2004] NZHRRT 48 (30 Sep. 2004).

398. Health Act, s. 22F(3)(a).

399. [2011] NZPrivCmr 6 (20 Jul. 2011).

that it would stop pursuing him. The Commissioner accepted that because the information held by the credit agency was not the complainant's personal information, he was not entitled to it under IPP 6.

§2. Exceptions to the Right of Access

I. The Discretion to Refuse Access to Personal Information

372. The phrase 'An agency may refuse access' is used in the introductory sections of all of the provisions that set out the reasons for refusing access to personal information in sections 49–53 of the Privacy Act. These provisions contain the only reasons for withholding personal information under the Act, and are therefore to be regarded as a code.[400] It should be noted, however, that the Act's savings provision applies as well, making the IPP 6 right of access subject to any limitations that may be provided for under other legislation.[401]

373. Where an agency proposes to withhold personal information on the basis of one of the reasons for refusing access, it must do so after an assessment of each item of information against the reason for withholding, and not on a broad 'class' or 'blanket' basis. This is the approach set out in the HC judicial review decision in *Kelsey v. Minister of Trade*,[402] which dealt with the analogous position under the Official Information Act 1982. Moreover, the point in time when the reason for refusing access is operative or else must exist is the date on which an agency makes the decision to refuse access.[403]

374. There is a discretion inherent in the expression 'An agency may refuse access', denoting that the grounds for refusing access are permissive. Thus, agencies may disclose personal information if they wish to (subject to any other statutory limitations that may exist),[404] but they would be justified in refusing access to the information if there is a good reason under the Act to do so. For example, in *Pointu v. Employrite Ltd*,[405] the Tribunal dealt with a case where the screening agency concerned refused to disclose information relating to a confidential job reference to the complainant under the 'evaluative material' exception.[406] While the Tribunal found that the agency had good reason to refuse access to the information, it went on to comment that the defendant was mistaken in believing that the exception *obliged* it to withhold the information. The Tribunal stated that the exception

400. Privacy Act, s. 46(1).
401. Privacy Act, s. 24(1)(b).
402. [2015] NZHC 2497 (13 Oct. 2015).
403. *Dotcom v. Crown Law Office* [2018] NZHRRT 7, (2018) 11 HRNZ 420, at para. 123; approved by the High Court on appeal in *Attorney-General v. Dotcom* [2018] NZHC 2564, [2019] 2 NZLR 277. This aspect of the decision was left undisturbed in the further appeal to the Court of Appeal in *Dotcom v. Attorney-General* [2020] NZCA 551 (10 Nov. 2020).
404. Privacy Act, s. 24(1).
405. [2002] NZHRRT 11 (1 Oct. 2002).
406. Privacy Act, s. 50.

allowed the defendant to refuse to disclose the information, but it could disclose the information and face the consequences should it choose to do so.[407] Conversely, neither the Privacy Commissioner nor the Tribunal would have the jurisdiction to question the exercise of an agency's discretion to refuse to disclose information once one of the exceptions is made out.[408]

II. Proceedings in Denied Access Cases

375. Sections 49–53 of the Act contains the various good reasons for refusing access to personal information. This raises the issue of how individuals can be certain whether or not an agency has a proper basis for refusing access to their information if they are unable to verify the agency's decision by actually accessing it. When a complaint is lodged with the Privacy Commissioner, the information sought to be withheld, and the good reasons claimed for withholding it, can be investigated by the Commissioner. Once a complaint is taken further and brought to the Tribunal personally by the aggrieved individual, however, the issue becomes more difficult, since the information in question can continue to be withheld from the individual concerned. This renders it problematic for requestors to argue that there is no proper basis for the agency to withhold their personal information.

376. To address this situation, section 109 of the Act ('Proceedings involving access to personal information') deals with the Tribunal's powers in proceedings involving access to personal information. This provision formalises Tribunal practice that has been followed in cases where an access request has been refused, and justifying why personal information has been refused in an open hearing would compromise the very interests that the agency wishes to protect. Accordingly, section 109 provides for closed hearings if it is necessary to have them. The Tribunal may require the agency concerned to produce the personal information to the members of the Tribunal, but to no other person; and it may allow the agency to give evidence and make submissions in the absence of other parties, all lawyers (if any) representing other parties, and all members of the public.

III. Protection of the Individual

377. Section 49 sets out the circumstances where access may be refused to protect the interests of the individual concerned or another individual. The grounds for withholding personal information are grouped together on the basis that they relate to the health, safety, and well-being of individuals or the public:

- Information may be refused if disclosure would be likely 'to pose a serious threat to the life, health, or safety of any individual, or to public health or public

407. *Pointu v. Employrite Ltd* [2002] NZHRRT 11 (1 Oct. 2002), at para. 46.
408. *M v. Ministry of Health* [1997] NZCRT 12, (1997) 4 HRNZ 79, at p. 87; and *M v. Police* [1997] NZCRT 13, (1997) 4 HRNZ 91, which were heard together.

safety'.[409] A 'serious threat' is defined as 'a threat that an agency reasonably believes to be a serious threat having regard to the likelihood of the threat being realised; and the severity of the consequences if the threat is realised; and the time at which the threat may be realised'.[410]

- Information may be refused where its disclosure would create a significant likelihood of serious harassment of an individual.[411]
- Information may be refused if its disclosure involves disclosing information about another person who is the victim of an offence or alleged offence, and the disclosure would cause that person significant distress, loss of dignity or injury to feelings.[412]
- Information may be refused when it relates to the physical or mental health of the individual concerned if, after consultation (where practicable) with the individual's medical practitioner, the agency is satisfied that disclosure of the information would be likely to prejudice the requestor's physical or mental health.[413]
- Information may be refused where the individual concerned is under the age of 16 and the disclosure of the information would be contrary to that individual's interest.[414]
- Information may be refused in respect of an individual who has been convicted of an offence or detained in custody where it would be likely to prejudice that individual's safe custody or rehabilitation.[415]

IV. Evaluative Material

378. Section 50 provides that an agency may refuse access in response to an IPP 6 request if the information requested is evaluative material where its disclosure, or disclosure of information identifying its supplier, would breach an express or implied promise that was made to the supplier and that was to the effect that the information or the identity of the supplier would be kept confidential.[416] 'Evaluative material' is defined as evaluative or opinion material compiled solely for the purposes of employment, continuance in employment, promotion, or appointment to office, or removal from employment or office; for the awarding or cancellation of

409. Privacy Act, s. 49(a)(i).
410. Privacy Act, s. 7(1).
411. Privacy Act, s. 49(1)(a)(ii).
412. Privacy Act, s. 49(1)(a)(iii).
413. Privacy Act, s. 49(1)(b). *See*, for example, *M v. Ministry of Health* [1997] NZCRT 12 (29 Apr. 1997), (1997) 4 HRNZ 79.
414. Privacy Act, s. 49(1)(c). In *O v. N (No 2)* [1996] NZCRT 4 (12 Mar. 1996), (1996) 3 HRNZ 636, at 645, the Tribunal suggested that 'interests' might denote 'best interests', in line with the United Nations Convention of the Rights of the Child, on the basis that this would be in accordance with general principles of statutory interpretation where New Zealand has relevant international obligations'.
415. Privacy Act, s. 49(1)(d). *See*, for example, *M v. Police* [1997] NZCRT 13 (29 Apr. 1997), (1997) 4 HRNZ 91.
416. Privacy Act, s. 50(1). *See*, for example, *O v. N* [1995] NZCRT 2 (29 May 1995), (1995) 2 HRNZ 501; *Westwood v. University of Auckland* [1997] NZCRT 14 (30 Apr. 1997), (1997) 4 HRNZ 107; *Pointu v. Employrite Ltd* [2002] NZHRRT 11 (1 Oct. 2002); *Director of Human Rights Proceedings v. NZ Institute of Chartered Accountants* [2015] NZHRRT 54 (18 Dec. 2015).

contracts, awards, scholarships, honours, or other benefits; or for the purposes of insurance. 'Evaluative material' does not include material that is compiled in the course of one's work, since protected material is compiled on the basis of a promise of confidentiality, not as a duty undertaken under a work contract.[417]

V. Security, Defence, and International Relations

379. Section 51 provides that an agency may refuse an access request if the disclosure of the information would be likely to prejudice: the security or defence of New Zealand, or its international relations; the entrusting of information to the New Zealand government on a basis of confidence by the government or any agency of any other country or any international organisation;[418] or the security or defence or international relations of its dependencies and associated states.

VI. Trade Secrets

380. Section 52 provides that an agency may refuse an access request if the information needs protection because disclosing it would reveal a trade secret,[419] or be likely to unreasonably prejudice the commercial position of the person who supplied the information or who is the subject of it.[420] The grounds for refusal are subject to a public interest balancing test, whereby the exception does not apply 'if, in the circumstances of the particular case, the withholding of that information is outweighed by other considerations that make it desirable, in the public interest, to make the information available'.[421]

381. In practice, section 52 is seldom invoked. The exception relating to prejudice to a person's commercial position can arise where an unsuccessful tenderer seeks access to information as to how far short the tender made was from that of the successful tenderer.

VII. Miscellaneous Reasons for Refusing Access

382. Section 53 provides for the remainder of good reasons for refusing an access request under IPP 6(1)(b).

---

417. Privacy Act, s. 50(2).

418. *See*, for example, *Kaiser v. Ministry of Agriculture and Forestry, Customs Department and the Department of Conservation* [2009] NZHRRT 10 (26 May 2009).

419. Privacy Act, s. 52(1)(a). *Case Note 36631* [2003] NZPrivCmr 14 (July 2003), where the Privacy Commissioner rejected a bank's claims that some of its documents constituted a 'trade secret'. The case note contains a discussion of what a 'trade secret' is in this context.

420. Privacy Act, s. 52(1)(b).

421. Privacy Act, s. 52(2).

A. Information Does Not Exist or Cannot Be Found

383. Section 53(a) contains two practical reasons for refusing access: that the information does not exist; and that despite reasonable efforts to locate it, it cannot be found. Cases in this area tend to arise because files have been mislaid.[422] In *Mitchell v. Police Commissioner*,[423] the Tribunal found that the search conducted for the information 'was mechanical rather than intelligent', and that some obvious lines of inquiry were not pursued. Accordingly, the Tribunal was not satisfied that a reasonable search had been made for the information.

384. Note that an agency has an obligation to transfer a request for personal information to another agency if it does not hold the information, but believes it to be held by another agency, or where the request is more closely connected with the functions or activities of another agency.[424]

B. Unwarranted Disclosure of Another's Affairs

385. Section 53(b) provides for the withholding of information where disclosure would involve the unwarranted disclosure of the affairs of another individual, living or dead. Accordingly, there are two limbs for refusing disclosure under this provision: first, the disclosure of the information would disclose the affairs of another person; and second, the disclosure would be unwarranted. This is one of the most common reasons for refusing access to personal information.

386. In *O v. N (No 2)*,[425] the Tribunal described the scope and application of this exception in the circumstances of that case as:

> the primary regulator of mixed information, i.e., information about two or more individuals. It means that an agency cannot delete information about a person other than the requester automatically. If the information is 'about' the requester, and that is a very wide net, then it can be withheld only if it would be an 'unwarrantable' disclosure of the 'affairs' of some other person of whom the information is also about.

387. An issue that arose in *Director of Human Rights Proceedings v. Commissioner of Police*,[426] was whether the assessment of what amounts to an 'unwarranted disclosure' should be approached objectively or subjectively. The Tribunal

422. *See*, for example, *Bartkus v. Parry Field and Co* [2000] NZCRT 22 (13 Sep. 2000); *Sansom v. Department of Internal Affairs* [2016] NZHRRT 17 (11 May 2016); *Yiasoumi v. Attorney-General* [2017] NZHRRT 12 (11 Apr. 2017).
423. [1994] NZCRT 3 (4 Nov. 1994); (1995) HRNZ 403; [1995] NZAR 274.
424. Privacy Act, s. 43(1).
425. [1996] NZCRT 4 (12 Mar. 1996), (1996) 3 HRNZ 636, at 650.
426. [2007] NZHRRT 22 (6 Nov. 2007).

appeared to favour an objective assessment, but where there are real concerns felt by the individual about the consequences of disclosure, a subjective approach may also be appropriate.

388. The Privacy Commissioner has commented on the general approach to be taken under this exception as follows:

> This requires agencies to balance the privacy interests of the person seeking the information against the interests of other people involved. Considerations such as the nature of the information, the purpose for which it was supplied, the purpose for which it was requested, and the extent of the requester's prior knowledge of the information might be relevant.[427]

389. Among factors that have favoured refusing to disclose information include a previous assurance that the individual would not be identified, such as in cases involving complainants and informants.[428] Among factors that have favoured disclosure of another individual's information in other cases is whether the requestor is already aware of the other individual's identity and the general content of the information concerned.[429] The starting point for any agency wishing to rely on section 53(b) will often be consultation with the individual who would be affected by the disclosure of his or her affairs.[430] If the other individual does not object to disclosure of their information, there will not be an issue under this exception. If the other individual opposes disclosure, however, other factors may be relevant to the agency's decision to disclose or withhold the information.

C. Prejudice to Maintenance of the Law

390. Section 53(c) provides that an agency may refuse to disclose personal information if it would be likely to prejudice the maintenance of the law by a public sector agency. The provision contains two limbs that are singled out in particular: first, prejudice to the prevention, investigation and detection of offences and, second, prejudice to the right to a fair trial. There have been a relatively large number of cases concerning the first limb of this exception.

391. The section 53(c) reason for refusing access is often invoked to protect the identity of informants. The Tribunal has accepted that the identity of informants is

---

427. *Case Note 15513* [1998] NZPrivCmr 5 (Feb. 1998).

428. *Director of Human Rights Proceedings v. Commissioner of Police* [2007] NZHRRT 22 (6 Nov. 2007); *Lohr v. Accident Compensation Corporation* [2016] NZHRRT 31 (29 Sep. 2016); *Case Note 93741* [2007] NZPrivCmr 9 (1 Jun. 2007); *Case Note 99971* [2008] NZPrivCmr 12 (1 Aug. 2008); *Case Note 207459* [2009] NZPrivCmr 17 (Oct. 2009); *Case Note 229963* [2011] NZPrivCmr 9 (9 Dec. 2011); *Case Note 236708* [2012] NZPrivCmr 11 (Dec. 2012).

429. *Case Note 15513* [1998] NZPrivCmr 5 (1 Feb. 1998); *Case Note 83694* [2006] NZPrivCmr 3 (Mar. 2006); *Case Note 84948* [2006] NZPrivCmr 4 (June 2006); *Case Note 942046* [2007] NZPrivCmr 3 (Mar. 2007); *Case Note 294247* [2019] NZPrivCmr 1 (22 Jan. 2019).

430. (1993) 10(2) CCNO 93.

personal information about the individual informed upon.[431] In one case, the Tribunal commented that 'we do not accept that it is possible to sever the connection between the information provided and its source because the two are so intimately connected. The information was provided generally as a result of what the informants saw, heard, or otherwise experienced'.[432] The section 53(c) exception has also been invoked to protect investigations while they are in progress,[433] and also on the basis that they would be likely to prejudice future investigations or detections of offences.[434]

392. The scope of section 53(c) is not limited to criminal matters, but can apply more widely to any public sector agency that deals with law enforcement issues, such as investigations of dishonesty or misconduct by public social welfare or accident insurance agencies,[435] and psychological reports held by the Department of Corrections for parole purposes.[436] In one case, the exception was invoked to protect the identity of people who commented on the requestor's suitability for a firearms licence after he applied for one from the police.[437]

D. Breach of Legal Professional Privilege

393. Section 53(d) provides that an agency may refuse to disclose information where disclosure would breach legal professional privilege.[438] There have been a relatively large number of cases on this exception. In *Adams v. Police*,[439] for example, the Tribunal found that the defendant properly withheld two legal opinions and a letter from outside legal advisers on the basis that they were subject to legal professional privilege. This was because they were communications between client and legal adviser.

---

431. *Hadfield v. Police* [1996] NZCRT (25 Jun. 1996), (1996) 3 HRNZ 115; *Nicholl v. Chief Executive Department of Work and Income* [2001] NZCRT 18 (31 Aug. 2001), upheld on appeal in *Nicholl v. Department of Work and Income* [2003] 3 NZLR 426; *Lohr v. Accident Compensation Corporation* [2016] NZHRRT 31 (23 Sep. 2016).
432. *Adams v. Police* [1997] NZCRT 16 (12 Jun. 1997), at p. 7.
433. *Case Note 0437* [1994] (not numbered); *Case Note 0845* [1994] NZPrivCmr 18 (31 Jan. 1994).
434. *Adams v. Police* [1997] NZCRT 16 (12 Jun. 1997); *Case Note 208123* [2010] NZPrivCmr 12 (June 2010).
435. *See*, for example, *Case Note 0107* [1994] NZPrivCmr 4 (31 Jan. 1994); *Case Note 0115* [1994] NZPrivCmr 5 (31 Jan. 1994); *Case Note 0549* [1994] NZPrivCmr 10 (31 Jan. 1994); *Case Note 0757* [1994] NZPrivCmr 16 (31 Jan. 1994); *Case Note 14554* [2001] NZPrivCmr 19 (Oct. 2001); *Case Note 80156* [2005] NZPrivCmr 2 (Mar. 2005); *Case Note 94010* [2007] NZPrivCmr 6 (Mar. 2007); *Lohr v. Accident Compensation Corporation* [2016] NZHRRT 31 (23 Sep. 2016).
436. *Case Note 290543* [2021] NZPrivCmr 7 (7 Apr. 2021).
437. *Case Note 93741* [2007] NZPrivCmr 9 (June 2007).
438. Legal professional privilege protects lawyer-client communications; communications between a lawyer and third parties, if made for the purpose of pending or contemplated litigation; and communications between the client and third parties, if made in order to obtain information to be submitted to the client's lawyer for the purpose of obtaining advice upon pending or contemplated litigation.
439. [1997] NZCRT 16 (12 Jun. 1997).

394. Where doubt arises as to the purpose for which a document has been brought into existence or a communication made, one applies the 'dominant purpose' test from the CA decision in *Guardian Royal Exchange Assurance v. Stuart*[440] to decide whether or not the privilege will apply. Thus, in a case involving a complaint against an insurance company for refusing to disclose a file on the complainant's claim for a stolen vehicle on the basis of legal professional privilege,[441] the Privacy Commissioner commented:

> the dominant purpose for the preparation of most of the documents on the file was to decide whether or not to accept the complainant's claim. I noted that if a decision was made to decline the claim and this decision became the subject of litigation then, no doubt, many of the documents would have been provided to the company's legal advisors to allow them to conduct or advise in respect of that litigation. However, it did not appear from the file that at the time the information was prepared litigation was reasonably apprehended; while facilitating the ability of the company's legal advisors to conduct litigation may have been an ancillary purpose for the preparation of the information, I did not consider it was the dominant purpose.

395. The section 53(d) exception has been invoked in a number of employment law disputes.[442] In one,[443] information contained in a draft report was able to be withheld under legal professional privilege since the lawyer's advice written in the margins was not finalised. The employer accepted that the privilege would not attach to the final report, which would take into consideration any comments made by the employee. In the result, however, the employee left the employment before the final report was produced, so the privilege applied to the report. The exception has also been successfully invoked by the police when they received advice from their in-house solicitor,[444] and when they decided on the basis of their legal section not to prosecute some people about whom the requestor had complained.[445]

396. Legal professional privilege, like any privilege, can be waived by the client. There are circumstances, however, where the existence or extent of the waiver may be disputed. In *Case Note 84948*,[446] for example, the Privacy Commissioner considered that legal professional privilege had been waived when during a settlement meeting one of the employer's solicitors told the complainant and her lawyer that she could get a copy of an email sought by her. Moreover, the substantive contents of the email had also been disclosed to the woman in the course of this meeting.

---

440. *Guardian Royal Exchange Assurance v. Stuart* [1985] 1 NZLR 596 (CA), at 602.
441. *Case Note 0305* [1994] NZPrivCmr 8 (31 Jan. 1994). *See also Case Note 20612* [2003] NZPrivCmr 16 (1 Jul. 2003); *Case Note 228045* [2012] NZPrivCmr 8 (1 Dec. 2012); and *Case Note 248835* [2015] NZPrivCmr 5 (24 Feb. 2015).
442. *Case Note 84948* [2006] NZPrivCmr 4 (1 Jun. 2006).
443. *Case Note 73919* [2006] NZPrivCmr 5 (1 Jun. 2006).
444. *Case Note 95812* [2007] NZPrivCmr 11 (1 Jun. 2007).
445. *Case Note 201228* [2009] NZPrivCmr 3 (1 Jan. 2009).
446. [2006] NZPrivCmr 4 (1 Jun. 2006).

E. Breach of a Condition Binding on a Library, Museum, or Archive

397. The section 53(e) reason for refusing access to personal information held in any library, museum, or archive is limited to where disclosure would breach a condition under which the material was placed in the institution. Personal information is otherwise available to a requestor.

F. Contempt of Court or the House of Representatives

398. The section 53(f) exception provides that an agency may refuse access if disclosure of the information would amount to contempt of court or of the House of Representatives.

399. Contempt of Court arises from actions that tend to obstruct or interfere with the orderly administration of justice, or impair the dignity of the court or respect for its authority. The section 53(f) ground for refusing access on the basis of contempt of court may overlap in some circumstances with the section 53(c)(ii) ground for refusing access, that disclosure of the information would be likely to prejudice the right to a fair trial. As noted by commentators, 'A fair trial means a trial conducted free from prejudice and in which the court tries a case impartially after considering all the available evidence which has been properly submitted.'[447] Where a publication is prejudicial to a fair trial, it is also contemptuous.[448] Thus, where a disclosure is thought to amount to a contempt of court and prejudices the right to a fair trial, the agency may rely on either or both section 53(c)(ii) and (f) for refusing disclosure. Under section 53(c)(ii), the legal test is whether the disclosure 'would be likely' to prejudice the right to a fair trial; that is, whether there is a 'real and substantial risk'. Under section 53(f), the test is whether the disclosure 'would constitute contempt of court'. Therefore, under either section, the information could be withheld if disclosure would amount to contempt, for in relation to section 53(c)(ii) it also 'would be likely' to prejudice the right to a fair trial.

400. Contempt of the House of Representatives[449] can arise when individuals disclose their own or others' submissions to a Parliamentary select committee before they have been considered by the select committee. Section 53(f) in particular serves to protect ministers and government officials who have confidential select

447. G Borrie and N Lowe, *The Law of Contempt* (London, 1973), at 35
448. *Case No 4* (1984) 5 CCNO 12 (GR Laking), at 19.
449. In *Rata v. The Attorney-General*, Wellington High Court, CP 213/94 (19 Mar. 1997), one of the few cases in the area, the plaintiff sought discovery of caucus records that recorded confidential matters that were discussed by a political party behind closed doors in the Parliament, but he failed on the ground that the information was protected by Parliamentary privilege, and thus their disclosure could amount to contempt of the House of Representatives. The confidential internal affairs of the legislature are protected by Parliamentary privilege until such time as matters are allowed to be made public.

committee documents circulated to them in the course of their duties from having to disclose them under the Privacy Act and thereby committing a contempt against the House of Representatives.

G. Information Available under Criminal Disclosure Act 2008

401. The section 53(g) exception provides that an agency may refuse access to personal information where the request is made by a defendant or a defendant's agent in a criminal matter, and is either for information that could be sought by the defendant under the Criminal Disclosure Act 2008, or that could be sought by the defendant under that Act and that has already been disclosed to, or withheld from, the defendant under that Act.

402. The purpose of the Criminal Disclosure Act is 'to promote fair, effective, and efficient disclosure of relevant information between the prosecution and the defence, and by non-parties, for the purposes of criminal proceedings'.[450] It establishes a four-fold disclosure regime that requires first initial, and then full disclosure by the prosecution; disclosure of certain information by the defence; and disclosure by third parties in certain circumstances. The section 53(g) exception in the Privacy Act therefore is in place to prevent duplication and avoid confusion in this area of the criminal law.

H. Request Is Frivolous or Vexatious or Information Requested Is Trivial

403. Section 53(h) of the Act provides that an agency may refuse disclosure where the request is frivolous or vexatious, or the information requested is trivial. The aim of this provision is to prevent abuse of the IPP 6 right by individuals whose aim is to harass or waste the time and resources of an agency.

404. The Privacy Commissioner and Tribunal have adopted the Ombudsmen's approach towards this provision,[451] the Commissioner noting that:

> for a request to be refused on the grounds that it is vexatious, the requester must be believed to be patently abusing the rights of access to information, rather than exercising those rights in a bona fide manner. [The provision] recognises the possibility of unbalanced, mischievous or malicious individuals bothering agencies with time-wasting requests. To determine whether a request is vexatious, the nature of the request in light of the surrounding circumstances needs to be considered.

---

450. Criminal Disclosure Act, s. 3(1).

451. *Case Note 18109* [1999] NZPrivCmr 14 (1 Aug. 1999), *Proceedings Commissioner v. Commissioner of Police* [2000] NZCRT 18 (10 Jul. 2000).

405. In *Dotcom v. Crown Law Office*,[452] the Tribunal stated that 'An information privacy request does not have to be justified by reasons, nor does the information sought need to be particularised.'[453] As 'everything' requests are the norm (requests for all personal information held by an agency), 'a lack of particularity is not, on its own, an indication that a request is vexatious'. The assessment of vexatiousness is an objective one.[454] The Tribunal went on to note that it should be 'manifestly clear', looking at all of the circumstances objectively, that a request is frivolous or vexatious or the information requested is trivial. In making this evaluation, an agency needs to realise that the requestor is unaware of the nature and content of the personal information that the agency holds. Likewise, the agency is ordinarily unaware of the reason for the information access request and its significance to the requester, so that 'an agency is not always in the best position to determine, objectively, what is in truth 'frivolous' or 'vexatious' or 'trivial'.[455] The Tribunal stated that the issue whether or not a request is 'vexatious' under this provision 'is highly fact specific and the assessment must be made in the context of the particular request and decision'.[456]

406. Repeated access requests under IPP 6 do not necessarily mean that that a request is vexatious. In *Proceedings Commissioner v. Commissioner of Police*,[457] the police withheld the information relating to the complainant's assailants on the basis that the request was frivolous or vexatious. The complainant was otherwise known to the police as someone who had lodged a number of complaints and requests for information over the years, often in relation to matters in which he was not personally involved. Neither the Privacy Commissioner accepted that this reason for withholding the information was valid, nor did the Tribunal. The Tribunal adverted to the Ombudsmen's approach in regarding repeated requests for the same information as that already provided to be vexatious, but here the Tribunal found that:

> it is clear that the information sought had not already been provided and that it was withheld from him principally because he had made a number of requests for other information which the defendant found to be burdensome and had been a nuisance to the defendant in other ways. Since this is not a valid basis for regarding a request as vexatious it cannot be upheld as justified in the circumstances of this case.[458]

452. [2018] NZHRRT 7 (26 Mar. 2018), Although the Tribunal's decision was overturned on appeal in [2018] NZHC 2564, the High Court largely agreed with the Tribunal's approach to the law but disagreed on the facts; and on further appeal, the Court of Appeal overturned that decision in *Dotcom v. Attorney-General* [2020] NZCA 551 (10 Nov. 2020).
453. *Ibid.*, at para. 36.4.
454. *Ibid.*, at para. 146.3.
455. *Ibid.*, at para. 147.6.
456. *Ibid.*, at para. 149.
457. [2000] NZHRRT 18 (10 Jul. 2000).
458. *Ibid.*, at p. 5.

407. In *Case Note 285353*,[459] an airline withheld personal information from a disgruntled customer on the basis that his requests were vexatious. The Privacy Commissioner formed the view that while his first request was not vexatious, his subsequent requests were, and his complaint in its entirely was not upheld on that basis. The complainant's bad behaviour deteriorated in the course of his dealings with the airline, and he became abusive and difficult to engage with. The Commissioner commented that an agency may not rely on the vexatious request exception 'just because a requester is difficult or even malicious. The request itself needs to be frivolous or vexatious'. Factors that could suggest that a request is vexatious include:

– many requests for the same information without any clear reason;
– using information from one request to demand more information – one request leading to another, and another;
– abusive or aggressive behaviour and no clear need for the information; and
– clear intent to use the request to divert the agency's resources or upset people.

408. In relation to the ground that 'the information requested is trivial', the Ombudsmen in their analogous freedom of information jurisdiction have noted that:[460]

– agencies should consider the nature of the information and what is known about the purpose of the request;
– information that seems trivial to an agency may be very important to a requester;
– agencies should consider consulting the requester, who may be able to clarify the terms of the request (so that truly trivial information is excluded), or their purpose in seeking the information. Such consultation is consistent with an agency's duty to provide reasonable assistance to requesters;[461]
– the volume of information at issue may also be relevant. It is usually no problem to supply a small amount of information, even if it does seem trivial. It may be more difficult, and not ultimately worth the effort, if there is a significant amount of trivial information at issue.

§3. Limitations on Making Personal Information Available

I. Imposition of Conditions

409. Section 54 of the Act provides that if an agency is entitled to refuse an IPP 6 request under sections 49–53, it may, instead of refusing access to the personal

459. [2018] NZPrivCmr 3 (Mar. 2018).
460. 'Frivolous, vexatious and trivial: A guide to s. 18(h) of the OIA [Official Information Act 1982] and s/ 17(h) of the LGOIMA [Local Government Official Information and Meetings Act 1987]' 16 Mar. 2019, at p. 12.
461. Compare s. 42 of the Privacy Act.

information, grant access subject to the imposition of conditions on the requestor's use of the information, or the disclosure of the information to any other person.

II. Information Contained in Documents

410. Section 55(1)–(2) of the Act provides that if there is a good reason under sections 49–53 to refuse to disclose some of the information in a document, the agency may grant access to other information contained in it by making a copy of the document available with any deletions and alterations it considers necessary. In respect of any withheld information, the agency must inform the requestor of the reasons for not making all of the information available, and of the requestor's right to complain to the Privacy Commissioner.

411. Section 55(3)–(4) of the Act provides that an agency must disclose to the requestor the grounds in support of withholding information if the reason for refusing access is the 'evaluative material' reason in section 50(1)(a). If the information is withheld for another reason, then the agency must disclose the grounds in support of the reason for withholding if the requestor has requested it. In either case, the availability of the grounds in support of the reasons for the decision to withhold is subject to not prejudicing the interests protected by section 50(1), and sections 49, 51, and 53. Withholding the grounds in support of a decision under section 52 (concerning trade secrets and an agency's commercial position), however, is subject to a public interest balancing test.

412. The term 'document' is defined in the Act 'as a document in any form, and includes':[462]

- any writing on any material;
- any information recorded or stored by means of any computer or other device, and any material subsequently derived from information so recorded or stored;
- any label, marking, or other writing that identifies or describes anything of which it forms part, or to which it is attached by any means;
- any book, map, plan, graph, or drawing;
- any photograph, film, negative, tape, or any device in which one or more visual images are embodied so as to be capable (with or without the aid of some other equipment) of being reproduced.

III. Ways in Which Personal Information May Be Made Available

413. Section 56 of the Act sets out the ways in which personal information contained in a document[463] may be made available to a requestor. The information may be made available in one or more of the following ways:

---

462. Privacy Act, s. 7(1).
463. *See* Part II, Ch. 3.1.3 and Part IV, Ch 2.3.2 above for the definition of 'document'.

- giving the requestor a reasonable opportunity to inspect the document;
- providing the requestor with a hard or an electronic copy of the document;
- arranging for the requestor to hear the sounds or view visual images where the document is in the form of a visual or aural medium;
- providing the requestor with a written transcript of the words recorded or contained in the document where the document contains sound or words in the form of shorthand writing or in codified form;
- giving, in any manner, an excerpt or summary of the document's contents;
- giving oral information about the document's contents.

414. IPP 6 covers personal information that is held not only in documentary form, but also information that is held in another person's memory, as the definition of 'personal information' extends wider than physically recorded form.[464] In the that case, persons holding information in their memory may be required to commit the information to writing to enable access.[465]

415. Unless there are good reasons for providing the information in another form, an agency must make personal information available in the way preferred by the requestor.[466] The good reasons for an agency to provide information in another form are that otherwise the efficient administration of the agency would be impaired; it would be contrary to a legal duty regarding the document; or it would prejudice an interest protected under the Act's grounds for refusing access. For example, impairment of the agency's efficient administration was accepted in one case where photocopies of an accident insurance recipient's files extending back for twenty years had been requested.[467] The Privacy Commissioner found that it was sufficient that the agency had invited the requestor to view his files, with an offer to photocopy any parts that he wanted to take away. In another case,[468] an employee who had been dismissed requested all of his work emails over a twelve-month period, which amounted to 12,000 emails and additional attached documents. The Commissioner accepted that it would impair efficient administration to comply with the request as framed, but the employee was advised that he could provide the employer with a specific list of information he wished to access.

416. If the agency does not provide information in the way preferred by the requestor, it must provide its reason for not doing so.[469] The requestor may request the grounds in support of the reason for not providing the information in the way preferred unless disclosure of the grounds would prejudice an interest protected by sections 49–53.[470]

---

464. *See* Part II, Ch. 3.1.3.
465. *See*, for example, the Tribunal case *L v. J* [1999] NZCRT 9 (26 Apr. 1999), (1999) 5 HRNZ 616.
466. Privacy Act, s. 56(2).
467. *Case Note 7602* [2007] NZPrivCmr 11 (1 Dec. 1997).
468. *Case Note 287145* [2017] NZPrivCmr 12 (Dec. 2017).
469. Privacy Act, s. 56(3)(a).
470. Privacy Act, s. 56(3)(b) and (4).

417. Access is required to be 'meaningful', as the Tribunal stated in *Naidu v. Royal Australasian College of Surgeons.*[471] To that end, the personal information must be 'intelligible' to requestors. The requirement that all information had to be intelligible was extrapolated from the Act's specification of the assortment of ways in which documents might be made available to the requestor,[472] as well as one of the purposes of the Act, which was the promotion and protection of individual privacy in general accordance with the OECD Guidelines.[473] Among these guidelines is the right of individuals to have data communicated to them 'in a form that is readily intelligible',[474] The Tribunal described this as 'an inherent aspect of the "meaningful accesses" standard'.[475] In the *Naidu* decision, the requestor, a physician, unsuccessfully applied for admission to a training programme in orthopaedic surgery. He was denied admission on the basis of his referee scores. He requested access to his file under IPP 6, but while he received a table summarising his referee scores, little meaningful information was disclosed as the scores lacked context. The Tribunal accepted that the formula or mechanism by which the referee scores were calculated should have been disclosed, as it was a 'condition precedent to being able to access personal information'.[476]

§4. Procedural Provisions

I. Making and Complying with an Access Request

418. IPP 6(3) provides that IPP 6 is subject to the procedural provisions relating to access to personal information in Part 4 of the Act.[477]

419. An IPP 6 access request may only be made by the individual concerned or that individual's representative.[478] The Act does not prescribe any particular form that such requests must take. There is no requirement that requestors of access requests must give reasons for their request, unless the request is urgent.[479] When determining the priority to be given to its response to an urgent request, the agency

471. [2018] NZHRRT 23 (14 Jun. 2018), at para. 36.
472. Under the predecessor provisions to s. 56(1)(c) and (d) under the Privacy Act 1993 (s. 42(1)(c) and (d)).
473. This was expressed in the long title to the Privacy Act 1993, but is currently found in s. 3(b) of the Privacy Act 2020.
474. OECD Recommendation of the Council concerning Guidelines Governing the Protection of Privacy and Transborder Flows of Personal Data, adopted 23 Sep. 1980, amended 11 Jul. 2013, Part 2, cl. 13(b)(iv).
475. *Naidu v. Royal Australasian College of Surgeons* [2018] NZHRRT 23 (14 Jun. 2018), at para. 40.
476. *Ibid.*, at para. 36.
477. These provisions are contained in subpart 2 ('Access to personal information').
478. Privacy Act, s. 40.
479. Privacy Act, s. 41(2). *See Koso v. Chief Executive, Ministry of Business, Innovation and Employment* [2014] NZHRRT 39 (29 Aug. 2014), (2014) 9 HRNZ 786; *Dotcom v. Crown Law Office* [2018] NZHRRT 7 (26 Mar. 2018); *Dotcom v. Attorney-General* [2020] NZCA 551 (10 Nov. 2020).

must consider it and the reason given for its urgency.[480] An agency is required to provide reasonable assistance to a person who wishes to make, or is making, an access request.[481] Where an agency does not hold the requested information but believes that it is held by another agency, or the agency believes that the information is more closely connected with the functions or activities of another agency, the agency must transfer the request.[482] If a transfer is made to another agency, the transferring agency must promptly, and no later than ten working days after the day the correction request was received, transfer the request to the other agency and inform the requestor of the transfer.[483] An agency has no duty to transfer a request if it has good cause to believe that the requestor does not want the request to be transferred to another agency. In that case, the agency must promptly, and no later than ten working days after the request was received, inform the requestor to that effect, as well as the name of the agency to which the request could be transferred.[484]

420. If the IPP 6 request has not been transferred, the agency must, as soon as is reasonably practicable, and no later than twenty working days after receiving the request, respond to it. The agency must notify the requestor whether it does not hold information in a way that enables the information to be readily retrieved;[485] whether the agency does not hold any personal information about the individual to whom the request relates;[486] whether access to the information, or some of it, is granted;[487] whether access to the information, or some of it, is refused;[488] or whether the agency neither confirms nor denies that it holds any personal information about the individual.[489] Where an agency decides to grant access to personal information, the notice given to the requestor must state the way the information is to be made available; the charge (if any) in respect of the request, and whether it is to be paid in advance; and the requestor's right to complain to the Privacy Commissioner about the charge.[490] After giving the notice and receiving any charge that is payable in advance, the agency is required to make the information available to the requestor.[491] An agency may only refuse an access request if it is able to rely on an exception set out in sections 49 to 53 (or if another law regulates or prohibits access to the information).[492] The requestor must be notified of the agency's reason

480. Privacy Act, s. 41(3).
481. Privacy Act, s. 42. *See Dotcom v. Attorney-General* [2020] NZCA 551 (10 Nov. 2020), at para. 79.
482. Privacy Act, s. 43(1)–(2). *See Dotcom v. Crown Law Office* [2018] NZHRRT 7; *Attorney-General v. Dotcom* [2018] NZHC 2564, [2019] 2 NZLR 277; *Dotcom v. Attorney-General* [2020] NZCA 551 (10 Nov. 2020).
483. Privacy At, s. 43(2).
484. Privacy Act, s 43(3)–(4).
485. Privacy Act, s. 44(2)(a). 'Readily retrieved' has been approached as meaning 'without undue difficulty': *see Case No 860* (1987) 8 CCNO 71 (J Robertson).
486. Privacy Act, s. 44(2)(b).
487. Privacy Act, s. 44(2)(c)(i).
488. Privacy Act, s. Privacy Act, s. 44(2)(c)(ii).
489. Privacy Act, s. Privacy Act, s. 44(2)(d).
490. Privacy Act, s. 45(1).
491. Privacy Act, s. 45(2).
492. Privacy Act, s. 46(1).

for its refusal, and the requestor's right to complain to the Privacy Commissioner in respect of the refusal.[493] Where an agency refuses a request on the basis of the 'evaluative material' exception,[494] requestors have a further right to be provided not only with the reason for the refused access, but also with the grounds in support of the reason[495] without first having to request it.[496] This position is different from the other grounds for withholding, where the requestor who has been refused access is provided with the reason, but must ask on their own initiative for the grounds in support of the reason.[497]

421. Section 47 empowers an agency to respond to a requestor that it neither confirms nor denies that it holds personal information that has been requested. The access request must be able to be refused on the basis of the section 49(1)(a)(i) or (d), section 51, section 52 or section 53(c) grounds for withholding, and the agency must be satisfied that the important interests protected by those provisions would be likely to be prejudiced if the agency confirmed whether or not it holds the information. If an agency invokes section 47, the requestor must be informed of the right to complain about the agency's response to the Privacy Commissioner. Complaints under section 47, all unsuccessful, have been made against the NZSIS,[498] the GCSB,[499] and the police (in relation to whether or not the complainant was under surveillance).[500]

422. An agency may extend the ten-working-day time limit in certain circumstances in relation to transfers of requests, and the twenty-working-day time limit in relation to responding to a correction request.[501] Any extension must be for a reasonable period, having regard to the circumstances.[502] Extensions may be made only on the basis that a large quantity of information must be searched through; consultations are necessary in order to make the decision; or complex issues are raised in processing the request.[503] An extension must be notified to the requestor within twenty working days after the day on which the request was received, giving the reasons for the extension and informing the requestor of the right to complain to the Privacy Commissioner.[504]

423. Section 57 of the Act sets out the responsibilities of an agency before making personal information available in response to an IPP 6 request. It requires an agency to take appropriate precautions to ensure that information is disclosed only

493. Privacy Act, s. 46(2).
494. Privacy Act, s. 50(1).
495. Subject to s. 46(4)(a).
496. Privacy Act, s. 46(3)(a).
497. Privacy Act, s. 46(3)(b).
498. *Case Note 0635* [1994] NZPrivCmr 15 (31 Jan. 1994); *Case Note 219773* [2010] NZPrivCmr 25 (16 Dec. 2010); *Case Note 284416* [2017] NZPrivCmr 5 (May 2017).
499. *Case Note 284416* [2017] NZPrivCmr 5 (May 2017).
500. *Case Note 202975* [2010] NZPrivCmr 19 (Sept. 2010).
501. Privacy Act, s. 48.
502. Privacy Act, s. 48(2).
503. Privacy Act, s. 48(1).
504. Privacy Act, s. 48(4).

to the requestor or the requestor's representative, and the agency must be satisfied of the requestor's identity.[505] If the request is made by a person as an agent of the individual, the requestor must have written authority to obtain the information, or be otherwise authorised by the individual to obtain it.[506] An agency must not give access to the information if it reasonably believes that the request is made under the threat of physical or mental harm.[507]

424. While the agency receiving an IPP 6 request has obligations of care in respect of giving access to personal information to a requestor, representative or agent, there is a penalty of up to $10,000 where a person: 'misleads an agency by impersonating an individual, or falsely pretending to be an individual or to be acting under the authority of an individual, for the purpose of … obtaining access to that individual's personal information'.[508]

II. Charges Relating to Access to Personal Information

425. A public sector agency may impose a charge for making personal information available, but only if the Privacy Commissioner has authorised it if satisfied that the agency would otherwise be commercially disadvantaged in comparison with a competitor in the private sector.[509] A private sector agency may impose a charge for providing assistance to a requestor,[510] but only if the information is made available in due course;[511] and also for making information available in compliance with a request.[512]

426. A charge must be reasonable, and regard may be had to the cost of labour and materials in making the information available, as well as any costs involved in making information available urgently.[513] An agency may require a charge to be paid in advance.[514]

427. Individuals may complain to the Privacy Commissioner over the amount of charge imposed. The Commissioner will investigate and attempt to secure a settlement of the matter, and if a settlement is unable to be achieved, the Commissioner

505. Privacy Act, ss 57(a) and (c).
506. Privacy Act, s. 57(d).
507. Privacy Act, s. 57(b).
508. Privacy Act, s. 212(2)(c)(i).
509. Privacy Act, s. 67(1).
510. Under s. 42 of the Act. *See* above, at 2.4.1.
511. Privacy Act, s. 66(1)(i).
512. Privacy Act, s. 66(1)(ii).
513. Privacy Act, s. 66(4). Urgent requests are provided for under s. 41 of the Act.
514. Privacy Act, s. 66(5).

may determine whether the charge has been improperly imposed or is unreasonable.[515] If the Commissioner finds that the charge is unreasonable, the Commissioner may determine the appropriate charge for the agency to impose.[516] The Commissioner's determination on charging 'is final and binding, and no proceedings may be commenced in the Tribunal by the parties in respect of that determination'.[517]

§5. LIABILITY FOR BREACH OF IPP 6

428. A breach of IPP 6 results in 'an interference with the privacy of an individual',[518] and will render the agency concerned liable to the remedies provided for in the Act.[519]

429. Some harm or loss is necessary for liability under all the IPPs except for IPPs 6 and 7. Instead, liability for 'an interference with the privacy of an individual' for breach of IPP 6 arises from any the following actions, without the necessity for proving any harm or loss, if the agency lacks a proper basis for making:

- a decision to refuse a request;[520]
- any other decision under Part 4 in relation to the request.[521]

A failure to comply with the time limits in Part 4 for responding to the request is deemed to be a decision to refuse the request under IPP 6,[522] as is undue delay in making information available after granting the request.[523]

515. Privacy Act, s. 93(2). Notification of any advance payment is provided for under s. 45(1)(b) once a decision to grant access has been made.
516. Privacy Act, s. 93(3).
517. Privacy Act, s. 93(5).
518. Privacy Act, s 69(1).
519. *See* below, at Part VIII, Ch. 4.
520. Privacy Act, s 69(3)(a).
521. Privacy Act, s 69(3)(c).
522. Privacy Act, s 69(4)(a).
523. Privacy Act, s 69(4)(b).

Chapter 3. Rights of Rectification

§1. IPP 7: 'Correction of Personal Information'

430. IPP 7 provides for the individual's entitlements relating to the correction of personal information. IPP 7 is a corollary to the IPP 6 right of access. IPP 7 in turn is connected with the duty of agencies under IPP 8 to ensure that personal information is accurate. As with the right to access in IPP 6, no harm or loss for the individual is required to be shown to establish liability for breach as an 'interference with the privacy of an individual'.[524] The term 'correct' is defined in the Act in relation to personal information, as 'to alter that information by way of correction, deletion, or addition, and *correction* has a corresponding meaning'.[525] The core obligation under IPP 7(2) is that an agency 'must, on request or on its own initiative, take such steps (if any) that are reasonable in the circumstances to ensure that, having regard to the purposes for which the information may lawfully be used, the information is accurate, up-to-date, complete, and not misleading.'[526]

431. An individual has two entitlements under IPP 7: first, to request the agency concerned to correct personal information;[527] and second, to provide a statement of correction and request that it be attached to the personal information concerned if the agency does not make the correction sought.[528] If the agency is unwilling to correct the information and has been provided with a statement of correction, it is required to 'take such steps (if any) that are reasonable in the circumstances to ensure that the statement of correction is attached to the information in a manner that ensures that it will always be read with the information'.[529] While an agency is not actually required to correct contested information under IPP 7, the attached statement of a correction sought but not made shows that the data subject contests the information. Moreover, under IPP 8, the agency may not use the information 'without taking such steps (if any) as are, in the circumstances, reasonable to ensure that, having regard to the purpose for which the information is proposed to be used, the information is accurate, up-to-date, complete, relevant, and not misleading'. IPP 7(5) provides for third-party notification of any correction to personal information, whether the agency itself has corrected information or has attached a statement of correction. The agency is required, so far as is reasonably practicable, to inform every person to whom the agency has disclosed the information. There is, however, no obligation to follow up the notification of correction to third parties to ensure that it has been acted upon.[530]

524. Privacy Act, s. 69(3)–(5).
525. Privacy Act, s. 7(1). On deletion of personal information, *see* Ch. 4 below on the right to erasure.
526. Privacy Act, s. 22, IPP 7(2).
527. Privacy Act, s. 22, IPP 7(1).
528. Privacy Act, s. 22, IPP 7(3).
529. Privacy Act, s. 22, IPP 7(4).
530. *Case Note 7327* [2002] NZPrivCmr 7 (June 2002).

432. In *Plumtree v. Attorney-General on behalf of the New Zealand Defence Force*,[531] the plaintiff successfully contested the accuracy of his personal information in the Tribunal, which ordered the agency to correct the information. IPP 7 does not include an express obligation that agencies must compulsorily correct personal information, but the Tribunal was able to make the order under the Act's remedies provision,[532] which includes the power to make 'an order that the defendant performs any acts specified in the order with a view to remedying the interference (with the privacy of an individual)'.

433. In a case investigated by the Privacy Commissioner,[533] the government agency holding personal information was found to have had no reasonable ground to consider it to be correct. The Commissioner considered that Immigration New Zealand (INZ) breached IPP 7 by refusing to correct the complainant's birth date. The refusal to correct the information had had serious repercussions on the complainant's ability to access various entitlements and services because he was documented as not being old enough to be eligible. INZ, however, refused to change the birth date on file, so all the complainant could obtain was a 'correction requested but not granted' note for his file. The Commissioner considered that INZ had no reasonable grounds for believing that the birth date on file was correct, despite medical evidence to the contrary. The Commissioner found that INZ breached both IPPs 7 and 8 ('Accuracy, etc., of personal information to be checked before use or disclosure'), but the matter was eventually settled after INZ was publicly 'named and shamed'.

434. Personal information is not limited to information in documentary form. The difficulty, if not impossibility, of correcting non-documentary information, however, is self-evident. In *Sissons v. Capper*,[534] the Tribunal dealt with a claim that the defendant breached IPP 7, *inter alia,* because he failed to correct information about the plaintiff that had been communicated orally to other members of a club. The Tribunal noted that the information concerned was 'held in the minds of the defendant and club members (if they still remember the original information (the plaintiff) seeks to correct)'.[535] In these circumstances, the Tribunal remarked that the nature of the information and the manner in which it was held raised difficulties in maintaining that IPP 7 had been breached. The Tribunal commented, 'We think it is almost impossible to assert a breach of IPP 7 in circumstances where the information sought to be corrected is held only in the minds of individuals constituting the agency concerned'.[536] Accordingly, the Tribunal found that it would be impossible to find that IPP 7 had been breached in the circumstances.

531. [2002] NZHRRT 10 (2 Oct. 2002).
532. The power was exercised under s. 85(1)(d) of the Privacy Act 1993, which was re-enacted as s. 102(2)(d) of the 2020 Act.
533. *Case Note 264435* [2015] NZPrivCmr 8 (18 Aug. 2015).
534. [1999] NZCRT 22 (10 Aug. 1999).
535. *Ibid.*, at p. 6.
536. *Ibid.*

435. A breach of IPP 7 will also be difficult to sustain where the information concerned is largely subjective in nature. In *Macdonald v. Healthcare Hawkes Bay and Morrison*,[537] the Tribunal commented:

> Information which has some subjective content will always be harder to correct than that which is neutral in tone or objectively able to be verified because subjective information is less open to objective analysis. What is true and accurate for one participant in a conversation may well not be so for another. We think this is the reason why agencies have the ability pursuant to IPP 7 to choose whether to correct information or attach a statement of correction to it. A statement of correction enables more than one perspective of an incident or a conversation to be included with personal information held by the agency.[538]

436. Similarly, in *Jones v. Waitemata District Health Board*, the Tribunal discussed the difficulty of establishing factually correct health information where 'information may well be in the form of an opinion or comment "about" the individual which may at some time become relevant in the clinical context alongside other health information'.[539]

§2. PROCEDURAL PROVISIONS

I. Making and Complying with a Correction Request

437. IPP 7(6) provides that IPP 7(1)–(4) are subject to the procedural provisions relating to the correction of personal information in Part 4 of the Act. These provisions are contained in subpart 2 ('Correction of personal information').

438. There are two types of correction requests: a request made under IPP 7(1) to correct personal information, and a request made under IPP 7(3)(b) to attach a statement of correction sought but not made to personal information.[540] IPP 7 correction requests may only be made by the individual to whom the information relates, or that individual's representative.[541] The Act does not prescribe any particular form that such requests must take. There is no requirement that requestors of correction requests must give reasons for their request, unless the request is urgent.[542] When determining the priority to be given to its response to such an urgent request, the agency must consider it and the reason given for its urgency.[543] An agency is required to provide reasonable assistance to a person who wishes to make, or is making, a correction request.[544] Where an agency does not hold the

537. [2000] NZCRT 35 (6 Dec. 2000).
538. *Ibid.*, at p. 3.
539. [2014] NZHRRT 52, at para. 40.
540. Privacy Act, s. 58(1).
541. Privacy Act, s. 59.
542. Privacy Act, s. 60(2).
543. Privacy Act, s. 60(3).
544. Privacy Act, s. 61.

requested information but believes that it is held by another agency, or the agency believes that the information is more closely connected with the functions or activities of another agency, the agency must transfer the request. If a transfer is made to another agency, the transferring agency must promptly, and no later than ten working days after the day the correction request was received, transfer the request to the other agency and inform the requestor of the transfer.[545] An agency has no duty to transfer a request if it has good cause to believe that the requestor does not want the request to be transferred to another agency. In that case, the agency must promptly, and no later than ten working days after the request was received, inform the requestor to that effect, as well as the name of the agency to which the request could be transferred.[546]

439. Where a correction request has not been transferred, the agency must respond to the request as soon as reasonably practicable, and no later than twenty working days.[547] In its response, an agency is required to notify the requestor of the action the agency has taken on the request. If the requestor is notified that the agency will not correct the information as requested, the requestor must also be notified of the agency's reason for its refusal, and the requestor's entitlements to provide a statement of the correction sought and to request that it be attached to the information concerned. The requestor must also be informed of the right to complain to the Privacy Commissioner concerning the refusal to correct the information.[548] When receiving a request for the attachment of a statement of correction under IPP 7(3)(b), an agency must decide whether to grant the request, and must notify the requestor whether or not it has attached the statement of correction.[549] The grounds for an agency's refusal to attach the statement are not specified. The only obvious basis for not attaching a statement of correction is implicit in IPP 7(4): where it is 'not reasonable in the circumstances' to attach such a statement 'in a manner that ensures that it will always be read with the information'. For example, there may be technical reasons rendering it impossible to attach a statement of correction. If the agency has not attached the statement of correction, the agency must inform the requestor of the right to complain to the Commissioner concerning the agency's refusal.

440. An agency may extend the ten-working-day time limit in certain circumstances for transfers of requests, and the twenty-working-day time limit for responding to a correction request.[550] Any extension must be for a reasonable period, having regard to the circumstances. Extensions may be made only on the basis that a large quantity of information must be searched through; consultations are necessary in order to make the decision; or complex issues are raised in processing the request.[551] An extension must be notified to the requestor within twenty working

545. Privacy At, s. 62(2).
546. Privacy Act, s 62(3)–(4).
547. Privacy Act, s. 63(1).
548. Privacy Act, s. 63(3).
549. Privacy Act, s. 64(1).
550. Privacy Act, s. 65.
551. Privacy Act, s. 65(1).

days after the day on which the request was received, giving the reasons for the extension and informing the requester of the right to complain to the Privacy Commissioner

441. It is an offence under the Act to mislead an agency through impersonation or falsely claiming to have the authority to act for an individual for the purpose, *inter alia*, of having that individual's information altered or destroyed. The offence carries a maximum fine of NZD10,000.[552]

II. Charges Relating to Correction of Personal Information

442. A charge may not be imposed for the correction of information under IPP 7(2). The NZLC commented as follows on the rationale for this: 'agencies should not be allowed to charge for correction, since it is in their own interests to ensure that the information they hold is correct'.[553] A charge, however, may be imposed by a private sector agency for providing assistance and for attaching a statement of correction to personal information,[554] and by a public sector agency if authorised to do so by the Privacy Commissioner.[555] The Law Commission accepted that a charge was appropriate for the attachment of statements of correction sought but not made by private sector agencies on the following basis:[556]

> The argument that it is in the agency's interest to hold correct information, and that it should therefore not be allowed to charge for correction, does not apply to statements of corrections sought but not made. Such statements are for the benefit of the individual concerned rather than the agency, and therefore the agency should be permitted to impose a reasonable charge for attaching a statement.

443. Any charge made must be reasonable.[557] Individuals may complain to the Privacy Commissioner concerning the amount of charge imposed for the correction of personal information. The Commissioner will investigate and attempt to secure a settlement of the matter, and if a settlement is unable to be achieved, the Commissioner may determine whether the charge has been improperly imposed or is unreasonable.[558] If the Commissioner finds that the charge is unreasonable, the Commissioner may determine the appropriate charge for the agency to impose.[559]

552. Privacy Act, s. 212(2)(c)(ii).
553. *Review of the Privacy Act 1993* (NZLC R123, 2011), at para. 3.99.
554. Privacy Act, s. 66(2)(b)(i) and (ii).
555. Privacy Act, s. 66(2)(a). The Privacy Commissioner may authorise this under s. 67 if the agency would otherwise be commercially disadvantaged in comparison with a competitor in the private sector. The definition of 'public sector agency' is contained in s. 7(1).
556. *Review of the Privacy Act 1993* (NZLC R123, 2011), at para. 100.
557. Privacy Act, s. 66(4).
558. Privacy Act, s. 93(2).
559. Privacy Act, s. 93(3).

The Commissioner's determination on charging 'is final and binding, and no proceedings may be commenced in the Tribunal by the parties in respect of that determination'.[560]

§3. LIABILITY FOR BREACH OF IPP 7

444. A breach of IPP 7 results in 'an interference with the privacy of an individual',[561] and will render the agency concerned liable to the remedies provided for in the Act.[562]

445. Some harm or loss is necessary for liability under all the IPPs except for IPPs 6 and 7. Instead, liability for 'an interference with the privacy of an individual' for breach of IPP 7 arises from any of the following actions, without the necessity for proving any harm or loss, if the agency lacks a proper basis for making:

– a decision to refuse a request;[563]
– any other decision under Part 4 in relation to the request.[564]

446. A failure to comply with the time limits in Part 4 for responding to the request is deemed to be a decision to refuse a request under IPP 7,[565] as is undue delay in correcting information after granting the request,[566] and undue delay in attaching a statement of correction after granting the request.[567]

560. Privacy Act, s. 93(5).
561. Privacy Act, s 69(1).
562. *See* below, at Part VIII, Ch. 4.
563. Privacy Act, s. 69(3)(b).
564. Privacy Act, s. 69(3)(c).
565. Privacy Act, s. 69(5)(a).
566. Privacy Act, s. 69(5)(b).
567. Privacy Act, s. 69(5)(c).

Chapter 4. Right to Erasure

§1. Introduction

447. There is no right to erasure or 'right to be forgotten' *per se* in the Privacy Act. There are, however, two IPPs that approach such a right, IPP 7 (correction of personal information) and IPP 9 (on retention of personal information), but it would be difficult to describe either of them as an entitlement to have personal information erased. There is also the availability of erasure as a remedy in appropriate circumstances where the Tribunal has found an interference with an individual's privacy.

§2. The Relevance to Erasure of the IPP 7 Right to Correct Personal Information

448. The term 'correction', as defined in section 7(1) of the Act, includes the deletion of personal information. There are a number of Privacy Commissioner case notes that deal with complaints about an agency failing to correct personal information under IPP 7 by way of deletion.

449. In the only Tribunal case on the issue,[568] the plaintiff unsuccessfully sought to delete personal information from his file. The Tribunal found that IPP 7 does not include a right to have information removed from a file, only to request correction (which includes deletion). An agency is not obliged to correct information unless satisfied, having regard to its purpose, that the correction is necessary to ensure that the information is accurate, up-to-date, complete, and not misleading. Where a request for correction is declined, the individual concerned may still request that a statement of the correction sought but not made be attached to the personal information at issue so that the two can be read together. The Tribunal also remarked that in a case such the one at hand, where the information was in large part subjective in nature, difficulties in correcting it will inevitably arise. The Tribunal commented that 'A statement of correction enables more than one perspective of an incident or a conversation to be included with personal information held by the agency.'[569]

450. In *Case Note 15376*,[570] the complainant asked a hospital to delete from its records information concerning her admission twenty-eight years earlier on the ground that it was inaccurate in terms of Rule 7 of the Health Information Privacy Code. The hospital refused to do so, but it did offer to attach a statement of correction sought but not made. The Privacy Commissioner considered that the hospital had good reason to maintain the complainant's medical records in their current state, and that therefore Rule 7 was not breached. The complainant asked whether the hospital, in the alternative, could 'seal' the admission notes, keeping only a reference in the file to the fact that there were sealed notes that could be opened only

568. *Macdonald v. Healthcare Hawkes Bay and Morrison* [2000] NZCRT 35 (6 Dec. 2000).
569. *Ibid.*, at 3.
570. [2001] NZPrivCmr 1 (Apr. 2001).

with her knowledge and consent. The Commissioner, however, did not consider this to be reasonable or practical for an organisation that dealt with a large number of medical records and the nature of its record filing system.

451. In *Case Note 256329*,[571] the complainant complained that she had been accused of being a 'dodgy trader' by an online community. Her personal information, which included her address, photos, bank account, and cell phone numbers, was posted on the community's website. She told the website administrators that the information about her was wrong and asked for it to be immediately removed, but her request was refused. They told the woman that they would only consider her request if she had evidence to show that the claims about her were wrong. The Privacy Commissioner was concerned about possible breaches of several IPPs, including IPP 7. The Commissioner raised the need for the website administrators to moderate comments, and advised them not to use anyone's full name or contact details without consent. The Commissioner also advised the administrators to ask people to provide proof of any potentially defamatory assertions so they could be tested for accuracy before being published. People should also be made aware that if they were named on the website they had a right of reply. If they asked for their personal information to be removed, that request should be responded to as soon as possible. In the result, the website voluntarily removed the information about the complainant.

452. In *Case Note 284027*,[572] the Privacy Commissioner considered that an insurance company did not breach the Act when it refused to delete a woman's personal information from its records. The complainant requested the deletion because she changed over to another insurer. She had not lodged any claims with the insurer concerned, and cancelled the policy after only two months. The insurer explained that the information was retained because a claim could still be made on the policy in certain circumstances. The Commissioner noted that an individual cannot compel an agency to delete information, because if an agency has collected information for a specific purpose, it is allowed to retain it for as long as it needs in order to meet that purpose.

§3. The Relevance to Erasure of the IPP 9 Limit on the Retention of Personal Information

453. IPP 9 ('Agency not to keep personal information for longer than necessary') provides that an agency that holds personal information must not keep it for longer than is required for the purposes that the information may lawfully be used. IPP 9 is a relatively weak principle, and its utility is arguable. It does not actually require the erasure or destruction of information once its purpose for being collected is 'spent'. In theory, information may always be 'lawfully used', if only for historical or statistical purposes. IPP 8 already deals with information having to be

571. [2016] NZPrivCmr 1 (Feb. 2016).
572. [2018] NZPrivCmr 1 (Jan. 2018).

up-to-date in relation to its proposed use. Moreover, the right to correction in IPP 7 covers the deletion of personal information (as 'correct' is defined in section 7(1)). IPP 7(2) provides for an entitlement to correction that requires an agency 'to ensure that, having regard to the purposes for which the information may lawfully be used, the information is up to date, complete, and not misleading.

454. There is no requirement in IPP 9 that an individual's permission is needed either to retain or destroy the information. The test of whether information may be kept is whether or not it may be required for the purposes for which it may be lawfully used, in which case one turns to IPP 10 governing the use of personal information.

455. There is some ambiguity surrounding IPP 9 that renders its real meaning problematic. At first glance, the substance of the principle does not appear to be entirely consistent with the marginal note 'Agency not to keep personal information for longer than necessary', because IPP 9 itself does not refer to the retention of personal information 'for longer than necessary'. The term 'necessary' in the marginal note is arguably intended to refer to retention 'for longer than *is required* for the purposes' for which it was collected. But IPP 9 does not expressly say this. It provides instead that the information may not be retained 'for longer than is required for the purposes for which the information may lawfully be used'. It cannot be that the information can be used for any purpose, so long as it is lawful. The only way this makes proper sense in the context of the other IPPs is if one takes the expression 'the purposes' as 'the purpose(s) for which the information was collected'. The definite article 'the' therefore assumes some importance here. It refers to the original purposes of collection of personal information that can still be lawfully used. The result of this ambiguity is that the case law is unclear, because it seems to confuse 'lawful purpose' with what IPP 9 actually says, 'lawful use' based on the purposes for collecting the personal information. As the NZLC observed in an issues paper, the Privacy Commissioner's interpretation of 'purposes for which the information may lawfully be used' as 'lawful purpose' amounts to 'arguably a somewhat different concept'.[573]

456. Only two cases dealing with IPP 9 have been successful. In one,[574] the complainant was an unsuccessful job applicant. The employer used a company that specialised in pre-employment screening of potential employees. The complainant complained that information collected by the screening company was being retained by it. The Privacy Commissioner considered that the employer was vicariously liable for breaching IPP 9. The form that it used to collect information about potential employees stated that all of the information collected would be retained by it indefinitely, and would form part of its own database for the purpose of determining that person's suitability for any position they applied for in the future. The Commissioner, however, remarked that' 'principle 9 is incompatible with indefinite retention'. The employer accepted this point, and instructed the screening company

573. *Review of the Privacy Act 1993* (NZLC IP17, 2010), para. 4.54.
574. *Case Note 218236* [2011] NZPrivCmr 4 (20 Jul. 2011).

to destroy the complainant's information. In the other successful IPP 9 case,[575] the complaint was against a business that operated in a shopping centre, where it offered a free photo shoot for children, with the option for parents to later purchase prints. The complainant took up the offer, but in the end did not purchase any photos. She was informed that the photos would be deleted, but two years later she discovered that they were being used in advertising material, including a large poster in a mall. The Commissioner considered that since the business told the complainant that the photos were only for her, it should have deleted them when she decided not to purchase them.

457. Two cases have dealt with the retention of an individual's personal information in the criminal law context. In *E F G v. Commissioner of Police,*[576] the Tribunal dealt with a claim that the police breached IPP 9 because they ought not to have been holding information about the plaintiff in relation to a charge of historic child abuse, because the court discharged him and issued a suppression order. The plaintiff's claim was dismissed on the basis that the police retained the information for the broad purpose of maintenance of the law including the prevention, investigation, and detection of offences. Despite the age of the information concerned, the Tribunal thought that 'it would be wrong, and potentially dangerous' were the police to dispose of the information concerned if it might in future be useful. The Tribunal commented that 'We are in no position to say whether or not the information at issue in this case had so clearly passed its "use by" date that it ought to have been removed' from the Police database.[577] Similarly, in a complaint investigated by the Privacy Commissioner,[578] it was found that the police had not breached IPP 9 for holding information about the complainant on its database concerning an alleged assault. The complainant believed the information was incorrect. The police maintained that they could retain the information indefinitely. The Privacy Commissioner commented:

> Most agencies do not have a lawful reason for keeping information indefinitely. However, the legitimate purpose of the Police database is to maintain a record of information to support the Police in their work of detecting, preventing, investigating and prosecuting crime. Where, as here, someone has alleged that a person has committed a criminal offence, the Police have an ongoing lawful purpose for retaining the information on their database.

458. The Privacy Commissioner also noted that the police were still subject to the other privacy principles, such as the need to check the accuracy of information it held before using it under IPP 8, and to provide for access and correction on request under IPPs 6 and 7.

---

575. 'Privacy Commissioner names photography agency for misleading practices' (18 Jan. 2017): no case note reference has been assigned, but it is available at: *privacy.org.nz/news-and-publications/statements-media-releases/privacy-commissioner-names-photography-agency/.*
576. [2006] NZHRRT 48 (21 Dec. 2006).
577. *Ibid.*, paras 77–78.
578. *Case Note 204195* [2009] NZPrivCmr 5 (Mar. 2009).

459. Two other unsuccessful complaints alleging a breach of IPP 9 were reported in the employment sphere. In one case,[579] a former employer was found to be entitled to retain information relating to the dismissal of an employee, even though the matter had been settled. The Commissioner noted that it was the employer's practice to retain personnel files for five years after an employee had left. The employer maintained that it was necessary to retain the information in case the former employee decided to take legal action. The Commissioner agreed that further legal action was possible, which justified retention of the information. In the other case,[580] the Commissioner considered that an agency had a lawful purpose for retaining information about an employment incident that had occurred many years earlier that resulted in the complainant's suspension. The employee was reinstated on the condition that the suspension and the reasons for it would be kept on his personal file for two years. Ten years later, he learned that the information had not been removed from his file. The employer complied with his request that it be removed. The employee was subsequently involved in another incident and was suspended pending an inquiry. In the course of the inquiry, the employee discovered that although the information concerning the earlier suspension was removed from his personal file, his employer still retained it in its files. The Commissioner considered that the employer had a lawful purpose that justified retention of the information, in that it had an interest in retaining information that was necessary for maintaining appropriate professional and personal standards. Moreover, the record of the employee's original reinstatement did not specify what would happen to the information after it had remained in his file for two years. There was no record of any agreement that the information would be destroyed or that the employer would refrain from using it in the future.

§4. Tribunal Orders to Erase or Take Down Personal Information

460. Section 102(2) of the Act provides for a number of remedies that the Tribunal may order in respect of an interference with an individual's privacy. These include orders under section 102(3)(d) and (e), which provide, respectively, 'that the defendant perform any acts specified in the order with a view to remedying the interference, or redressing any loss or damage suffered by the aggrieved individual … as a result of the interference'; and 'any other relief that the Tribunal considers appropriate'. The Tribunal has made orders for erasure under these provisions in several decisions that dealt with the collection or disclosure of personal information that amounted to an interference with an individual's privacy.

461. In *Armfield v. Naughton*,[581] the Tribunal found breaches of the Act's collection principles arising from the operation of CCTV surveillance when two neighbouring families had a falling out. The defendant's surveillance system included three cameras facing the plaintiff's residence, and had an unobstructed view into the

579. *Case Note 5532* [1996] NZPrivCmr 3 (Nov. 1996).
580. *Case Note 13066* [1998] NZPrivCmr 10 (1 Apr. 1998).
581. [2014] NZHRRT 48 (6 Oct. 2014).

entire front, side and rear sections of the property. The plaintiffs were concerned about what information had been collected about them, and the purpose for which it would be used. Among the orders made by the Tribunal was one that required the defendant to erase or destroy all personal information held by him about the plaintiffs.

462. In *Hammond v. Credit Union Baywide*,[582] the defendant, the plaintiff's former employer, breached IPP 11 by disclosing information about her. The plaintiff had made a cake for a dinner party attended by former co-workers. The top of the cake was decorated with obscene insults directed at their employer. The plaintiff uploaded a picture of this cake on to her Facebook page, which had an activated privacy setting that only allowed the plaintiff's 150 or so 'friends' to have access to it. The defendant's manager, learning about the cake, put pressure on an employee and took a screenshot of the photograph. He then sent the screenshot to several human resources agencies in the region to warn them against employing the plaintiff. The Tribunal's remedies included an order that the defendant request that the email sent to these agencies and any screenshot of the cake be deleted from their records. Written confirmation was to be sought from each agency that this request had been complied with. The defendant was to supply a report to the Tribunal and the plaintiff within thirty days detailing the steps taken to comply with this order, as well as the responses received by the defendant.

463. In *Director of Human Rights Proceedings v. Slater*,[583] the Tribunal found that the defendant, a blogger, repeatedly breached IPP 11 by disclosing the complainant's email correspondence, photographs, and a video, all of which were contained on a hard drive that came into the defendant's possession without the complainant's authority. The disclosures were made repeatedly over a six-month period on the defendant's blog, causing the plaintiff distress. Among its remedies, the Tribunal made a takedown order that provided that the defendant 'erase, destroy, takedown, and disable any personal information' about the plaintiff on the defendant's websites, or any other website under his direction or control.[584] The Tribunal noted that while the restraining order it made barred future disclosures of personal information, it did not deal with 'the enduring nature of material already published on the Internet'.[585]

582. [2015] NZHRRT 6 (2 Mar. 2015).
583. *Ibid.*, at 162.
584. *Ibid.*, at para. 162.
585. *Ibid.*, at para. 158.

Chapter 5. Right to Restriction

§1. Introduction

464. There is no right to 'restriction of processing' under the Privacy Act, in the GDPR sense of 'the marking of stored personal data with the aim of limiting their processing in the future'.[586] The only entitlement under the Act that involves the 'marking' of personal information is where a statement of correction sought but not made is attached to personal information under IPP 7(4), when the agency concerned is not willing to correct it. This right, however, does not limit future processing; it only ensures that the individual's statement of correction will always be read together with the information held by the agency. The right also requires the agency concerned to inform every other person to whom the agency has disclosed the information, so far as this is reasonably practicable.[587]

465. The only right approaching a right to restriction is when proceedings against an agency are already on foot in the Tribunal in respect of an interference with the plaintiff's privacy based on breach of one or more of the IPPs, and the plaintiff applies for an interim order, or where one of the remedies sought by the plaintiff in the Tribunal is an order restraining an agency's continued or repeated action that breaches the IPPs. Neither of these remedies, however, necessarily involves marking personal data to limit processing in the future.

§2. Interim Orders by the Tribunal

466. The Tribunal has the power to make interim orders in matters before it where it has the power to make any final determination.[588] The criterion for granting such orders is that the Tribunal must be satisfied 'that it is necessary in the interests of justice to make the order to preserve the position of the parties pending a final determination of the proceedings'. In deciding whether or not to grant such an order, the Tribunal considers the relative strength of the parties' cases, the balance of convenience, the conduct of the parties, and undertakings as to damages.[589]

586. General Data Protection Regulation, Art. 4(3).
587. Privacy Act, s. 22, IPP 7(5).
588. Human Rights Act 1993, s. 95(1). The Tribunal is established under s. 93 of the Human Rights Act.
589. *See*, for example the Human Rights Act discrimination case *Hosking v. Wellington City Transport Ltd (t/a Stagecoach Wellington)* [1995] NZCRT 7, (1995) 1 HRNZ 542. The interim order there was made to restrain the defendant from taking delivery of any additional buses that were not wheelchair-friendly pending determination of the substantive issue. No interim orders have yet been made in the Tribunal's Privacy Act jurisdiction.

§3. Tribunal May Make Restraining Orders

467. The Act lacks any provision for any order in the nature of injunctive relief *per se* except in relation to situations where an interference with an individual's privacy involves a continuing or repeated action.[590] Thus, the specific action in question must have already breached one or more of the IPPs. The remedy is not available when a breach is merely apprehended, however reasonable that apprehension may be. There must be some prior or continuing breach.

468. In *E F G v. Commissioner of Police*,[591] the plaintiff succeeded in his claim that the Police Vetting Centre breached IPP 8 ('Accuracy, etc., of personal information to be checked before use or disclosure') by disclosing a database notation to his employer that misleadingly suggested that he had sexually abused two young girls. In fact, the HC had discharged him and ordered his name and any identifying details to be suppressed. The Tribunal ordered that the police be restraining from disclosing the notation in the future when it received vetting requests concerning the plaintiff. The Tribunal was concerned that:

> the Police may have been sticking to a position that the noting will be released without either (a) giving fresh and appropriate consideration to whether that is justified having regard to the kind of work that is in contemplation, or (b) reflecting on whether what is revealed by the noting is justified having regard to the other information on the Police file, or (c) considering what the effect of the High Court's name suppression order is in the circumstances.[592]

469. The Tribunal qualified the scope of this restraining order as follows:

> We do not know what information the Police file for the 1992 trial contains. If there is information on that file or elsewhere that meets the standard in Principle 8, and which the Police consider ought to be disclosed to a prospective employer, then (assuming that the Police are satisfied that it can properly be disclosed notwithstanding the High Court name suppression order) the order we have made will not prevent disclosure. Our order is limited only to any future disclosure of the noting.[593]

470. In *Hammond v. Credit Union Baywide (t/as NZCU Baywide)*,[594] the defendant breached IPP 11 ('Limits on disclosure of personal information') by disclosing information about the plaintiff, its former employee. The plaintiff had made an obscenely decorated cake that was insulting to her former employer and she uploaded a picture of it on to her Facebook page. The defendant's human resources manager accessed the plaintiff's Facebook page and took a screenshot of the cake. He telephoned other human resources agencies in the region to warn them against

590. Privacy Act, s. 102(2)(b).
591. [2006] NZHRRT 48 (21 Dec. 2006).
592. *Ibid.*, at para. 109.
593. *Ibid.*, at para. 111.
594. [2015] NZHRRT 6 (2 Mar. 2015).

employing the plaintiff. At the same time, the other agencies were sent screenshots of the cake, and the defendant's CEO sent an internal email to staff that disclosed the circumstances in which the plaintiff had earlier resigned. The email acknowledged that although employers should not normally talk about such personnel matters, it was appropriate here because of the plaintiff's 'public display of her views towards Baywide on Facebook'. The defendant accepted that all of these communications breached IPP 11. The Tribunal's remedies included an order restraining the defendant from continuing or repeating the breaches of IPP 11, or from engaging in, or causing or permitting others to engage in, conduct of the same kind as that constituting the breaches.

471. In *Director of Human Rights Proceedings v. Slater*,[595] the Tribunal found that the defendant, a blogger, repeatedly breached IPP 11 over a period of six months by disclosing the complainant's personal information contained in a hard drive that came into the defendant's possession without the complainant's authority. The Tribunal accepted that the plaintiff suffered significant humiliation, significant loss of dignity, and significant injury to his feelings as a result,[596] and made an order restraining the defendant from continuing or repeating the interferences with the complainant's privacy, or from engaging in or causing or permitting others to engage in, conduct of the same kind.

595. [2019] NZHRRT 13 (12 Mar. 2019).
596. In terms of the Privacy Act provision that is now s 69(2)(b).

Chapter 6. Profiling

§1. Lack of Specific Regulation of Profiling

472. There are neither any provisions on profiling in the Privacy Act, nor are there any reported cases dealing with the practice. Any regulation of such practices would need to be made under the existing IPPs. Given that the Act is harm-based, some harm to the individual would need to be shown in addition to breach of one or more of the IPPs, which have numerous exceptions, such as in relation to maintenance of the law and public safety.[597]

§2. Possible Avenues for Regulating Profiling under the Act

473. The IPPs that are most relevant to profiling are IPPs 1 ('Purpose of collection of personal information'), IPP 3 ('Collection of information from subject'), and IPP 10 ('Use of personal information').

474. IPP 1 prohibits an agency from collecting personal information unless it is done so for a lawful purpose connected with a function or activity of the agency, and the collection is necessary for that purpose. There are no exceptions to this principle. There is an open question as to how closely defined a 'purpose' needs to be for the requirements of the Privacy Act, as the Act is silent on the level of detail required for describing purpose. The issue then arises as to whether collecting information to compile a database of personal information can be a 'purpose' in and of itself under the Act, or whether it is too general and lacking in specificity if the ultimate purpose(s) for the collection of the information, and the identity of its users, are as yet undetermined at the time of collection. In some circumstances, the purposes may not necessarily be known until the information is processed and on-sold. Moreover, IPP 1 requires that the personal information that is collected must be 'necessary' for the purpose of its collection, which is problematic if the specific purpose(s) for the collection has yet to be determined. Where the information is being collected on a 'just in case it can be used or on-sold' basis, this is arguably inconsistent with the requirements of IPP 1 and its role in establishing the whole framework in respect to the handling, use, and disclosure of personal information.

475. Collecting personal information in connection with profiling therefore appears to raise an important conceptual and policy issues in some, if not most, circumstances, as to how the Act should apply where the purpose is itself to collect as much personal information as possible, just in case it might be of some use, before any more specific purpose has been determined. At the core of the issue is whether the collection of personal information itself can constitute a legitimate purpose in terms of IPP 1. The background to and underlying policy of the Act suggests that the collection of personal information itself cannot constitute a valid 'purpose'

597. *See*, for example, Privacy Act, s. 22, IPP 10(1)(e) and (f) ('Limits on use of personal information').

under IPP 1, because the concept of 'purpose' is supposed to operate as a *limitation* on the collection of personal information, not as a *justification* for its collection. It would be perverse if the minimality principle were to be used to confer legitimacy on the collection of a large amount of personal information. Therefore, the collection of personal information for profiling under the Act arguably cannot be done for open-ended purposes, but it must be done with an already-determined purpose. As the specific purpose(s) for the profiling (as well as the future users of the information collected) often have yet to be determined as at the time of collecting the personal information, profiling without any purpose other than the profiling itself would arguably breach IPP 1.

476. Furthermore, IPP 3(1) requires that when an agency collects personal information directly from the individual concerned, it must take reasonable steps in the circumstances to ensure that the individual is aware of a number of matters, including:

- the fact that the information is being collected;
- the purpose for which it is being collected;
- its intended recipients;
- the name and address of the agency that is collecting and holding the information;
- if the collection of the information is authorised by law, which law authorises it and whether or not the supply of the information is voluntary or mandatory;
- the consequences of not providing the information;
- and the rights of access to, and correction of, the information pursuant to IPPs 6 and 7.

477. The steps to make individuals aware of the above matters must be taken before personal information is collected. If they are not, the steps must be taken 'as soon as practicable' afterwards.[598] In *Boyle v. Manurewa RSA Incorporated*,[599] the Tribunal held that an agency cannot rely upon principle 3(2) to retrospectively justify a new recipient of an individual's personal information. The Tribunal stated that 'we regard it as wrong to suggest that an agency might be able to comply with IPP 3 by simply informing an individual after collecting personal information that the information is going to be used for a purpose that was not identified at the time of collection'.[600] Authorisation for the change would be required.

478. Again, as with IPP 1, a problem arises with the setting out of a sufficiently specific 'purpose' for the collection of personal information in connection with profiling. The intended recipients and their contact details may also be uncertain at the time of collection. There are a number of exceptions to the IPP 3(1) notification

598. Privacy Act, s. 22, IPP 3(2).
599. [2003] NZCRT 16 (12 Jun. 2003).
600. *Ibid.*, at para. 44.

requirements. Although several of these may be relevant to profiling, the application of most of them appears to be problematic. Non-compliance with IPP 3(1) is relevantly permitted where the agency believes, on reasonable grounds, that:

- 'non-compliance would not prejudice the interests of the individual concerned'.[601] The problem with this ground is that non-compliance could very much affect the interests of the individual concerned, or the individual concerned may simply not wish their sensitive information to be disclosed to agencies they may not anticipate or wish to hold it. Moreover, application of this ground would involve the circularity of assuming that individuals would not be prejudiced by not being informed of matters of which they have a right to be informed. As the Tribunal observed in *Boyle v. Manurewa RSA Incorporated*:[602]

  > Principle 3 sets the standard which agencies that collect personal information must meet when they are collecting information directly from an individual. A significant purpose of setting that standard is to protect the autonomy of individuals who are asked to give personal information … . The obvious reason for these obligations is to give the individual concerned some ability to make an informed choice about whether or not to provide the information.

- 'non-compliance is necessary … to avoid prejudice to the maintenance of the law by any public sector agency, including prejudice to the prevention, detection, investigation, prosecution, and punishment of offences; or for the enforcement of a law that imposes a pecuniary penalty; or for the protection of public revenue'.[603]
- 'compliance would prejudice the purposes of the collection',[604] and 'compliance is not reasonably practicable in the circumstances of the particular case'.[605] It seems highly unlikely that the Act would have intended to allow profiling on bases such as these two exceptions.

Given that a 'purpose' for which personal information has been obtained is required before it can be used under IPP 10, a breach of IPP 1 would also seem to affect the legitimacy of its future use unless an exception to IPP 10 applies. Permissible exceptions to IPP 10 most relevantly include situations where the agency reasonably believes:

- that the purpose for which the information will be used is directly related to the purpose in connection with which the information was obtained.[606]

601. Privacy Act, s. 22, IPP 3(4)(a).
602. [2003] NZCRT 16 (12 Jun. 2003), at para. 42.
603. Privacy Act, s. 22, IPP 3(4)(b)(i)–(iii).
604. Privacy Act, s. 22, IPP 3(4)(c).
605. Privacy Act, s. 22, IPP 3(4)(d).
606. Privacy Act, s. 22, IPP 10(1)(a).

- that the source of the information is a publicly available publication, and in the circumstances it would not be unfair or unreasonable to use the information.[607]
- that the use of the information for another purpose is necessary to avoid prejudice to the maintenance of the law by a public sector agency, including prejudice to the prevention, detection, investigation, prosecution, and punishment of offences; for the enforcement of a law that imposes a pecuniary penalty; or for the protection of public revenue; or the conduct of legal proceedings.[608]
- that the use of the information for another purpose is necessary to prevent or lessen a serious threat to public health or safety, or the life or health of an individual.[609]

§3. Sanctions for Profiling in Breach of the IPPs

479. A key obstacle standing in the way of regulating profiling, and indeed other breaches of IPP 1 and other IPPs, is the requirement of showing that a breach of an IPP has caused the individual concerned some harm or loss.[610] For example, there is one Privacy Commissioner case note on automated decision-making involving the automated transfer of inaccurate information between a debt collector and a credit reporter, in breach of the IPP 8 requirement of checking personal information for accuracy before use, but the complaint failed because of the absence of any harm caused to the complainant as a result of the breach.[611] This renders any legal sanction for breach of an IPP arising out of the collection, holding, use, or disclosure of personal information in connection with profiling difficult to envision, and the absence of reported cases in the area reflects this reality. Aside from its procedures relating to breaches of the IPPs, the Act does not otherwise contain a process whereby information processing that systematically breaches the IPPs, but does not result in harm or loss to an individual, can be regulated, even where the breach is high-profile and made on a large scale. Available remedies appear to be limited to the making by the Privacy Commissioner of a public statement on the matter,[612] or undertaking an inquiry into the issue.[613]

480. The Act, as re-enacted in 2020, however, has a new but as yet untested compliance jurisdiction,[614] whereby the Privacy Commissioner may issue a compliance notice when, *inter alia*, the Commissioner considers that there has been a breach of one or more of the IPPs in relation to an individual.[615] No evidence of

607. Privacy Act, s. 22, IPP 10(1)(d). The expression 'publicly available publication' is defined in s. 7(1).
608. Privacy Act, s. 22, IPP 10(1)(e)(i)–(iv).
609. Privacy Act, s. 22, IPP 10(1)(f)(i)–(ii). The expression 'serious threat' is defined in s 7(1).
610. Privacy Act, s. 69(2)(b).
611. *Case Note 205558* [2010] NZPrivCmr 1 (Mar. 2010).
612. Privacy Act, s. 17(1)(d).
613. Privacy Act, s. 17(1)(i).
614. Privacy Act, Part 6, Subpart 2 ('Compliance notices').
615. Privacy Act, s. 123(2)(a).

harm or loss under section 69(2)(b) is required to be proved for the issuing of a compliance notice. The agency that receives such a notice is required to remedy the breach,[616] and the Commissioner may take enforcement proceedings in the Tribunal.[617] This possibly removes the obstacle that must be overcome when complaining of a breach of any of the IPPs, including those that could relate to the use of personal information for profiling.

616. Privacy Act, s. 125(1)(c).
617. Privacy Act, s. 130.

Chapter 7. Right to Object

§1. The Right to Object under IPP 3

481. The Act does not recognise a true right of opposition or objection consistent with European standards. It is largely limited to opposing the collection of personal information *ab initio*, when it is being collected directly from the individual concerned. IPP 3 deals with the collection of personal information from the individual concerned, and it provides for particular obligations of notification that should take place before personal information is collected, or if that is not practicable, as soon as practicable after the information is collected.[618] Among the matters that individuals are required to be informed under IPP 3(1) are:

(e) if the collection of the information is authorised or required by or under law, –
  (i) the particular law by or under which the collection of the information is authorised or required; and
  (ii) whether or not the supply of the information by that individual is voluntary or mandatory; and
(f) The consequences (if any) for that individual if all or any part of the requested information is not provided.

482. A right of objection to the collection or other processing of personal information is implicit at this stage, and there is nothing to prevent a data subject from complaining about the subsequent processing of personal information if there has been a breach of the IPPs, or where there is some other legal basis for the objection, such as another statutory or common law right (such as a contractual right). Only two reported cases deal with complaints investigated by the Privacy Commissioner about breaches of IPP 3 involving a denied opportunity to object to the collection of personal information.

483. In one case,[619] the complainant alleged that while fishing, he was asked numerous intrusive questions by a Department of Conservation (DOC) enforcement officer. There were relevant fishing regulations that required anglers to provide their name, address, and fishing licence details when required by a DOC officer. The Privacy Commissioner found that the DOC officer breached IPP 3(1)(e) because the complainant was not advised whether or not answers were required under law, and IPP 3(1)(f) was breached because the officer did not advise the complainant of the consequences if information was not provided. In the result, however, no breach of the Act was found because the fisherman had suffered no harm or loss as a result of the breaches. In the other case,[620] the President of a club with national affiliations objected that the national body required club members to provide personal information, such as their names and addresses, as a condition of membership. The Privacy Commissioner, however, considered that this was permissible because the club's

618. Privacy Act, s. 22, IPP 3(2).
619. *Case Note 43927* [2003] NZPrivCmr 10 (May 2003)).
620. *Case Note 19399* [2002] NZPrivCmr 1 (Jan. 2002).

constitution provided that the information was to be collected, what the purpose of the collection was, and who the recipients would be. The practice of circulating membership details, and details of the recipients of that information, was also highlighted in the standard membership nomination form.

484. Where personal information has been collected from third parties, there is no right to object to its collection. Collection of personal information from third parties is permitted if an exception to IPP 2 applies ('Source of personal information'). One of the exceptions deals with the situation where the individual concerned has authorised the collection of information from someone else, but there are a number of other exceptions in IPP 2 that do not involve such consent. If individuals want to object to the processing of their data when it has been collected from a third party, they must resort to the complaints and conciliation processes of the Privacy Commissioner under the Act. Thus, the individual can lodge a complaint against the person who collected, held, used or disclosed the information contrary to the IPPs, so long as there is some harm or loss in terms of s. 69(2) of the Act.

§2. Direct Marketing

I. Introduction

485. Except in relation to spam and telecommunications, New Zealand law does not contain a specific legal obligation for the provision of an opting-out for direct marketing use, but industry self-regulation measures provide some degree of protection for individuals.

II. The Act and Direct Marketing

486. The Privacy Act does not contain specific provisions that regulate direct marketing *per se*. Direct marketing is treated under the Act in the same way as other forms of information handling. Accordingly, any direct marketing activities must conform to the IPPs in s. 22 of the Act.

487. IPP 2(1) requires agencies to collect personal information from the individual concerned unless an exception in IPP 2(2) applies. In particular, direct marketers could collect personal information about individuals from a source other than the individual concerned if the agency reasonably believes that the information is in a publicly available publication, such as a public register, a telephone directory or a website that is accessible to the general public.[621] When an exception to IPP 2(1) applies, the individual's authorisation is not required.

488. IPP 3 requires that when information is being collected from an individual, agencies must advise the individual of the fact that information is being collected;

621. Privacy Act, s. 22, IPP 2(2)(d).

the purpose for its collection; the intended recipients of the information; the contact details of the agency that is collecting the information and the agency that will hold the information; and the consequences (if any) for the individual of not providing the information. IPP 3 therefore provides individuals with the opportunity of opting out at the time information is being collected. Once the information has been collected, the purpose limitation principle applies, which enables individuals to maintain some form of control over the future use (IPP 10) and disclosure (IPP 11) of their information by complaining under the Act if the purpose for the collection or the recipients of the information change.

489. IPP 10 would require that personal information may not be used for direct marketing if that was not a purpose for which the information was obtained unless the agency reasonably believes that its use for direct marketing is directly related to the purpose in connection with which the information was obtained; the individual concerned authorises use for this purpose; or the source of the information is a publicly available publication.

490. Direct marketers can buy, rent or exchange personal information, but in order for such information to be disclosed, the agency providing it must reasonably believe under IPP 11 that disclosure of the information is one of the purposes in connection with which the information was obtained or is directly related to the purposes in connection with which it was obtained; disclosure is authorised by the individual concerned; or the source of the information is a publicly available publication.

491. IPP 7 entitles individuals to request correction of their personal information. Individuals must be informed of this right when their personal information is collected from them under IPP 3. Agencies must take such steps (if any) to correct information as are, in the circumstances, reasonable to ensure that, having regard to the purposes for which the information may lawfully be used, the information is accurate, up-to-date, complete, and not misleading. Where an agency has corrected information, or attached a statement of correction sought but not made,[622] it must, if reasonably practicable, inform each person or body or agency to whom the personal information has been disclosed of the steps taken.[623] The term 'correct' is defined in the Act as including the alteration of personal information by way of deletion or addition.[624]

492. While on its face, IPP 7 entitles individuals to request deletion of personal information from a direct marketer's list, and requires the agency to decide whether or not to accept such a request, the Privacy Commissioner has considered that 'it is unlikely that an agency can be obliged to delete accurate information under the principle.'[625] The Commissioner's reasoning was as follows:

622. Privacy Act, s. 22, IPP 7(4).
623. Privacy Act, s. 22, IPP 7(5).
624. Privacy Act, s. 7(1).
625. *Necessary & Desirable: Privacy Act 1993 Review* (Dec. 1998), para. 2.9.9.

> The principle has as its primary focus the correction of inaccurate information rather than the deletion of information which it is alleged should not be used for a particular purpose. In that sense, it might be characterised as a data quality entitlement rather than a limit upon use. One might therefore argue that principle 7 is appropriately used for removing a name from a marketing list where the individual's details were placed on the mailing list through error but not because the details were obtained in breach of principle 3 or 11.[626]

493. In one case,[627] a couple who had been on a mailing list and requested that their names be removed, complained that they subsequently received a marketing letter after the company claimed to have removed their names from the list. The Privacy Commissioner investigated this complaint under Principle 7 as a failure to correct information by way of deletion when requested. He found that although the company removed the couple's names from its internal database, it failed to pass on the couple's request to another company that supplied it with information from publicly available sources for its mailing database. The couple was advised to write directly to the other company to be removed from its database.

494. The Privacy Commissioner has observed that direct marketing complaints are common, and often involve an agency failing to act upon a request to delete a person from a mailing list,[628] or using personal information obtained for one purpose for another purpose.[629] Most of these complaints have been resolved by the agency simply removing the individual's name off a list rather than going through an elaborate enquiry into how the details came to be included on an agency's marketing list by investigating compliance with IPPs 1 to 4, 10, and 11, on collection (IPPs 1 to 4), use (IPP 10), and disclosure (IPP 11).[630] Direct marketing complaints thus tend to be resolved more often through the Commissioner's assistance in conciliating complaints than through invoking strict legal rights.

495. A few cases that have been investigated by the Privacy Commissioner have been reported in case notes. In one case, a customer objected that a company sent him a brochure advertising another company's products without his authorisation.[631] The Commissioner found that the customer had agreed to the company using the customer's information to inform him of related services. Accordingly, the company's action was covered under IPPs 3 and 10, which relate, respectively, to informing individuals of the proposed use, and the actual use, of personal information. The Commissioner, however, cautioned the company that 'when it marketed another company's products, those products had to be very closely connected with the services it offered. If the link was not as close as it was in this case, and a reasonable customer might not expect to be contacted about the product, I would not necessarily be able to conclude that marketing the product was provided for by the

626. *Ibid.*, para. 2.9.10.
627. *Case Note 96103* [2007] NZPrivCmr 13 (June 2007).
628. *Ibid.*, para. 2.9.8.
629. *Ibid.*, para. 2.9.13.
630. *Necessary & Desirable: Privacy Act 1993 Review* (Dec. 1998), para. 2.9.12.
631. *Case Note 13682* [1998] NZPrivCmr 4 (Feb. 1998).

subscriber contract'. In another reported case,[632] a customer was transferring from one telephone company to another, and complained that information in the transfer agreement was used by the former telephone company for marketing purposes. The Commissioner, however, found that the information had not been obtained from the transfer agreement, but from other company records that it was entitled to use for marketing purposes under the original subscriber agreement with the complainant. Another case turned on the complainant's agreement to publication of his email address online, which resulted in him receiving spam.[633] The complainant had made a submission to a local council, and the submission process required submitters to accept its terms and conditions for online submissions. Those terms included acknowledgment and a waiver that personal information would be made public on the council's website. The Commissioner considered that by accepting the terms, the complainant consented to the publication of his information online.

496. In a case involving an association,[634] the complaint was that a list of its members' names and addresses had been collected by a travel agency for marketing purposes without the members' permission. The Commissioner, however, found that the agency had been given the information by a member of the association who had arranged a package tour for members. The agency had not collected the information, and it reasonably believed that the member had supplied the list with the authorisation of those on it. Since the information had not been 'collected' in terms of the Act's definition (which excludes the receipt of unsolicited information), the IPPs relating to collection did not apply to the agency complained against. In another case,[635] a member of a club complained that it supplied his personal details to a direct mailing company and as a result he received unsolicited mail from insurance companies. The Commissioner found that there had been no breach of IPP 3 regarding informing members of the purposes for the collection of the information, as there had been an earlier club resolution to release members' contact information to a direct mailing company for the purpose of providing targeted advertising material to its members. All club members were advised of this resolution. The Commissioner also found that the disclosure of the information was permissible because it was one of the purposes for collecting the information. The Commissioner suggested, however, that the club should inform members when they renewed their memberships that their contact information was provided to the direct mailing company, and that club members be allowed to opt out. The Commissioner also suggested that it was preferable to invite members to opt in.

---

632. *Case Note 17281* [2001] NZPrivCmr 7 (June 2001).
633. *Case Note 256547* [2015] NZPrivCmr 4 (24 February).
634. *Case Note 4784* [2001] NZPrivCmr 20 (Nov. 2001).
635. *Case Note 10141* [2008] NZPrivCmr 14 (Aug. 2008).

III. Telecommunications Information Privacy Code

497. The Telecommunications Information Privacy Code 2020, a code of practice issued under the Privacy Act, limits the type of information that can be gathered and the use to which it can be put. The code applies to network operators, telecommunications service providers, directory publishers and enquiry agencies, Internet service providers, call centres that provide call centre services on contract to another agency, and mobile telephone retailers.[636]

498. The code only permits the use of telecommunications information for direct marketing with the data subject's consent. Rule 10(1)(b) of the Code ('Limits on use of telecommunications information') provides that 'A telecommunications agency that holds telecommunications information that was obtained in connection with one purpose must not use the information for any other purpose unless the agency believes on reasonable grounds … that the use of the information for that other purpose is authorised by the individual concerned, provided that if the other purpose is for direct marketing the individual has been advised that he or she may withdraw such authorisation at any time'. Moreover, r. 10(2) of the code provides that 'A telecommunications agency must not use traffic information obtained as a result of interconnection, wholesaling or similar arrangements between network operators for the purposes of direct marketing to an individual who is not a subscriber of the agency without the authorisation of that individual.' The use of telecommunications information by a telecommunications agency for direct marketing therefore is on an opt-out basis for subscribers, and on an opt-in basis for non-subscribers.

IV. Credit Reporting Privacy Code

499. The Credit Reporting Privacy Code 2020, a code of practice issued under the Privacy Act, provides that credit information held by credit reporters may not be used for marketing or direct marketing purposes.[637] This includes facilitating marketing or direct marketing by a credit providing subscriber or other agency, or developing a tool or service for credit providing subscribers or providing such a tool or service, for the purpose assisting them to assess the likelihood than an individual might accept an offer of credit or insurance in relation to credit, or variation of credit or insurance, or otherwise to target individuals for offers of credit or insurance. The purpose of this provision is to strengthen and broaden 'the existing prohibitions on the use of credit information by credit reporters for marketing or the facilitation of marketing by others'.[638]

---

636. Clause 4(2).
637. Rule 10(3).
638. Office of the Privacy Commissioner, *Amendment No 13 to Credit Reporting Code 2004*, Information Paper, 6 Nov. 2018, p. 4.

500. A credit reporter may only use credit information to remove names from a direct marketing list supplied by a subscriber under certain conditions:[639]

Pre-screening to remove names from subscriber marketing lists (Rule 10(3))

A credit reporter may use credit information to remove names from a direct marketing list supplied by a subscriber if the following 4 conditions are all met:

Condition 1: The subscriber

The subscriber must be a credit provider that is either –

(a) an externally regulated credit provider; or
(b) a member of a self-regulatory association that binds members to responsible marketing practices.

Condition 2: The list

The list submitted to the credit reporter for pre-screening must –

(a) be warranted by, or on behalf of, the subscriber to have been compiled in compliance with the Act;
(b) omit the names of any individuals who have been registered with the New Zealand Marketing Association indicating that they do not wish to receive unsolicited marketing; and
(c) be used only for direct marketing related to the provision of credit by the subscriber.

Condition 3: Criteria for removal

The removal of names is based upon criteria agreed in advance between the credit reporter and the subscriber with the purpose of excluding individuals who represent an adverse credit risk and would be ineligible to receive the direct marketing.

Condition 4: Assurance of limitation of use

The credit reporter has a process in place to ensure that

(a) the requirements of condition 2(a) and (b) are met; and
(b) information derived from the list is not retained or used by the credit reporter for the purpose of credit reporting; and
(c) the list, after the removal of names, is –
    (i) used only for the purpose of the direct marketing permitted under condition 2(c); and
    (ii) not disclosed directly to the subscriber.

639. Credit Reporting Privacy Code 2020, Sch. 10.

V. Anti-spam Legislation

501. The Unsolicited Electronic Messages Act 2007, which deals with spam, covers email, instant messaging, and texting of a commercial nature that has a New Zealand link.[640] The legislation prohibits the use of address-harvesting software or a harvested-address list for the sending of spam.[641] It seeks to ensure that electronic messages are sent only to customers who have consented to receiving them by requiring commercial electronic messages to include a functional unsubscribe facility to enable the recipient to instruct the sender that no further messages are to be sent to the recipient.[642] The Act provides for enforcement mechanisms and effective remedies.

VI. Industry Self-Regulation of Direct Marketing

A. Code of Practice for Direct Marketing

502. The New Zealand Marketing Association is an industry body that has a Code of Practice for Direct Marketing in New Zealand.[643] All marketers are expected to comply with the code's principles. The code contains a number of provisions that relate to privacy, including an opt-out right for individuals,[644] as well as a free process for the resolution of complaints by consumers. It promises prompt resolution of complaints against its members. If a complaint is made against a non-member, the Marketing Association attempts to reach a satisfactory resolution if it can. The shortcoming of the scheme is that it is voluntary, but it nevertheless has over 400 corporate entities as members.

503. Principle 4 provides that 'Marketers will carry out their business in a way that is socially responsible.' This includes compliance with the name removal registers maintained by the Marketing Association, namely, the 'Do Not Mail' and 'Do not call' lists.[645] Consumers must have the opportunity to opt out of receiving marketing information that they have not requested, and marketers must have a system in place that enables them to honour such requests. Marketers also must not allow individuals to provide details of others, such as friends, colleagues, or family members, for receiving marketing offers without their permission.[646] They must also ensure that the third-party lists they use comply with the Privacy Act.[647] Principle

640. Unsolicited Electronic Messages Act, s. 9.
641. Unsolicited Electronic Messages Act, s. 13.
642. Unsolicited Electronic Messages Act, s. 11.
643. Available at https://marketing.org.nz/resources/code-of-practice-direct-marketing. It was last reviewed in Feb. 2014.
644. Marketing Association, Code of Practice for Direct Marketing in New Zealand, Principle 4 ('Marketers will carry out their business in a socially responsible manner'), cl. 4(b).3 ('Opting out').
645. *See* below at 7.2.6.2.
646. *Ibid.*, at cl. 4(b.).4 ('Marketing list referrals').
647. *Ibid.*, at cl. 4(b).5 ('Third-party lists').

5 provides that 'Marketers will uphold high standards of business practice to generate consumer trust.' This includes the requirement that organisations must have fair and effective procedures in place to handle consumer complaints, and these must be available free of charge and without jeopardising the consumer's right to seek legal redress. If consumers are not satisfied with the way an organisation has handled a complaint, they must be told how to contact the Marketing Association.

B. Do not Mail and Do Not Call Registers

504. The Marketing Association operates free Do Not Mail and Do Not Call Services in order to decrease the number of unwanted unsolicited phone calls and mailings to individual consumers. The association contends that responsible marketers would not want to bother consumers who have indicated that they do not wish to receive information about products or services. Accordingly, marketers regularly receive an updated copy of the Association's Do Not Mail and/or Do Not Call registers. However, because not every company is a member of the association, it cannot guarantee a stop to all mailings or phone calls. Moreover, listing will not stop communications from organisations with which the consumer has an existing relationship, such as a bank or telephone company. Forms for getting on the registers are available online or by writing to the Marketing Association.[648] The Marketing Association website states that the do not mail list contains over 100,000 records, and the do not call list contains over 160,000 records.[649]

C. Data Warranty Register

505. The Marketing Association also operates a Data Warranty Register, whereby owners of lists guarantee that a list that is compiled, rented, or sold for direct marketing purposes complies with the legal requirements of the Privacy Act, name suppression requirements, and the Marketing Association's Codes of Practice and Best Practice Guidelines. Data owning companies participating in the scheme must complete a warranty contract, under which the company agrees to comply with the warranty conditions. If the Marketing Association is satisfied that the company fulfils the required warranty conditions, the data owner is accepted for the Data Warranty Register. Once accepted, the data owner can communicate this status to their prospective data users. Verification that a database is approved by the Marketing Association can be checked on the association's website.

648. At www.marketing.org.nz.
649. Website accessed 7 Mar. 2021.

Chapter 8. Other Data Subject Rights

§1. General

506. The principal data subject rights are covered in the preceding chapters. There are a few other entitlements conferred upon the data subject (or 'individual concerned' as more usually referred to in New Zealand privacy law) under the codes of practice issued under the Privacy Act. Selected rights are conferred upon individuals under other laws where these are of similar character to data protection rights.

§2. Other Data Subject Rights under Privacy Act 2020

507. Codes of practice issued under section 32 of the Privacy Act may, among other things, modify the IPPs or prescribe how the IPPs are to be complied with. Code may thereby confer additional rights upon data subjects. The clearest examples of such additional data subject rights can be found in the Credit Reporting Privacy Code 2020, Health Information Privacy Code 2020 and Telecommunications Information Privacy Code 2020.

I. Credit Reporting Privacy Code 2020

508. The Credit Reporting Privacy Code 2020 confers the following rights upon data subjects that are additional to those in the IPPs:

- Access to a generated credit score: Rule 6(2) and access to the general methodology used to create the credit score: Rule 6(4).
- To be given a written summary of rights: Rules 6(5) and 7(3).
- Suppression of credit information where subject may be a victim of fraud: Rule 11, Schedule 8.

II. Health Information Privacy Code 2020

509. The Health Information Privacy Code 2020 confers the following rights upon data subjects that are additional to those in the IPPs:

- A right to veto routine disclosure of the subject's presence in hospital: rule 11(1).
- A right to veto disclosure to news media of the subject's details as an accident victim in hospital: rule 11(1).

III. Telecommunications Information Privacy Code 2020

510. The Telecommunications Information Privacy Code 2020 confers the following rights upon data subjects that are additional to those in the IPPs:

- To refuse consent (without charge) to having details in a telecommunications subscriber directory: Rule 11(1) and Schedule 2.
- To block (without charge) the display of calling line identity on a per-line basis for both incoming and outgoing calls: Schedule 3.

§3. Data Subject Rights under Other Enactments

511. There follows a summary of selected privacy-type rights that confer entitlements upon data subjects.

I. Adult Adoption Information Act 1985

512. The Adult Adoption Information Act 1985 is, in effect, a subject access law in a specialist area relating to sensitive information. The Adult Adoption Information Act 1985 confers the following rights upon data subjects that are additional to those in the IPPs:

- Birth parent (of a person adopted before 1 March 1986) may restrict access to identifying information on original birth certificate: section 3.
- Adult adopted person may apply for original birth certificate: section 4.
- Access by birth parents to identifying information relating to an adult adopted person: section 8.
- Access by adult adopted persons to identifying information relating to either or both of that person's birth parents: section 9.

II. Assisted Human Reproductive Technology Act 2004

513. The Assisted Human Reproductive Technology Act 2004 requires the creation and retention of certain records and creates a subject access regime to the information. As it concerns genetically related people the personal information might be said to relate to multiple individuals.

514. In the following summary of the data subject rights, terms have the following meanings:

- donor means a person from whose cells a donated embryo is formed or from whose body a donated cell is derived;
- donor offspring means a person formed from a donated embryo, or a donated cell, that is derived wholly or partly from the donor's body;

– provider means a person who, in the course of a business, performs, or arranges the performance of, services in which donated embryos or donated cells are used.

515. The Assisted Human Reproductive Technology Act 2004 confers the following rights upon data subjects that are additional to those in the IPPs:

– Access by donors to information about them kept by providers: s. 49.
– Access by donor offspring to information about donors kept by providers and Registrar-General: s. 50.
– Right by donor offspring to provide updated and corrected information that must be retained by providers: s. 56.
– Access by donor offspring to information about them kept by providers or Registrar-General: s. 57.
– Access to information about siblings of donor offspring: section 58.
– Donor offspring 18 years or older may consent to disclosure of identifying information to donor: s. 59.
– Access by donors to information about donor offspring kept by providers: s. 60.
– Access by donors to information about donor offspring kept by Registrar-General: s. 61.

III. Criminal Records (Clean Slate) Act 2004

516. The Criminal Records (Clean Slate) Act 2004 addresses the processing of criminal history data in relation to old convictions. The Criminal Records (Clean Slate) Act confers the following right upon data subjects that are additional to those in the IPPs:

– Right of eligible individual to lawfully respond any question asked of him or her about his or her criminal record that he or she has no criminal record: section 14.

IV. Health Act 1956

517. The Health Act 1956 confers the following right upon data subjects that are additional to those in the IPPs:

– A right by the data subject to have a health services provider transfer information to the subject or another provider: section 22F.

518. Section 22F of the Health Act creates, in effect, both a subject access and a data portability right.

V. Official Information Act 1982

519. The Official Information Act 1982 confers the following rights upon data subjects that are additional to those in the IPPs:

- Right of access by person to reasons for decisions affecting that person: section 23.
- Right of subject access to personal information by a body corporate: section 24.

Part V. Duties of Controllers and Processors

Chapter 1. National Rules Regarding Duties of Controllers

§1. Terminology

520. The Privacy Act 2020, in common with the predecessor 1993 Act, does not use the terms 'controller' or 'processor' instead including both concepts within the broad term 'agency'. However, several provisions in the Act operate to vary obligations among classes of agency in ways that broadly align with the European concepts of controller and processor.

521. In particular, s. 11 provides that if an agency (A) holds information as an agent for another agency (B) (e.g., the information is held by A on behalf of B for safe custody or processing) then for the purposes of this Act, the personal information is to be treated as being held by B, and not A. Expressed in those terms, principal B may be considered the controller in European terms and agent A the processor.

§2. Privacy Act, Section 11: Personal Information Treated as Being Held by Another Agency in Certain Circumstances

522. The full section 11 provides:

11 Personal information treated as being held by another agency in certain circumstances

(1) This section applies if an agency (**A**) holds information as an agent for another agency (**B**) (e.g., the information is held by A on behalf of B for safe custody or processing).
(2) For the purposes of this Act, the personal information is to be treated as being held by B, and not A.
(3) However, the personal information is to be treated as being held by A as well as B if A uses or discloses the information for its own purposes.
(4) For the purposes of this section, it does not matter whether A –
  (a) is outside New Zealand; or
  (b) holds the information outside New Zealand.
(5) To avoid doubt, if, under subsection (2), B is treated as holding personal information, –

(a) the transfer of the information to A by B is not a use or disclosure of the information by B; and
(b) the transfer of the information, and any information derived from the processing of that information, to B by A is not a use or disclosure of the information by A.

523. Expressed in those terms, principal B may be considered the controller in European terms and agent A the processor. (For that reason, the 'controller/processor' terminology is used in this chapter.) Both types of entity are referred to as agencies in the Act. Generally, the controller will be deemed to hold information for the purposes of the Act and thus have the duty to comply with the IPPs (section 11(1) and (2)). However, the personal information is to be treated as being held by A as well as B if A uses or discloses the information for its own purposes (section 11(3)).

§3. Duty on Agency to Appoint a Privacy Officer

524. Section 201 provides that an agency must appoint a privacy officer whose responsibilities include, among other things, 'encouraging the agency to comply with the IPPs' and 'ensuring that the agency complies with the provisions of this Act' (section 201(1)(a) and (d)). This is an obligation that applies to both controllers and processors.

§4. Responsibility of the Controller

525. Beyond the duty to appoint a privacy officer, there is neither explicit obligation on controllers in the Act equivalent to art. 24(1) of the GDPR to 'implement appropriate technical and organisational measures to ensure and to be able to demonstrate that processing is performed in accordance with this regulation' nor are there any statutory duties on controllers to implement 'data protection by design and by default' of the kind in art. 25 GDPR. The omission of obligations to have compliance measures and to be able to demonstrate compliance, sometimes referred to as accountability mechanisms, arguably falls short not only of GDPR standards but also of standards applicable in instruments adopted by APEC and OECD, of which New Zealand is a member.

526. Article 32 of the APEC Privacy Framework (2015) provides that:

> A personal information controller should be accountable for complying with measures that give effect to the [APEC Information Privacy Principles].

527. Article 44 of the APEC Privacy Framework provides that member economies should consider encouraging personal information controllers to develop and implement privacy management programmes for all personal information under their control.

528. Similarly, art. 14 of the OECD Privacy Guidelines (2013) provides that 'A data controller should be accountable for complying with measures which give effect to the principles stated above.' Article 15 anticipates controllers having in place privacy management programmes and being prepared to demonstrate compliance upon request.

§5. Credit Reporting Privacy Code 2020

529. Section 32 of the Privacy Act 2020 empowers the Privacy Commissioner to issue a code of practice which may, among other things, prescribe how the IPPs are to be applied or complied with. The Credit Reporting Privacy Code 2020 requires credit reporters to implement an accountability model of compliance that mirrors the approaches recommended in art. 14 of the OECD Privacy Guidelines (2013), art. 44 of the APEC Privacy Framework (2015) or art 24. of the GDPR (2016). Credit reporting is a business that creates heightened privacy risks to individuals.

530. Clause 8 of the code requires a credit reporter to provide the Commissioner annually with a report, prepared with the involvement of an independent person, which is to reflect the outcome of the credit reporter's systematic reviews, and monitoring activities, undertaken under specific obligations prescribed in relation to the security safeguards and accuracy principles (Rules 5(2) and 8(3)) and to provide certain other assurances in relation to code compliance (*see* Schedule 7 of the code).

Chapter 2. National Rules Regarding Joint Controllers

§1. Terminology

531. The Privacy Act 2020, in common with the predecessor 1993 Act, does not use the terms 'controller' or 'processor', but instead includes both concepts within the broad term 'agency'. However, several provisions in the Act operate to vary obligations among classes of agency in ways that broadly align with the European concepts of controller and processor.

532. In particular, s. 11 provides that if an agency (A) holds information as an agent for another agency (B) (e.g., the information is held by A on behalf of B for safe custody or processing) then for the purposes of this Act, the personal information is to be treated as being held by B, and not A (but *see* discussion of section 11(3) below). Expressed in those terms, principal B may be considered the controller in European terms and agent A the processor. (For that reason, the 'controller/ processor' terminology is used in this chapter.)

§2. Privacy Act, Section 11(3): Personal Information Treated as Being Held by Both Controller and Processor in Certain Circumstances

533. Section 11 provides:

11 Personal information treated as being held by another agency in certain circumstances

(1) This section applies if an agency (**A**) holds information as an agent for another agency (**B**) (for example, the information is held by A on behalf of B for safe custody or processing).
(2) For the purposes of this Act, the personal information is to be treated as being held by B, and not A.
(3) However, the personal information is to be treated as being held by A as well as B if A uses or discloses the information for its own purposes.
(4) For the purposes of this section, it does not matter whether A –
  (a) is outside New Zealand; or
  (b) holds the information outside New Zealand.
(5) To avoid doubt, if, under subsection (2), B is treated as holding personal information,-
  (a) the transfer of the information to A by B is not a use or disclosure of the information by B; and
  (b) the transfer of the information, and any information derived from the processing of that information, to B by A is not a use or disclosure of the information by A.

534. Expressed in those terms, principal B may be considered the controller in European terms and agent A the processor. Generally, the controller will be deemed to hold information for the purposes of the Act and thus have the duty to comply with the IPPs (section 11(1) and (2)). However, the personal information is to be treated as being held by both agency A as well as B if A uses or discloses the information for its own purposes (section 11(3)).

§3. Duty on Both Controllers and Processors to Appoint a Privacy Officer

535. Section 201 provides that an agency must appoint a privacy officer whose responsibilities include, among other things, 'encouraging the agency to comply with the IPPs' and 'ensuring that the agency complies with the provisions of this Act' (section 201(1)(a) and (d)). This is an obligation that applies to both controllers and processors.

§4. Privacy Act, Section 120(4): Liability in Respect of Breach Notification Obligations

536. Part 6 of the Act sets out requirements in relation to notifiable privacy breaches. Sections 114 and 115 set out obligations to notify the privacy commissioner and affected individuals of notifiable privacy breaches. Civil or criminal liability may attach to an agency for a failure to meet the obligations. Section 120 applies to processes and proceedings under this Act relating to the obligations under section 114 or section 115 and provides:

> **120 Liability for actions of employees, agents, and members of agencies**
>
> (1) This section applies to processes and proceedings under this Act relating to the obligations under section 114 or 115.
> (2) An employee or a member of an agency is not liable in those processes or proceedings if anything done or omitted by them results in the employer or agency failing to notify the Commissioner or an affected person (or their representative) or give public notice of a notifiable privacy breach.
> (3) For the purpose of those processes and proceedings, anything done or omitted by an employee or a member of an agency is to be treated as being done or omitted by the employer or agency.
> (4) For the purpose of those processes and proceedings, anything done or omitted by an agent of another agency is to be treated as being done or omitted by both the agent and the principal agency.
> (5) However, the extent of liability of an agent is affected by whether they hold personal information that is the subject of a notifiable privacy breach. *See* the definition of privacy breach in section 112 and *see* section 11, which applies and which provides that information held by an agent is to be treated as being held by the principal agency unless section 11(3) applies.

537. Relevantly, section 120(4) provides for joint liability where 'anything done or omitted by an agent of another agency is to be treated as being done or omitted by both the agent and the principal agency'. However, *see* also section 120(5) which refers back to section 11(3). In other words, by reason of section 11(3), the agent will not be considered to hold the information of the principal agency and thus be liable along with the principal agency unless it uses or discloses the information for its own purposes.

Chapter 3. National Rules with Regard to Processors

§1. Terminology

538. The Privacy Act 2020, in common with the predecessor 1993 Act, does not use the terms 'controller' or 'processor' instead including both concepts within the broad term 'agency'. However, several provisions in the Act operate to vary obligations among classes of agency in ways that broadly align with the European concepts of controller and processor.

539. In particular, section 11 provides that if an agency (A) holds information as an agent for another agency (B) (e.g., the information is held by A on behalf of B for safe custody or processing) then for the purposes of this Act, the personal information is generally to be treated as being held by B, and not A. Expressed in those terms, principal B may be considered the controller in European terms and the agent B the processor.

§2. Privacy Act, Section 11(2): Personal Information Generally Treated as Being Held by Controller Rather Than Processor

540. Section 11 provides:

> **11 Personal information treated as being held by another agency in certain circumstances**
>
> (1) This section applies if an agency (A) holds information as an agent for another agency (B) (for example, the information is held by A on behalf of B for safe custody or processing).
> (2) For the purposes of this Act, the personal information is to be treated as being held by B, and not A.
> (3) However, the personal information is to be treated as being held by A as well as B if A uses or discloses the information for its own purposes.
> (4) For the purposes of this section, it does not matter whether A –
> (a) is outside New Zealand; or
> (b) holds the information outside New Zealand.
> (5) To avoid doubt, if, under subsection (2), B is treated as holding personal information,-
> (a) the transfer of the information to A by B is not a use or disclosure of the information by B; and
> (b) the transfer of the information, and any information derived from the processing of that information, to B by A is not a use or disclosure of the information by A.

541. Expressed in those terms, principal B may be considered the controller in European terms and agent A the processor. Generally, the controller will be deemed to hold information for the purposes of the Act and thus have the duty to comply with the IPPs (section 11(2)). However, there is an exception: personal information is to be treated as being held by both agency A as well as B if A uses or discloses the information for its own purposes (section 11(3)).

§3. Duty on Both Controllers and Processors to Appoint a Privacy Officer

542. Section 201 provides that an agency must appoint a privacy officer whose responsibilities include, among other things, 'encouraging the agency to comply with the IPPs' and 'ensuring that the agency complies with the provisions of this Act' (section 201(1)(a) and (d)). This is an obligation that applies to both controllers and processors.

§4. Privacy Act, Section 120(4): Liability in Respect of Breach Notification Obligations

543. Part 6 of the Act sets out requirements in relation to notifiable privacy breaches. Sections 114 and 115 set out obligations to notify the privacy commissioner and affected individuals of notifiable privacy breaches. Civil or criminal liability may attach to an agency for a failure to meet the obligations. Section 120 applies to processes and proceedings under this Act relating to the obligations under section 114 or section 115 and provides:

> **120 Liability for actions of employees, agents, and members of agencies**
>
> (1) This section applies to processes and proceedings under this Act relating to the obligations under section 114 or 115.
> (2) An employee or a member of an agency is not liable in those processes or proceedings if anything done or omitted by them results in the employer or agency failing to notify the Commissioner or an affected person (or their representative) or give public notice of a notifiable privacy breach.
> (3) For the purpose of those processes and proceedings, anything done or omitted by an employee or a member of an agency is to be treated as being done or omitted by the employer or agency.
> (4) For the purpose of those processes and proceedings, anything done or omitted by an agent of another agency is to be treated as being done or omitted by both the agent and the principal agency.
> (5) However, the extent of liability of an agent is affected by whether they hold personal information that is the subject of a notifiable privacy breach. *See* the definition of privacy breach in section 112 and *see* section 11, which applies and which provides that information held by an agent is to be treated as being held by the principal agency unless section 11(3) applies.

544. Relevantly, section 120(4) provides for joint liability where 'anything done or omitted by an agent of another agency is to be treated as being done or omitted by both the agent and the principal agency'. However, *see* also section 120(5) which refers back to section 11(3). In other words, by reason of section 11(3), the agent will not be considered to hold the information of the principal agency and thus be liable along with the principal agency unless it uses or discloses the information for its own purposes.

Chapter 4. Security Obligations

§1. General

545. The Privacy Act sets out general security obligations in the IPPs, particularly IPP 5. The Act supplements those general obligations in particular provisions in the Act and by code of practice. When there is a privacy breach, which will often involve a breach of security obligations, there may be an obligation to notify the Privacy Commissioner or affected individuals.

§2. General Obligation Regarding Security of Personal Information in the IPPs

546. IPP 5 ('Storage and security of personal information') provides that an agency that holds personal information must ensure that the information is protected by reasonable security to safeguard it against loss and unauthorised loss, access, use, modification, disclosure, and other misuse, and that if it is necessary for the information to be given to a person in connection with the provision of a service to the agency, everything reasonably within the power of the agency is done to prevent unauthorised use or disclosure of the information.

547. IPP 5 draws on the security safeguards principle of the OECD Guidelines which provides that 'Personal data should be protected by reasonable security safeguards against such risks as loss or unauthorised access, destruction, use, modification or disclosure of data.'

548. IPP 6 ('Access to personal information') provides that it is subject to the provisions of Part 4 which includes section 57. Section 57(c) provides that an agency that receives an IPP 6 access request:

> must ensure, by the adoption of appropriate procedures, that any information intended for a requestor is received –
>
> (i) only by that requestor
> (ii) if the request is made by a requestor as the representative of an individual, only by the requestor or the individual.

549. IPP 13 applies in respect of unique identifiers. The obligations in IPP 13(4)(b) in relation to the disclosure and display of unique identifiers may also be characterised as security obligations. IPP 13(1) provides that 'agency (A)' may assign a unique identifier to an individual for use in its operations. IPP 13(4) adds that:

> [Agency] A must take any steps that are, in the circumstances, reasonable to ensure that –

(a) a unique identifier is assigned only to an individual whose identity is clearly established; and
(b) the risk of misuse of a unique identifier by any person is minimised (for example, by showing truncated account numbers on receipts or in correspondence).

550. The obligation in paragraph (a) of IPP 13(4) is a data quality or accuracy obligation while paragraph (b) requires safeguards to be taken against the risk of misuse, particularly to minimise risks of identity fraud.

§3. Privacy Act Codes of Practice

551. Codes of practice issued under section 32 of the Act may, among other things, modify the application of an IPP by prescribing more stringent standards and may prescribe how an IPP is to be complied with.

552. The only code of practice to make any substantial modifications to the security obligations in IPP 5 is the Credit Reporting Privacy Code 2020. Rule 5 of the code substitutes for IPP 5 and prescribes how the principle is to be complied with by providing in Rule 5(2) that, without limiting the IPP 5 obligations:

> A credit reporter must take the following measures to safeguard the credit information it holds against unauthorised access or misuse:
>
> (a) develop written policies and procedures to be followed by its employees, agents and contractors; and
> (b) impose access authentication controls such as the use of passwords, credential tokens or other mechanisms; and
> (c) provide information and training to ensure compliance with the policies, procedures and controls; and
> (d) ensure that a subscriber agreement is in place before disclosing information under rule 11(2); and
> (e) monitor usage and regularly check compliance with the agreement, policies, procedures and controls and the requirements of this code; and
> (f) identify and investigate possible breaches of the agreement, policies, procedures and controls; and
> (g) take prompt and effective action in respect of any breaches that are identified; and
> (h) systematically review the effectiveness of the policies, procedures and controls and promptly remedy any deficiencies; and
> (i) maintain an access log.

§4. Mandatory Privacy Breach Notification to Privacy Commissioner

553. Section 114 of the Privacy Act provides that an agency must notify the Privacy Commissioner as soon as practicable after becoming aware that a notifiable privacy breach has occurred.

554. Section 112 defines 'notifiable privacy breach' as: a 'privacy breach' that it is reasonable to believe has caused serious harm to an affected individual or individuals or is likely to do so.

555. 'Privacy breach', in relation to personal information held by an agency, is defined to mean (i) unauthorised or accidental access to, or disclosure, alteration, loss, or destruction of, the personal information; or (ii) an action that prevents the agency from accessing the information on either a temporary or permanent basis.

556. A notifiable privacy breach does not include a privacy breach if the personal information that is the subject of the breach is held by an agency who is an individual and the information is held solely for the purposes of, or in connection with, the individual's personal or domestic affairs.

§5. Mandatory Privacy Breach Notification to Individual Concerned

557. Section 115 of the Privacy Act provides that an agency must notify an affected individual as soon as practicable after becoming aware that a notifiable privacy breach has occurred. However, the obligation is subject to exceptions that may waive the obligation or allow for delayed notification or substitute public notification for personal notification.

558. 'Affected individual' is defined, in relation to personal information that is the subject of a privacy breach, to mean the individual to whom the information relates and includes an individual inside or outside New Zealand.

559. Section 113 sets out factors that must be considered by an agency when assessing whether a privacy breach is likely to cause serious harm. This section provides:

> When an agency is assessing whether a privacy breach is likely to cause serious harm in order to decide whether the breach is a notifiable privacy breach, the agency must consider the following:
>
> (a) any action taken by the agency to reduce the risk of harm following the breach:
> (b) whether the personal information is sensitive in nature:
> (c) the nature of the harm that may be caused to affected individuals:

(d) the person or body that has obtained or may obtain personal information as a result of the breach (if known):
(e) whether the personal information is protected by a security measure:
(f) any other relevant matters.

Chapter 5. Privacy Officer

§1. Designation of Privacy Officer: General

560. Section 201 of the Privacy Act 2020 requires an agency to appoint at least one privacy officer and continues an obligation first imposed in the Privacy Act 1993. This person would deal with requests for access to, and correction of, information and work with the Privacy Commissioner when a complaint was made and otherwise encourage or ensure the agency's compliance with the Act.

561. The obligation is on all 'agencies' (a term that encompasses both controllers and processors) and so is a more broadly applicable requirement than is the EU requirement under art 37 of the GDPR to designate a data protection officer only in any case where:

(a) the processing is carried out by a public authority or body;
(b) the core activities of the controller or the processor consist of processing operations which, by virtue of their nature, their scope and/or their purposes, require regular and systematic monitoring of data subjects on a large scale; or
(c) the core activities of the controller or the processor consist of processing on a large scale of special categories of data or personal data relating to criminal convictions and offences.

562. The 1993 Act required that a privacy officer be appointed from 'within that agency'. The 2020 Act changed the obligation to appoint individuals 'within or outside the agency'. The change resulted from recommendations from the Privacy Commissioner in 1998 and the Law Commission in 2011. The change to enable outsiders to perform the role was expected to add flexibility and enable agencies to obtain the support of people with greater expertise to perform the role. The Law Commission noted that it could make more sense for smaller agencies to pay an outside consultant to perform the privacy officer role than appointing someone from within the agency.

563. An agency may be required by the Privacy Commissioner to supply the name and contact details of the agency's privacy officer under section 202. A failure by an agency to supply details as required under section 202, or actually to appoint a privacy officer as required by section 201 if one had not been designated, would constitute a breach of the Act for which the Privacy Commissioner could issue a compliance notice under section 124.

564. Section 201(2) provides that an agency is not required to appoint a privacy officer where the agency 'is an individual who is collecting and holding personal information solely for the purposes of, or in connection with, the individual's personal or domestic affairs'.

§2. Designation of Privacy Officer: Government Entities

565. In common with most obligations in the Privacy Act, the obligation under section 201 to appoint a privacy officer applies equally to all agencies in the public and private sectors. However, two particular public sector contexts may be noted.

566. Section 201(3) provides that in relation to the functions of a 'departmental agency', the responsibility under the section lies with the departmental agency. Section 7 of the Act provides that 'departmental agency' has the meaning given in section 5 of the Public Service Act 2020. Section 5 of the Public Service Act 2020 provides that:

> *departmental agency* means any of the agencies that are listed in the first column of the table in Part 2 of Schedule 2, and that are each part of the corresponding host department stated in the second column of that table

567. Part 2 of Schedule 2 provides a list of departmental agencies and their host departments. For example, the Ministry for Ethnic Communities is listed against the Department of Internal Affairs as the host department. Thus, in the example of the Ministry for Ethnic Communities, the departmental agency must appoint a privacy officer and cannot simply rely upon the Department of Internal Affairs having appointed a privacy officer.

568. In November 2013, the government announced the creation of a Government Chief Privacy Officer (GCPO) position. The announcement emphasised that it was important that New Zealanders have confidence in government agencies to do all they can to ensure personal information is kept safe. The creation of the GCPO followed a series of high-profile privacy breaches in the state sector.

569. The GCPO position does not purport to be a privacy officer appointed under the Privacy Act. Rather the role leads an all-of-government approach to privacy to raise public sector privacy maturity and capability. The GCPO supports government agencies to meet their privacy responsibilities and improve their privacy practices.

§3. Designation of Privacy Officer: Overseas Agencies Carrying on Business in New Zealand

570. The obligation to appoint a privacy officer falls upon an 'agency'. This term is defined in section 7 to mean 'a person described in section 4 to whom this Act applies'. Section 4(1)(b) applies the Act to 'an overseas agency (B), in relation to any action taken by B in the course of carrying on business in New Zealand in respect of personal information collected or held by B'. Accordingly, overseas agencies 'carrying on business in New Zealand' must appoint a privacy officer.

571. The expression 'carrying on business in New Zealand' is made clearer by section 4 concerning the application of the Act. Section 4(1)(b) provides that the Act applies to 'an overseas agency (B), in relation to any action taken by B in the course of carrying on business in New Zealand in respect of personal information collected or held by B'. Section 4(2) and (3), elucidates the meaning of 'carrying on business in New Zealand' in terms of section 4(1)(b) as follows:

> (2) For the purposes of subsection (1)(a) and (b), it does not matter –
> (a) where the personal information is, or was, collected by the agency; or
> (b) where the personal information is held by the agency; or
> (c) where the individual concerned is, or was, located.
> (3) For the purposes of subsection (1)(b), an agency may be treated as carrying on business in New Zealand without necessarily –
> (a) being a commercial operation; or
> (b) having a place of business in New Zealand; or
> (c) receiving any monetary payment for the supply of goods or services; or
> (d) intending to make a profit from its business in New Zealand.

§4. Tasks of Privacy Officer

572. Section 201(1) of the Privacy Act provides that the privacy officer's responsibilities include:

(a) encouraging the agency to comply with the IPPs;
(b) dealing with requests made to the agency under this Act;
(c) working with the Commissioner in relation to investigations conducted under the privacy Act in relation to the agency; and
(d) ensuring that the agency complies with the provisions of the Privacy Act.

Part VI. Codes of Conduct and Certification

§1. General

573. A key feature of New Zealand's Privacy Act is the ability to issue codes of practice to modify the IPPs in certain situations. This provides New Zealand's privacy law with particular flexibility and the ability to provide greater or lesser stringency in appropriate cases.

574. In addition to the codes of practice issued under the Privacy Act there are certain specialised codes issued under other enactments that have the same status as Privacy Act codes.

575. As a new innovation in the 2020 Act, that did not exist under the 1993 Act, there is provision to recognise internationally recognised schemes for protecting personal information as 'prescribed binding schemes.'

§2. Privacy Act Framework for Codes of Practice

576. Section 32 of the Privacy Act provides for the Privacy Commissioner to issue codes of practice. A code of practice may modify the application of the IPPs by prescribing standards that may vary from those provided by the IPPs or by exempting particular actions from the IPPs. A code may also prescribe how the IPPs are to be applied or complied with.

577. A code of practice may apply to: any specified information or class of information; any agency or class of agency; any activity or class of activity; or any industry, profession or calling or class of industry, profession or calling. It may also regulate information matching in the private sector, set guidelines in respect of charges and make provision for various administrative and mechanical aspects of that code of practice. A code of practice may not limit or restrict the circumstances in which individuals are entitled to exercise their entitlements under IPPs 6 and 7.

§3. Codes Issued under the Privacy Act

578. Six codes of practice have been issued under the Privacy Act 2020:

(1) Civil Defence National Emergencies (Information Sharing) Code 2020.
(2) Credit Reporting Privacy Code 2020.
(3) Health Information Privacy Code 2020.
(4) Justice Sector Unique Identifiers Code 2020.
(5) Superannuation Schemes Unique Identifier Code 2020.
(6) Telecommunications Information Privacy Code 2020.

I. Civil Defence National Emergencies (Information Sharing) Code 2020

579. The Civil Defence National Emergencies (Information Sharing Code) 2020 seeks to assist with the management of the response to a national emergency and to assist with the recovery from a national emergency.

580. The code provides additional legal authority for any agency to collect, use, and disclose personal information about an individual involved in a national emergency if it is for a permitted purpose related to the government management of the response to, or recovery from, a national emergency and any disclosure is to a public sector agency or an agency involved in the response or recovery or to a person responsible for the individual.

581. The code replaced the Civil Defence National Emergencies (Information Sharing Code) 2013. The 2013 code was based upon the Christchurch Earthquake (Information Sharing) Code 2011 (Temporary). The 2011 code drew substantially upon Part VIA of the Australian Privacy Act 1988 (Dealing with personal information in emergencies and disasters).

582. Following the Christchurch earthquake on 22 February 2011, and the declaration of a state of national emergency on 23 February, the Privacy Commissioner issued the 2011 code on 24 February to assist in the response. The code came into effect at 5 pm on 24 February 2011 and, after extensions, expired on 30 June 2011..

583. On 26 March 2020 a state of national emergency was declared over the whole of New Zealand, owing to the impact of COVID-19, pursuant to section 66 of the Civil Defence Emergency Management Act 2002. The state of national emergency was subsequently extended by a series of further declarations to 13 May 2020. The 2013 code automatically applied to assist with management and recovery of the emergency by virtue of clause 3 of the code.

II. Credit Reporting Privacy Code 2020

584. In policy terms, the objectives of the code include to apply standards that are more stringent than the IPPs to credit reporters and thereby to enhance consumer rights and protections in a high privacy risk environment. In practical terms, the code is more prescriptive than the IPPs in order to make privacy principles effective and enforceable in a context of massive information sharing for secondary purposes.

585. The code regulates the information handling of agencies that carry on the business of reporting to other agencies, for payment, information relevant to the assessment of creditworthiness of individuals. The code does this by prescribing standards that are more stringent than the IPPs and prescribing how the IPPs are to be complied with. The code is innovative in a number of ways and imposes certain information requirements not found directly in the IPPs or in other codes such as collection and retention limits, consumer information obligations and temporary 'freezes' on third-party access.

586. The Credit Reporting Privacy Code 2020 is more stringent than the IPPs in nearly every respect. The two exceptions would seem to be Rules 12 and 13 which mainly replicates IPPs 12 and 13 although Rule 13 allows for otherwise prohibited use of the driver licence number (subject to strict controls) and so may be considered to be less stringent than the IPP.

III. Health Information Privacy Code 2020

587. The code has twin objectives to provide more stringent standards to meet community expectations in the handling of sensitive health information and also to facilitate the retention and sharing of health information in the provision of healthcare.

588. The code regulates the information of health agencies by prescribing standards that are more stringent than the IPPs in some places (e.g., prioritising the use of individual authorisation over use of disclosure exceptions) and less stringent than the IPPs in others (e.g., by creating additional exceptions for disclosure of health information).

589. The code replaced the Health Information Privacy Code 1994. The 1994 code replaced a temporary code issued in 2013.

IV. Justice Sector Unique Identifiers Code 2020

590. The code seeks to assist in the effective administration of justice by enabling core law enforcement authorities to share and reassign the unique identifiers assigned to individuals. The code replaced the Justice Sector Unique Identifier Code 1998.

591. In particular, the NZ Police make every effort to establish the true identity of a person at the time of entering the criminal justice system. Once a person's identity is established, they may have their fingerprints and photograph taken which is then linked to the originating identity. On charging an offender, police will assign a Person Record Number (PRN) to that person that can then be used and shared by other justice sector agencies.

592. The code modifies IPP 13 by allowing, in accordance with a schedule, reassignment of certain justice sector unique identifiers by identified justice sector agencies for stated purposes.

V. Superannuation Schemes Unique Identifier Code 2020

593. The code facilitates the sharing of unique identifiers assigned by agencies to individuals in relation to their working lives with agencies involved in the provision of retirement income to those individuals. The code replaced the Superannuation Schemes Unique Identifier Code 1995.

594. The code modifies IPP 13 to enable unique identifiers assigned by employers or unions to be reassigned.

VI. Telecommunications Information Privacy Code 2020

595. The code replaced the Telecommunications Information Privacy Code 2003. The 2003 code was introduced to address compliance difficulties that the industry anticipated having with the 1993 Act and to facilitate privacy protections with the introduction of new data services.

596. The code is particularly focused upon telecommunications network operators and service providers but also has wider application to, for example, directory publishers, ISPs, and mobile telephone retailers. The code's rules relax a number of the IPPs to facilitate certain telecommunications industry practices and network requirements. It also creates some telecommunications-specific protections, such as requiring directory publishers to include entries only with subscriber authorisation. Several schedules prescribe how the code must be complied with.

§4. Public Register Codes of Practice under Family Violence Act 2018

597. The Privacy Act 1993 provided extensive regulation of public registers, through a set of public register privacy principles (PRPPs), and provided for broad ranging public register codes of practice. The 2020 Act did not include the PRPPs and made no provision for public register codes of practice. However, provision continued to be included in the Family Violence Act 2018 for the Privacy Commissioner to issue narrowly focused public register codes of practice in relation to the processes for obtaining directions under that other Act that identifying information on public register not be publicly available.

598. Section 256 of the Family Violence Act 2018 provides:

> **Application of certain provisions of Privacy Act 2020**
>
> Sections 33 to 37 of the Privacy Act 2020 apply, so far as applicable and with all necessary modifications, to the issuing of a code of practice under section 255, and to a code of practice issued under section 255, as if the issuing were done, or, as the case may be, the code were issued, under that Act.

599. Accordingly, the Commissioner would follow the Privacy Act notification, public submission and issue processes if issuing a public register code under the Family Violence Act.

§5. Statutory Codes of Conduct under Social Security Act 2018 and the Public and Community Housing Management Act 1992

600. There are two 'codes of conduct' issued under other enactments that are treated 'as if' they were issued under the Privacy Act. These codes have the benefit of prescribing binding privacy rules for departmental use of intrusive powers to obtain information but are issued by the department concerned and not the independent Privacy Commissioner.

601. The two codes of conduct are issued under, respectively, the Social Security Act 2018 and the Public and Community Housing Management Act 1992. Each of these codes of conduct are issued by the Ministry of Social Development, after consultation with the Privacy Commissioner, to govern the use of certain statutory powers to obtain information and documents.

602. Complaints of breach of either code of conduct may be taken to the Privacy Commissioner and Parts 5 and 6 of the Privacy Act 2020 apply to the complaint 'as if the code of conduct were a code of practice issued under section 32 of the Act' (refer: clause. 12, Schedule 6, Social Security Act 2018; section 141 Public and Community Housing Management Act 1992).

603. Clause 10, Schedule 6, of the Social Security Act further elaborates on the relationship between the code of conduct and Privacy Act codes of practice making it clear that in the event of conflict codes of practice prevail over codes of conduct. Clause 10, Schedule 6, of the Social Security Act and section 140 Public and Community Housing Management Act also provide for the issue of regulations which would prevail over any Privacy Act code of practice.

§6. Prescribed Binding Schemes

604. New Zealand does not have a statutory certification scheme as such. However, IPP 12 does anticipate 'prescribed binding schemes' under which an internationally recognised scheme for protecting personal information might be formally recognised for the purposes of cross-border transfers. Prescribed binding schemes would almost certainly involve a certification process for the enforcement bodies and participants.

605. IPP 12 sets out the requirements on agencies for disclosure of personal information outside New Zealand. The principle allows an agency to disclose personal information to a foreign person or entity only for certain enumerated exceptions. Exception (d) allows an agency to disclose if it:

> believes on reasonable grounds that B is a participant in a prescribed binding scheme.

606. Section 7 defines 'binding scheme' as:

> *binding scheme* means an internationally recognised scheme in which the participants agree to be bound by –
>
> (c) specified measures for protecting personal information that is collected, held, used, and disclosed; and
> (d) mechanisms for enforcing compliance with those measures

607. 'Prescribed binding scheme' is defined in IPP 12 (3) to mean a binding scheme specified in regulations made under section 213. The regulation-making section provides:

> **213 Regulations: prescribed binding schemes**
>
> (1) The Governor-General may, by Order in Council made on the recommendation of the responsible Minister given after consultation with the Commissioner, make regulations prescribing binding schemes for the purpose of IPP 12(1)(d).
> (2) The Minister may recommend the making of regulations under subsection (1) only if the Minister is satisfied that the binding schemes require a foreign person or entity to protect personal information in a way that, overall, provides comparable safeguards to those in this Act.

608. Provision has been made to recognise an internationally recognised scheme as a prescribed binding scheme to enable New Zealand to, if it chooses at some point, to join the APEC CBPRs. New Zealand at this stage has taken no decision to join the APEC CBPRs and has not issued any regulations to specify any binding scheme in regulations.

609. The APEC CBPRs System is an accountability-based system that facilitates privacy-respecting data flows among APEC economies. Participating companies are required to adhere to the standards established by the APEC CBPR system and to domestic laws in the economies in which they operate. All APEC CBPR System certified companies have their privacy policies and practices evaluated by an approved independent third-party verifier (known as an 'Accountability Agent'). Accountability agents monitor and enforce companies' compliance with the APEC CBPR programme requirements. In appropriate cases, they are also required to report non-compliance to Privacy Enforcement Authorities.

610. The scheme has four main components:

(1) Recognition criteria for organisations wishing to become an APEC CBPR system certified Accountability Agent.
(2) Intake questionnaire for organisations that wish to be certified as APEC CBPR system compliant by a third-party CBPR system certified Accountability Agent.
(3) Assessment criteria for use by APEC CBPR system certified accountability agents when reviewing an organisation's answers to the intake questionnaire.
(4) A regulatory cooperative arrangement (the CPEA) to ensure that each of the APEC CBPR system programme requirements can be enforced by participating APEC economies.

611. A Joint Oversight Panel (JOP) administers the APEC CBPR system. Decisions about an organisation's eligibility to be an Accountability Agent are made by APEC economies.

612. The APEC CBPR System, finalised in 2011, only applies to personal information controllers ('controllers'), as the APEC Privacy Framework (the Framework), pursuant to which the CBPR System was created, also applies only to controllers. However, a complementary APEC scheme, PRP, is designed to help personal information processors demonstrate their ability to assist controllers in complying with relevant privacy obligations. The PRP also helps controllers identify qualified and accountable processors. The PRP intake questionnaire sets forth the baseline requirements of the PRP against which an APEC-recognised Accountability Agent will assess a processor seeking recognition. To receive such recognition, the processor must meet this set of requirements.

Part VII. International Transfers

Chapter 1. General Principles

§1. General

613. As a general characterisation, New Zealand privacy law provides that personal information held in New Zealand (including information received from overseas) should only be disclosed to another country if the information will be subject to comparable safeguards to those in the Privacy Act 2020. That general characterisation is modified by a number of exemptions, exceptions, and qualifications.

614. The relevant law is contained in IPP 12 (Disclosure of personal information outside New Zealand) and Part 8 (Prohibiting onward transfer of personal information received in New Zealand from overseas). These two sets of provisions operate separately from each other. IPP 12 is a new feature in the 2020 Act whereas Part 8 is carried over from the 1993 Act.

§2. Disclosure of Personal Information Outside New Zealand

615. IPP 12 provides that 'An agency (A) may disclose personal information to a foreign person or entity (B) in reliance on IPP 11(1)(a), (c), (e), (f), (h), or (i) only if' one of six conditions apply. Those conditions are:

(1) the individual concerned authorises the disclosure to B after being expressly informed by A that B may not be required to protect the information in a way that, overall, provides comparable safeguards to those in this Act; or
(2) B is carrying on business in New Zealand and, in relation to the information, A believes on reasonable grounds that B is subject to this Act; or
(3) A believes on reasonable grounds that B is subject to privacy laws that, overall, provide comparable safeguards to those in this Act; or
(4) A believes on reasonable grounds that B is a participant in a prescribed binding scheme; or
(5) A believes on reasonable grounds that B is subject to privacy laws of a prescribed country; or
(6) A believes on reasonable grounds that B is required to protect the information in a way that, overall, provides comparable safeguards to those in this Act (for example, pursuant to an agreement entered into between A and B).

616. Conditions (2) to (6) can be said to represent the different ways that personal information transferred out of New Zealand can continue to be protected in a way that, overall, provides comparable safeguards to those in this Act, namely:

- Continuing to be subject to the Act by reason of its extraterritorial reach.
- Being subject to privacy laws that, overall, provide comparable safeguards.
- Receiving protection under a prescribed binding scheme.
- Being subject to foreign privacy laws that have been prescribed as providing comparable safeguards.
- The foreign person or entity is legally required to protect the information in a way that, overall, provides comparable safeguards.

617. By contrast, condition (1) covers the situation where the information might not be subject to comparable protections. In such a case the individual concerned may give an informed authorisation for the transfer to proceed.

618. In addition to the situation anticipated in condition (1), there are several circumstances where there an information transfer out of New Zealand may not be required to be subject to comparable safeguards. For instance:

- Where an enactment requires personal information to be made available to a foreign person or entity (section 24(1)(a)).
- Where an entity is exempt from the Act entirely (*see* section 8(b)) or from IPP 12 (e.g., an individual holding information for personal or domestic affairs: section 27(2)).
- Where a disclosure is made under IPP 11(1)(b) (disclosure to the individual concerned), IPP 11(1)(d) (sourced from a publicly available publication) or IPP 11(1)(g) (disclosure necessary to enable an intelligence and security agency to perform its functions).
- Where a disclosure is made in reliance on IPP 11(1)(e) or (f) (in relation to maintenance of the law and health and safety) and it is not reasonably practicable to comply with IPP12(1).
- Where an authorisation is obtained from the Privacy Commissioner under section 30(1)(d).

619. IPP 12 can be enforced in the usual manner as with other IPPs such as by way of issue of a compliance notice under section 123.

§3. Prohibiting Onward Transfer of Personal Information Received in New Zealand from Overseas

620. The object of Part 8 is to empower the Privacy Commissioner in exceptional cases to prohibit the onward transfer of personal information received from overseas. It replicates Part 11A of the 1993 Act. The power to prohibit transfers is intended to meet the expectations of New Zealand's trading partners whose own laws limit cross-border transfers. For example, the general prohibition of data transfers from EU countries to third countries in GDPR art. 44 expressly includes onward transfers of personal data from the third country to another third country.

621. Section 193 of the Privacy Act 2020 provides that the Privacy Commissioner may prohibit onward transfer of personal information received in New Zealand from overseas if satisfied that the information will be transferred to a jurisdiction where it will not be subject to a law providing comparable safeguards to the Privacy Act and the transfer would be likely to breach the privacy principles set out in the OECD Guidelines. In exercising this discretion, the Commissioner must consider whether the proposed transfer would be likely to affect any individual, the desirability of facilitating the free flow of information between New Zealand and other countries, and any international guidelines relevant to transborder data flows.

622. The prohibition may be effected by service on an agency of a transfer prohibition notice. The prohibition may be appealed to the HRRT. Section 197 provides that an offence is committed when there is a failure or refusal to comply with a transfer prohibition notice served by the Privacy Commissioner. Such an offence attracts a fine of up to $10,000.

Chapter 2. Transfers in the Context of International Agreements

§1. Relationship of IPP 12 and Other New Zealand Law

623. IPP 12 ('Disclosure of personal information outside New Zealand') does not limit or affect any New Zealand enactment that authorises or requires personal information to be made available or any provision contained in any New Zealand Act that regulates the manner in which personal information may be obtained or made available (section 24(1) Privacy Act 2020).

624. Accordingly, a New Zealand statute such as the Mutual Assistance in Criminal Matters Act 1992 is unaffected by IPP 12. The Mutual Assistance in Criminal Matters Act governs both requests made by New Zealand to other countries and requests made by other countries to New Zealand. New Zealand has made a number of commitments at an international level as to how it will provide assistance to foreign countries in criminal matters. The enactment of the 1992 Act gave effect to some of New Zealand commitments in this area. The Act has been amended to give effect to later commitments that have been made.

§2. Transfer Prohibition Notices Not Available If Information Required by International Instrument

625. Section 193 of the Privacy Act provides that the Privacy Commissioner may prohibit a transfer of personal information from New Zealand to another country in certain circumstances. However, section 193(3) provides that:

> Subsection (1) does not apply if the transfer of the information, or the information itself, is –
>
> (a) required or authorised by or under any enactment; or
> (b) required by any convention or other instrument that imposes international obligations on New Zealand.

§3. Comprehensive and Progressive Agreement for Trans-Pacific Partnership

626. The Comprehensive and Progressive Agreement for Trans-Pacific Partnership (CPTPP) is a 2018 free trade agreement involving eleven countries in the Asia-Pacific region, including New Zealand, Australia, Brunei Darussalam, Canada, Chile, Japan, Malaysia, Mexico, Peru, Singapore, and Vietnam.

627. The Electronic Commerce chapter includes obligations on personal information protection at art 14.8. Article 14.11 addresses cross-border transfers and provides:

Article 14.11: Cross-Border Transfer of Information by Electronic Means

4. The Parties recognise that each Party may have its own regulatory requirements concerning the transfer of information by electronic means.
5. Each Party shall allow the cross-border transfer of information by electronic means, including personal information, when this activity is for the conduct of the business of a covered person.
6. Nothing in this Article shall prevent a Party from adopting or maintaining measures inconsistent with paragraph 2 to achieve a legitimate public policy objective, provided that the measure:
   (c) is not applied in a manner which would constitute a means of arbitrary or unjustifiable discrimination or a disguised restriction on trade; and
   (d) does not impose restrictions on transfers of information greater than are required to achieve the objective.

Part VIII. Enforcement

Chapter 1. Supervisory Authorities

§1. Privacy Commissioner under Privacy Act 2020

628. The Privacy Commissioner is New Zealand's independent supervisory authority.

629. Section 13 of the Privacy Act 2020 continued the position of Privacy Commissioner, first established under the Privacy Commissioner Act 1991 and later consolidated into the 1993 Act. Section 20 provides that the Privacy Commissioner must act independently in performing functions or exercising powers under the Act or other enactments.

630. New Zealand's first statutory privacy commissioner was created in 1976 under the Wanganui Computer Centre Act 1976. The Wanganui Computer Centre Privacy Commissioner was one of the earliest statutory privacy authorities anywhere in the world. The Wanganui Computer Centre Act 1976 was repealed by the 1993 Act with unfinished matters completed by the Privacy Commissioner.

631. The Privacy Commissioner is a corporation sole and both an 'independent Crown entity' and a 'board' for the purposes of the Crown Entities Act 2004. The Commissioner is appointed by the Governor-General on the recommendation of the Minister of Justice.

632. Although the Privacy Act references only the Privacy Commissioner, the Commissioner together with the Commissioner's staff are generally known as the Office of the Privacy Commissioner. The Commissioner can delegate functions to staff under section 73 of the Crown Entities Act.

633. Section 28(1)(b) of the Crown Entities Act provides that the Privacy Commissioner, as a statutory entity that is an independent Crown entity, is 'appointed by … the Governor-General, on the recommendation of the responsible minister'. The 'responsible minister' is the Minister of Justice (Privacy Act, section 7). Independent Crown entities are described in section 7 of the Crown Entities Act. They are bodies corporate that are established under an Act and generally independent of government policy. They are named in Part 3 of Schedule 1 to the Crown Entities Act.

634. The Commissioner is subject to the ombudsmen's jurisdiction under the Ombudsmen Act 1975. The Privacy Commissioner is also subject to the Official Information Act. However, the coverage of that legislation is limited by para (j) of the definition of 'official information' in the Official Information Act 1982, which provides that the term:

> Does not include information contained in any correspondence or communication that has taken place between the office of the Privacy Commissioner and any department or Minister of the Crown or organisation and that relates to any investigation conducted by the Privacy Commissioner under the Privacy Act 2020, other than information that came into existence before the commencement of that investigation.

635. As a member of a 'board' of a statutory entity under the Crown Entities Act, the Privacy Commissioner owes the following statutory duties under sections 53–57 of that Act:

- Duty to comply with this Act and entity's Act: a member must not contravene, or cause the contravention of, or agree to the entity contravening, this Act or the entity's Act.
- Duty to act with honesty and integrity: a member must, when acting as a member, act with honesty and integrity.
- Duty to act in good faith and not at expense of an entity's interests: a member must, when acting as a member, act in good faith and not pursue his or her own interests at the expense of the entity's interests.
- Duty to act with reasonable care, diligence, and skill: a member must, when acting as a member, exercise the care, diligence, and skill that a reasonable person would exercise in the same circumstances taking into account the nature of the statutory entity, the nature of the action and the position of the member and the nature of the responsibilities undertaken by him or her.
- Duty not to disclose information: generally (and subject to exceptions) a member who has information in his or her capacity as a member that would not otherwise be available to him or her must not disclose that information to any person, or make use of, or act on, that information, except in the performance of the entity's functions; or as required or permitted by law.

636. Subject to section 39 (Removal of members of independent Crown entities), non-compliance with any of the individual duties may lead under to removal under section 59. Detailed conflict-of-interest disclosure rules appear in sections 62–72 of the Crown Entities Act. Section 30(2) of the Crown Entities Act and section 15 of the Privacy Act constrain the Commissioner in holding certain other offices.

637. The Crown Entities Act 2004 and Public Finance Act 1989 apply to the Privacy Commissioner and create a system of monitoring and accountability for an independent Crown entity. The principal features of this system include the following:

- The Privacy Commissioner annually agrees upon a Statement of Expectations with the responsible minister which is presented to Parliament.
- The Privacy Commissioner reports every four months to the minister in relation to progress against the Statement of Expectations.
- The Privacy Commissioner reports annually on activities, with accounts audited by Audit New Zealand, and the annual report is presented to Parliament.
- Parliament's Justice Committee annually conducts a review of the Privacy Commissioner's performance in the previous financial year and current operations.

638. Section 206 of the Privacy Act requires the Privacy Commissioner and the Commissioner's staff to maintain secrecy in respect of all matters that come to their knowledge in the exercise of their functions under the Privacy Act. The Commissioner may disclose such matters as in his or her opinion ought to be disclosed for the purposes of giving effect to the Act, but this does not extend to information that might prejudice certain important public interests that are listed in the provision.

§2. Statutory Entities Having an Enforcement Role under Privacy Act 2020

639. It is useful to note the following two statutory entities that have a role, alongside the Privacy Commissioner, in interpreting, applying, and enforcing the Privacy Act: Director of Human Rights Proceedings and HRRT.

640. The Director of Human Rights Proceedings (or 'Director') is appointed under section 20A of the HR Act, and may take civil proceedings before the HRRT against any person, and in relation to any action of that person, that is an interference with the privacy of an individual. The Director may also bring proceedings on behalf of an affected class of persons.

641. The Privacy Commissioner does not take cases to the Tribunal but instead refers cases to the Director who may initiate proceedings. Section 97(1) of the 2020 Act provides that Director may commence proceedings in Tribunal applies where a complaint or matter is referred by the Privacy Commissioner to the Director under the following provisions:

- Section 78: when the Commissioner decides to refer the complaint without conducting an investigation. This is where the Commissioner is unable to secure a settlement or a satisfactory assurance that the agency's action will not be repeated; a settlement has not been complied with; or the action that is the subject of the complaint was done in breach of any term of settlement or an assurance previously secured.
- Section 84: when the Commissioner decides to refer the complaint or matter without conducting any further investigation. This is where the Commissioner is unable to secure a settlement or a satisfactory assurance that the agency's action

will not be repeated; a settlement has not been complied with; or the action that is the subject of the complaint was done in breach of any term of settlement or an assurance previously secured.
- Section 91(5)(b) or (6): when the Commissioner has completed an investigation into an IPP 6 access complaint that has not been resolved despite the Commissioner's best endeavours to secure a settlement or an assurance, or the action that is the subject of the complaint or investigation was done in breach of any term of settlement or assurance previously secured.
- Section 94(4)(a) or (5): when the Commissioner has completed an investigation (other than one that falls under section 91, which relates to an IPP 6 access complaint, or section 93, which relates to a charging complaint), but the complaint or matter has not been resolved, the action that is the subject of the complaint or investigation was done in breach of any term of settlement or assurance previously secured.

642. The HRRT or Tribunal means the HRRT continued by section 93 of the HR Act (Privacy Act, section 7). One of the purposes of the specialist Tribunal is 'to provide a forum to which all can have general access without the costs normally associated with proceedings in the courts of general jurisdiction'.[650] The Tribunal is made up of the Chairperson or a Deputy Chairperson together with two other persons appointed by the Chairperson for the purposes of each hearing from a panel maintained by the minister.

643. For complaints to be brought to the HRRT, they must first be dealt with by the Privacy Commissioner. Sections 97 and 98 of the Privacy Act 2020 are the 'gateway' provisions through which claims must pass if they are to be determined by the HRRT. Section 97 relates to the commencement of Tribunal proceedings by the Director of Human Rights Proceedings, and section 98 relates to the commencement of Tribunal proceedings directly by aggrieved individuals or their representative.

§3. Entities Recognised in Privacy Act in Enforcement Context

644. Although neither themselves supervisory authorities under the Privacy Act, nor entities created by the Privacy Act, several other classes of entities might usefully be noted in relation to the disposition of Privacy Act complaints.

645. The classes of entities fall within three broad categories:

(1) Entities to whom individuals might, or should, take their complaints instead of taking them to the Privacy Commissioner.
(2) Entities to whom individuals might, or should, take their complaints before taking them to the Privacy Commissioner.
(3) Entities to whom the Privacy Commissioner might transfer a complaint.

---

650. *Child Poverty Action Group Inc v. Attorney-General* [2005] NZHRRT 28 (15 Sep. 2005).

646. The first category of entities to which individuals might take their complaints instead of taking them to the Privacy Commissioner. Examples would include:

> Complaints against entities that are exempt under section 8 from being agencies under the Privacy Act e.g., a court or tribunal in relation to its judicial functions where a privacy complaint might be taken to the Judicial Conduct Commissioner; or a news entity, to the extent that it is carrying on news activities where a privacy complaint might be taken to the Broadcasting Standards Authority or the NZ Media Council.
>
> Circumstances in which the Commissioner may decide not to investigate complaint under section 74 such as where there is an adequate remedy or right of appeal that it would be reasonable for the complainant to pursue.

647. The second category of entities to which individuals might take their complaints before taking them to the Privacy Commissioner. Examples would include:

> Circumstances in which the Commissioner may decide not to investigate complaint under section 74 unless the step had first been taken such as (a) taking the matter up with the agency concerned, or (b) exhausting an available alternative dispute resolution process (such as the Banking Ombudsman).

648. The final category of entities that might dispose of Privacy Act complaints are those to which the Privacy Commissioner may transfer the case. Examples would include:

> Domestic transfers under section 75 to an Ombudsman, the Health and Disability Commissioner, the Inspector-General of Intelligence and Security or the Independent Police Conduct Authority.
>
> International transfer under section 76 to an overseas privacy enforcement authority.

§4. Authorities under Other Statutory Schemes for Protecting Privacy

649. There are several statutes that include, within a wider regulatory scheme, provision for privacy remedies or enforcement. The bodies that operate those schemes might be conceivable be considered to have the character of ‘supervisory authorities’ for quasi-privacy laws albeit that privacy be only a part of the bodies’ functions and none have all the attributes of an independent national supervisory authority.

650. The Broadcasting Standards Authority established under the Broadcasting Act 1989 operates a regulatory scheme that involves setting standards, including for privacy, and operating a complaints process under which individuals may obtain redress for breach.

651. The Department of Internal Affairs enforces the Unsolicited Electronic Messages Act 2007 which has a number of characteristics in common with a data protection law.

652. Netsafe is the 'approved agency' under the Harmful Digital Communications Act 2015 which provides remedies for persons harmed by harmful digital communications. Netsafe's role falls short of either a regulator (or rule setter) or enforcer but its educative and mediation functions are similar to those exercised by privacy authorities.

653. Finally, it may be noted that there is provision in the IPP 12 in the Privacy Act to recognise 'prescribed binding schemes.' If such a scheme were to be approved there would likely be both certification bodies and enforcement bodies performing functions similar in some respects to a supervisory authority.

Chapter 2. Composition

§1. Privacy Commissioner Is a Corporation Sole

654. Section 13(2)(a) of the Privacy Act 2020 provides that the Privacy Commissioner is a 'corporation sole'. A corporation sole is an individual person who represents an official position which has a single separate legal entity.

§2. Deputy Privacy Commissioner

655. There is provision to appoint a Deputy Privacy Commissioner in section 14 of the Act. Such an appointment is by the Governor-General on the recommendation of the responsible minister. Part 2 of the Crown Entities Act 2004, except section 46, applies to the appointment and removal of a Deputy Commissioner in the same manner as it applies to the appointment and removal of the Commissioner.

Chapter 3. Competence, Tasks and Powers

§1. General

656. The Privacy Commissioner has competence across all aspects of the Privacy Act, including its extraterritorial application. The Privacy Act enumerates a broad range of tasks for the Commissioner as is usual for a national data protection authority.

657. The Commissioner's more significant powers include rule setting of a legislative-type, through issue of codes of practice, complaints handling mainly of an Ombudsman-type, though with powers to make some binding orders.

§2. Competence of Privacy Commissioner

658. The Privacy Commissioner is competent in relation to all actions of an agency where the Privacy Act 2020 applies (refer section 4).

659. In summary, this means that the Commissioner is competent in relation to any action taken by:

(a) a New Zealand agency in respect of personal information collected or held by it whether or not the agency is, or was, present in New Zealand;
(b) an overseas agency in the course of carrying on business in New Zealand in respect of personal information collected or held by it; or
(c) an individual who is not ordinarily resident in New Zealand in respect of personal information:
  (i) collected by that individual while present in New Zealand, regardless of where the information is subsequently held by that individual or where the individual to whom the information relates is, or was, located;
  (ii) held by that individual while present in New Zealand (but not collected by that individual while present in New Zealand), regardless of where the individual to whom the information relates is, or was, located.

660. Section 4(3) provides that an agency may be treated as carrying on business in New Zealand without necessarily:

(a) being a commercial operation;
(b) having a place of business in New Zealand;
(c) receiving any monetary payment for the supply of goods or services; or
(d) intending to make a profit from its business in New Zealand.

661. The Privacy Commissioner is not competent in relation to bodies exempted from the definition of 'agency' such as a court or Tribunal in relation to its judicial functions in their judicial capacity (*see* Act, section 8).

§3. Privacy Commissioner Tasks

662. Section 17(1) of the Privacy Act 2020 enumerates the Privacy Commissioner's functions as follows:

> The functions of the Commissioner are:
>
> (a) to exercise the powers, and carry out the functions and duties, conferred on the Commissioner by or under this Act or any other enactment:
> (b) to provide advice (with or without a request) to a Minister, a Parliamentary Under-Secretary, or an agency on any matter relevant to the operation of this Act:
> (c) to promote, by education and publicity, an understanding and acceptance of the information privacy principles and of the objectives of those principles:
> (d) to make public statements in relation to any matter affecting the privacy of individuals:
> (e) to receive and invite representations from members of the public on any matter affecting the privacy of individuals:
> (f) to consult and co-operate with other persons and bodies concerned with the privacy of individuals:
> (g) to examine any proposed legislation (including subordinate legislation) or proposed government policy that the Commissioner considers may affect the privacy of individuals, including any proposed legislation that makes provision for either or both of the following:
> (i) the collection of personal information by a public sector agency:
> (ii) the sharing of personal information between public sector agencies (including parts of public sector agencies):
> (h) to monitor the use of unique identifiers:
> (i) to inquire generally into any matter, including any other enactment or any law, or any practice or procedure, whether governmental or non-governmental, or any technical development, if it appears to the Commissioner that the privacy of individuals is being, or may be, infringed (for powers of the Commissioner in relation to inquiries, *see* section 203):
> (j) to undertake research into, and to monitor developments in, data processing and technology to ensure that any adverse effects of the developments on the privacy of individuals are minimised:
> (k) to give advice to any person in relation to any matter that concerns the need for, or desirability of, action by that person in the interests of the privacy of individuals:
> (l) when requested to do so by an agency, to conduct an audit of personal information maintained by that agency for the purpose of ascertaining whether the information is maintained according to the information privacy principles:
> (m) to monitor the operation of this Act and consider whether any amendments to this Act are necessary or desirable:
> (n) to report to the responsible Minister on the results of –

(i) any examination conducted under paragraph (g):
(ii) the monitoring undertaken under paragraph (h):
(iii) the research and monitoring undertaken under paragraph (j):
(iv) the monitoring and consideration undertaken under paragraph (m):

(o) to report to the Prime Minister on –
(i) any matter affecting the privacy of individuals, including the need for, or desirability of, taking legislative, administrative, or other action to give protection or better protection to the privacy of individuals:
(ii) the desirability of New Zealand accepting any international instrument relating to the privacy of individuals:
(iii) any other matter relating to the privacy of individuals that, in the Commissioner's opinion, should be drawn to the Prime Minister's attention:

(p) to gather any information that will assist in carrying out the functions in paragraphs (a) to (o).

663. Examples of the functions in paragraph (a) conferred on the Commissioner by or under the Act that are not expressly listed in section 17 include the receipt of breach notifications, handling of complaints and issue of codes of practice.

664. Examples of functions in paragraph (a) conferred on the Commissioner by other enactments include various statutory consultations and the handling of complaints submitted under other laws.

665. Section 17(2) mentions, as a function of the Commissioner, the publishing of reports. Section 18 accords an advisory function upon the Commissioner in relation to prescribing binding schemes and countries that provide comparable safeguards to those in this Act for the purpose of IPP 12.

§4. Privacy Commissioner Powers

666. The Privacy Commissioner has a range of investigative, corrective, authorisation, and advisory powers.

667. The Commissioner's principal investigative powers include:

- Hear and obtain information from any person and make any inquiries: sections 81(2), 128, 194.
- Use best endeavours to secure a settlement of a complaint and secure a satisfactory assurance: under various sections.
- Call a compulsory conference: section 85.
- Issue a summons: section 86.
- By notice require information and documents: section 87.

- Require agency to supply information about privacy officer or information holdings: section 202.

668. The Commissioner's principal corrective powers include:

- Issue a code of practice: section 32.
- Refer a complaint or a matter that is the subject of an investigation to the Director of Human Rights Proceedings: under various sections.
- Make an access direction, section 92.
- Make a charging determination: section 93.
- Determine a complaint or investigation: section 94.
- Report on an investigation into an intelligence and security agency, including reporting to Prime Minister: section 95.
- Report breach of duty or misconduct: section 96.
- Publish the identity of an agency that has notified the Commissioner of a notifiable privacy breach: section 122.
- Issue a compliance notice: section 124.
- Publish details of compliance notice: section 129.
- Report on approved information sharing agreement: sections 151, 159.
- Prohibit a transfer of personal information from New Zealand to another country: section 193.

669. The Commissioner's principal authorisation powers include:

- Authorise collection, use, storage, or disclosure of personal information otherwise in breach of IPP 2 or IPPs 9 to 12: section 30.
- Issue a code of practice: section 32.
- Make a charging determination: section 93.
- Authorise public sector agency to impose charge: section 67.

670. The Commissioner's principal advisory powers include:

- To provide advice to a minister, a Parliamentary Under-Secretary, or an agency on any matter relevant to the operation of this Act: section 17(1)(b).
- To give advice to any person in relation to any matter that concerns the need for, or desirability of, action by that person in the interests of the privacy of individuals: section 17(1)(k).
- To report to the responsible minister or Prime Minister: section 17(1)(n) and (o).
- To provide advice to the responsible minister on whether a binding scheme requires a foreign person or entity to protect personal information in a way that, overall, provides comparable safeguards to those in the Act: section 18(1).
- To provide advice to the responsible minister on whether the privacy laws of a country, overall, provide comparable safeguards to those in the Act: section 18(2).
- To be consulted on proposed information sharing agreement: section 150(1)(a).

Chapter 4. Remedies

§1. The Human Rights Review Tribunal

671. A breach of the IPPs in the Privacy Act or a code of practice issued under it amounts to an 'interference with the privacy of an individual'.[651] Such an interference occurs only when there has been a breach of an IPP accompanied by some harm or loss to the individual concerned.[652] In relation to the IPPs relating to subject access and correction, however, no harm or loss is required to be shown.[653]

672. The IPPs are not enforceable in a court of law, with the one exception of the right to access one's personal information under IPP 6 when it is held by a public sector agency.[654] This entitlement is both directly legally enforceable and may alternatively be pursued through the processes provided for under Privacy Act if the individual concerned so chooses. The latter option is the preferred one as it is free of charge. There are no filing or hearing fees in the HRRT.

673. All complaints under the Privacy Act are required to be dealt with by the Privacy Commissioner at first instance. Where there has been no resolution to the complaint, the complainant may pursue the claim in the Tribunal[655] personally, or, as is less often the case, by the Director of Human Rights Proceedings on a referral by the Privacy Commissioner.[656]

§2. Representation

I. Self-Represented Litigants

674. There is no requirement that a claimant must be represented by a lawyer in the Tribunal. Most complainants represent themselves, and the Tribunal makes due allowance for this in its procedure.[657] It has been noted that in approximately 75% of the cases filed with the Tribunal, one or more of the litigants are self-represented 'either by choice or by necessity'.[658]

651. Privacy Act, s. 69(1), (2), and (3).
652. Privacy Act, s. 69(2)(b).
653. Privacy Act, s. 69(3).
654. Privacy Act, s. 31. *See also R v. Wong-Tung* (1996) 2 HRNZ 272 (Court of Appeal) and *Jaffe v. Bradshaw* (1998) 16 CRNZ 122 (High Court).
655. Known as the Complaints Review Tribunal until 31 Dec. 2021.
656. Privacy Act, s. 94(4)(a) and s. 97.
657. *See*, for example, *Coates v. Springlands Health Limited* [2007] NZHRRT 17 (5 Oct. 2007).
658. *Waxman v. Pal (Application for Non-Publication Orders)* [2017] NZHRRT 4 (25 Jan. 2017), at para. 69.

II. Class Actions

675. The Director of Human Rights Proceedings has the power to bring proceedings in the Tribunal on behalf of a class of aggrieved individuals where an agency has acted in a way that has affected the class and that is an interference with the privacy of an individual.[659]

676. Class actions may also be brought by a 'representative lawfully acting on behalf of a class of aggrieved individuals'.[660] As was observed in a Law Commission report, 'This would allow such persons and agencies like Consumer NZ or the Children's Commissioner to lay complaints.'[661]

§3. Miscellaneous Powers of the Tribunal

677. The Tribunal has the power to make a variety of orders, including interim orders in matters where it has the power to make any final determination.[662] The criterion for granting such orders is that the Tribunal must be satisfied that it is necessary in the interests of justice to make the order to preserve the position of the parties pending a final determination of the proceedings.

678. The Tribunal also has the power to suppress details about a case on an interim or permanent basis, and to hold a hearing, in whole or in part, in private if the circumstances warrant it.[663]

§4. Costs

679. The Tribunal has the power to make an award of costs against either party.[664] The general rule concerning costs in the Tribunal has traditionally been that costs should follow the event, and that the unsuccessful party should make a reasonable contribution to the legal costs of the successful party.[665] The decision as to the quantum of a costs award is a discretionary one for the Tribunal, but as with all judicial discretions, the discretion must be exercised in a principled manner. There is extensive case law on costs awards in the Tribunal, with a variety of factors taken into account, such as whether the complainant had rejected a reasonable settlement

---

659. Privacy Act, s. 97(6).
660. Privacy Act, s. 98(1).
661. New Zealand Law Commission, *Review of the Privacy Act 1993* (NZLC R123, 2011), at para. 6.57.
662. Human Rights Act, s. 95(1).
663. Human Rights Act, s. 107(3).
664. Privacy Act, s. 110(1).
665. *See*, for example, the early case *O v. N (No 2)* [1996] NZCRT 4 (12 Mar. 1996), (1996) 3 HRNZ 636, at 654.

offer; whether the complainant unreasonably prolonged proceedings or made unreasonable or untenable claims; or whether the case was withdrawn or abandoned shortly before the hearing, causing unnecessary preparation costs to be incurred by the defendant.

680. The presumption that costs should ordinarily follow the event changed with a 2014 Tribunal decision that was subsequently endorsed on appeal by the HC.[666] The Tribunal's current approach is to take the human rights nature of its jurisdiction into account where appropriate in exercising its discretion to award costs. This is so that the imposition of costs awards does not have a chilling effect on the entitlement of individuals to vindicate their rights. Such an approach is viewed as being particularly appropriate where individuals are challenging decisions or actions by the state or large institutional agencies.[667] The court's view was that an unsuccessful bona fide plaintiff should neither be punished by a costs order 'for bringing a claim that was important to him and about which he was genuine', nor should such claimants be 'unduly discouraged'.[668]

§5. Appeals

681. Appeals to the HC from Tribunal decisions are heard by a HC judge together with two panel members of the Tribunal[669] if the appeal concerns or includes a question of fact.[670]

682. Appeals may be made from the HC to the CA on a question of law only.[671] The appellant must seek leave to appeal from the HC. If leave is not granted, the CA may grant special leave to appeal 'if in the opinion of the court the question of law involved in the appeal is one which, by reason of its general or public importance or for any reason, ought to be submitted to the CA for decision'. Appeals to the Supreme Court from the CA are made on the same basis.[672]

---

666. *Andrews v. Commissioner of Police* [2014] NZHRRT 31 (5 Aug. 2014), upheld on appeal in *Commissioner of Police v. Andrews* [2015] NZHC 745 (17 Apr. 2015).
667. *See*, for example, the subsequent case of *Lohr v. Accident Compensation Corporation (Costs)* [2016] NZHRRT 36 (17 Nov. 2016), where the plaintiff failed entirely in his IPP 6 access claim against the state accident insurance corporation, but the successful defendant's application for costs nevertheless failed.
668. *Commissioner of Police v. Andrews* [2015] NZHC 745 (17 Apr. 2015), at para. 80.
669. The Tribunal consists of the Chairperson, who must have legal credentials, and two lay members chosen from a panel of up to twenty members.
670. Human Rights Act, s. 126(1).
671. Human Rights Act, s. 124.
672. Senior Courts Act 2016, s. 68.

§6. REMEDIES

I. Declarations

683. The Tribunal has the power to issue declarations.[673] This remedy is the one that is granted most often, sometimes in combination with other remedies. A declaration is a discretionary remedy. Thus, even if the Tribunal or Court finds that a particular state of affairs exists, it need not make a declaration to that effect. This can occur if there is some form of disentitling conduct, or there is merely a *de minimis* breach.[674] Disentitling conduct might include misleading or other improper behaviour,[675] or inordinate delay in pursuing a case.[676] The general approach, however, is that a declaration should not ordinarily be denied.

684. It should be noted that the HC has a quite separate jurisdiction in respect of declarations. The Privacy Commissioner can refer a matter to the Director of Human Rights Proceedings for the purpose of deciding whether a declaratory judgment or an order of the HC under the Declaratory Judgments Act 1908 should be obtained. This is a general power and is not exercised within the complaints jurisdiction.[677]

II. Restraining Orders

685. The Tribunal lacks the power to issue an injunction *per se*, where action is merely apprehended, but it can make orders restraining interferences with an individual's privacy where a continuing or repeated action is involved.[678]

III. Damages

A. Introduction

686. The Tribunal has the power to make an order for compensatory damages,[679] which may be awarded under any one or more of several heads of loss. There must be a causal connection to warrant damages in the sense that the defendant's act or omission was a contributing or material cause of the plaintiff's harm or

673. Privacy Act, s. 102(2)(a).
674. *Taylor v. Chief Executive, Department of Corrections* [2018] NZHRRT 35 (31 Jul. 2018).
675. *Geary v. New Zealand Psychologists Board* [2011] NZHRRT 19 (19 Sep. 2011); *Geary v. New Zealand Psychologists Board* [2012] NZHC 384, [2012] NZLR 414.
676. *Te Wini v. Askelund* [2015] NZHRRT 21 (15 Jun. 2015); *Deeming v. Whangarei District Council* [2015] NZHRRT 55 (22 Dec. 2015).
677. Privacy Act, s. 204.
678. Privacy Act, s. 102(2)(b). *See*, for example, *Hammond v. Credit Union Baywide (t/as NZCU Baywide)* [2015] NZHRRT 6 (2 Mar. 2015), *Director of Human Rights Proceedings v. Slater* [2019] NZHRRT 13 (12 Mar. 2019).
679. Privacy Act, s. 102(2)(c).

loss.[680] The Tribunal's damages awards are currently limited to a maximum of $350,000,[681] which is the same limit that applies to the DC, the lowest forum in the New Zealand judicial hierarchy. In one decision, the Tribunal awarded damages of $168,070.88,[682] which approached its then statutory limit of $200,000. Where proceedings are brought on behalf of more than one individual, the Tribunal may award damages to each individual.[683]

687. The Tribunal can refer a matter to the HC for a monetary remedy that is higher than the statutory limit if the plaintiff has made a claim for a higher amount.[684] Alternatively, the monetary jurisdiction of the Tribunal may be increased if the parties themselves agree to it.[685]

688. The Tribunal lacks the power to award exemplary damages.[686] There is, however, a separate penalty regime,[687] but penalties are not available for interferences with an individual's privacy.

B. Damages for Pecuniary Loss

689. Damages are available for pecuniary loss suffered as a result of the transaction or activity out of which the privacy interference arose.[688] In one case, the plaintiff was awarded compensation for lost income as a result of being forced to resign from her employment.[689]

690. Reasonable expenses incurred by the individual for the purpose of the transaction or activity out of which the privacy interference arose may also be awarded.[690] Damages under this head of loss have been awarded for previously incurred legal costs.[691]

---

680. *Dotcom v. Crown Law Office* [2018] NZHRRT 7 (26 Mar. 2018).
681. Privacy Act, s. 111, via s. 92Q of the Human Rights Act 1993.
682. *Hammond v. Credit Union Baywide* [2015] NZHRRT 6 (2 Mar. 2015).
683. Privacy Act, s. 103(2).
684. Sections 92R-92U of the Human Rights Act.
685. Section 92W of the HR Act. The parties might agree to this to avoid the higher legal costs involved in pursuing a case in the High Court.
686. *Dotcom v. Crown Law Office* [2018] NZHRRT 7 (26 Mar. 2018), at [253].
687. *See* Ch. 6 below.
688. Privacy Act, s. 103(1)(a).
689. *Hammond v. Credit Union Baywide* [2015] NZHRRT 6 (2 Mar. 2015) ($38,350).
690. Privacy Act, s. 103(1)(b).
691. *Proceedings Commissioner v. Health Waikato* [2000] NZCRT 3 (14 Mar. 2000), (2000) 6 HRNZ 274 ($1,000, on appeal); *DAS v. Department of Child, Youth and Family Services* [2000] NZHRRT 24 (13 Sep. 2000) ($1,000); *Proceedings Commissioner v. Health Waikato Limited* (2000) 6 HRNZ 274 ($1,000, awarded by the High Court on appeal from a Tribunal decision); *NOP v. Chief Executive, Ministry of Business, Innovation and Employment* [2014] NZHRRT 16 (17 Apr. 2014) ($2,500); *Director of Human Rights Proceedings v. Schubach* [2015] NZHRRT 4 (19 Feb. 2015) ($1,374.25); *Hammond v. Credit Union Baywide* [2015] NZHRRT 6 (2 Mar. 2015) ($15,543.10).

C. Damages for Loss of a Benefit

691. Damages are available for loss of any benefit, whether or not of a monetary kind, which the affected individual might reasonably have been expected to obtain but for the privacy interference.[692]

692. Damages have been awarded under this head for loss of the benefit of using information in legal proceedings, where access under IPP 6 had been wrongly denied;[693] lost benefit of peace of mind by withholding information needed for legal obligations;[694] lost benefit of paying income-related rent while a welfare beneficiary;[695] lost benefit due to 'career regression' due to forced resignation from a job;[696] and loss of a good credit rating due to inaccurate information provided to a debt collection agency.[697]

D. Damages for Emotional Harm

693. Damages may also be awarded to an individual for 'humiliation, loss of dignity, and injury to the feelings'.[698] This is by far the most commonly awarded head of damages for breach of the IPPs.

694. The conventional test for damages for humiliation, loss of dignity, and injury to feelings under the Act is subjective, not objective.[699] The focus is thus on how the particular individual was affected, not how a 'reasonable person' would have felt.

695. There are two classes of awards for 'humiliation, loss of dignity, and injury to the feelings': those made where there has been a breach of IPP 6 (access) or IPP 7 (correction), and the associated administrative provisions dealing with access and

692. Privacy Act, s. 103(1)(c).
693. *Proceedings Commissioner v. Health Waikato Limited* [2000] NZCRT 3; (2000) 6 HRNZ 274 ($5,000 awarded by the High Court on appeal); *Jans v. Winter* [2003] NZHRRT 21 (27 Jun. 2003) ($15,000); *Director of Human Rights Proceedings v. Grupen* [2010] NZHRRT 22 (19 Nov. 2010) ($5,000, upheld on appeal); *Director of Human Rights Proceedings v. Schubach* [2015] NZHRRT 4 (19 Feb. 2015) ($5,000); *Watson v. Capital and Coast District Health Board* [2015] NZHRRT 27 (13 Jul. 2015) ($5,000); *Dotcom v. Crown Law Office* [2018] NZHRRT 7 (26 Mar. 2018) ($30,000, overturned on appeal, but on further appeal in *Dotcom v. Attorney-General* [2020] NZCA 551 (10 Nov. 2020) the award was remitted back to Tribunal for reconsideration); *Patel v. Dean* [2020] NZHRRT 37 (31 Aug. 2020) ($5,000).
694. *Director of Human Rights Proceedings v. Hamilton* [2012] NZHRRT 24 (1 Nov. 2012) ($5,000, concerning accounting services); *Director of Human Rights Proceedings v. Valli & Hughes* [2014] NZHRRT 58 (15 Dec. 2014) ($5,000, concerning income tax obligations).
695. *Holmes v. Housing New Zealand Corporation* [2014] NZHRRT 54 (3 Nov. 2014).
696. *Hammond v. Credit Union Baywide* [2015] NZHRRT 6 (2 Mar. 2015) ($16,177.78).
697. *Taylor v. Orcon Ltd* [2015] NZHRRT 15 (14 May 2015) ($10,000).
698. Privacy Act, s. 103(1)(d).
699. *AB v. Chief Executive, Ministry of Social Development* [2011] NZHRRT 16 (23 Jun. 2011), at para. 30; *Hammond v. Credit Union Baywide* [2015] NZHRRT 6 (2 Mar. 2015), at paras 170.5 and 177.2.

correction;[700] and those where there have breaches of the other IPPs.[701] The difference between awards in the two classes of damages for emotional harm is that the second class must involve '*significant* humiliation, *significant* loss of dignity, or *significant* injury to feelings'. This functions as a filtering mechanism to limit claims of *de minimis* harm. Awards under the first class need not involve 'significant' emotional harm (or indeed any harm at all), as they involve legal entitlements of access to and correction of personal information, and so by their very nature will commonly involve emotional harm of some degree. Thus, awards for the first class of breach can involve emotional harm that is short of 'significant', and in some cases only nominal damages may be awarded.

E. Quantum of Damages for Emotional Harm

696. Damages for emotional harm 'are fact-driven and vary widely'.[702] In recent years, the Tribunal has taken the position that awards fall into roughly three bands: the less serious cases, which attract awards of up to $10,000; the more serious cases, which fall in the range between $10,000 and $50,0000; and the most serious category of case, where awards will be in excess of $50,000. The highest amount of damages for emotional harm to date has been $98,000, which was for several harmful disclosures of personal information by a former employer.[703] In a subsequent case, $70,000 was awarded for online disclosures of personal information by a blogger.[704] The highest awards among the older cases was $40,000, awarded for disclosures of sensitive health information by an alcohol treatment clinic,[705] and $20,000, for a denied access request involving the deliberate deception of the plaintiff and the Privacy Commissioner where the withheld information concerned unanswered allegations of child abuse.[706]

697. The HC has held that the Tribunal is not bound by the amount of damages sought by a plaintiff, but that it can award a higher amount where appropriate. This is on the basis that the Tribunal has a 'special statutory jurisdiction' based on equity and good conscience,[707] and that 'the Privacy Act should be interpreted and applied in a manner which is not legalistic and does not place barriers, especially of a technical nature, between the claimant and a just outcome'.[708]

700. Privacy Act, s. 69(3).
701. Privacy Act, s. 69(2).
702. *Hammond v. NZCU Baywide* [2015] NZHRRT 6 (2 Mar. 2015), at para. 76.
703. *Hammond v. NZCU Baywide* [2015] NZHRRT 6 (2 Mar. 2015).
704. *Director of Human Rights Proceedings v. Slate*r [2019] NZHRRT 13 (12 Mar. 2019).
705. *Hamilton v. The Deanery 2000 Ltd* [2003] NZHRRT 28 (29 Aug. 2003).
706. *L v. N* [1997] NZCRT 11 (14 Apr. 1997), (1997) 3 HRNZ 721.
707. Human Rights Act, s. 105.
708. *Chief Executive of the Ministry of Social Development v. Holmes* [2013] NZHC 672, [2013] NZAR 780, at paras 106 and 108.

IV. Order to Remedy Interference with Privacy or Redress Any Loss or Damage

698. The Tribunal has the power to order the defendant to remedy an interference with an individual's privacy or redress any loss or damage suffered by individual as a result of the interference.[709]

699. This provision has been used to order an agency to disclose information to the individual concerned where an IPP 6 access request has been denied;[710] to correct[711] or delete[712] personal information; and take down personal information from a website.[713] In one denied access case, which involved unexplained referee scores, the Tribunal ordered the defendant College of Surgeons to provide 'meaningful access' by disclosing the formula or mechanism by which the referee scores were calculated so as to make the information intelligible.[714]

V. Other Relief

700. The Tribunal has the power to grant 'such other relief as the Tribunal thinks fit'.[715] This provision has been used to apply for a remedy not expressly provided for under the Privacy Act, such a written apology from a defendant.[716] An application for an apology was denied in one case, however, because the Tribunal doubted the worth and sincerity of any apology: this was because of the passage of time since the breaches, and the employees responsible for the breaches were no longer working for the defendant, who continued to maintain that it had complied with the Privacy Act.[717]

701. In recent years, the Tribunal has issued Privacy Act training orders against defendants,[718] but it is doubtful that the Tribunal has the power to do so. Early

709. Privacy Act, s. 102(2)(d).
710. *Dijkstra v. New Zealand Police* [2006] NZHRRT 16 (25 May 2006); *Director of Human Rights Proceedings v. Schubach* [2015] NZHRRT 4 (19 Feb. 2015); *Watson v. Capital and Coast District Health Board* [2015] NZHRRT 27 (7 Jul. 2015); *Turner v. Itchyfoot Pty Ltd* [2021] NZHRRT 27 (9 Jun. 2021).
711. *Plumtree v. Attorney-General on behalf of the New Zealand Defence Force* [2002] NZHRRT 10 (2 Oct. 2002).
712. *Armfield v. Naughton* [2014] NZHRRT 48 (6 Oct. 2014).
713. *Director of Human Rights Proceedings v. Slater* [2019] NZHRRT 13 (12 Mar. 2019).
714. *Naidu v. Royal Australasian College of Surgeons* [2018] NZHRRT 23 (14 Jun. 2018).
715. Privacy Act, s. 102(2)(e).
716. *L v. N* [1997] NZCRT 11 (14 Apr. 1997), (1997) 3 HRNZ 721; *W v. Director-General of Social Welfare* [1998] NZCRT 12 (1 Aug. 1998).
717. *Cook v. Manawatu Community Law Centre* [2021] NZHRRT 10 (15 Feb. 2021).
718. *Hammond v. Credit Union Baywide* [2015] NZHRRT 6 (2 Mar. 2015); *Taylor v. Orcon Ltd* [2015] NZHRRT 15 (14 May 2015); *Director of Human Rights Proceedings v.* Crampton [2015] NZHRRT 35 (29 Jul. 2015); and *Deeming v. Whangarei District Council* [2015] NZHRRT 55 (22 Dec. 2015).

Tribunal cases found that the Tribunal lacked the jurisdiction to do so.[719] Moreover, unless the relationship between the plaintiff and defendant is a continuing one, it can hardly be considered 'relief' or a 'remedy' as far as the plaintiff is concerned.

§7. Relevance of the Defendant's Conduct

702. It is not a defence to maintain that the interference with an individual's privacy was unintentional or without negligence, but the Tribunal is required to take the defendant's conduct into account in deciding what, if any, remedy to grant. The defendant's conduct may be mitigating, such as prior consistent dealings with the plaintiff;[720] early admission of breach and an early apology;[721] the defendant having to deal with plaintiff's confusing requests for information;[722] and supporting an employee when a complaint was being pursued against the employer.[723]

703. The defendant's conduct may also be an aggravating factor where actions are deliberate or there is bad faith. Conduct that has been considered in this context include deliberately concealing information from and misleading an individual;[724] misleading the Privacy Commissioner during an investigation;[725] acting in an uncooperative and confrontational manner;[726] disclosing an individual's health information to the media;[727] and exposure of the plaintiff to extreme ridicule and contempt on the defendant's blog.[728]

704. There is no express provision that requires the Tribunal to take the plaintiff's or complainant's conduct into account (aside from deciding costs), but the Tribunal's equity and good conscience jurisdiction[729] enables it to do so in appropriate cases.[730]

719. *W v. P* [1999] NZCRT 2 (16 Feb. 1999), which followed an analogous High Court decision in *NZ Van Lines Ltd v. Proceedings Commissioner* [1995] 1 NZLR 100, at 109, where it was questioned whether a training order could be considered a remedy or relief in respect of a plaintiff.
720. *L v. L*, High Court Auckland AP95-SW01 (31 May 2002).
721. *Feather v. Accident Compensation Corporation* [2003] NZHRRT 29 (4 Sep. 2003); *Williams v. Accident Compensation Corporation* [2017] NZHRRT 26 (21 Jul. 2017) *Taylor v. Chief Executive, Department of Corrections* [2018] NZHRRT 35 (31 Jul. 2018); *Marshall v. Idea Services Ltd (Privacy Act)* [2020] NHRRT 13 (18 May 2020).
722. *Steele v. Board of Trustees of Salisbury School* [2012] NZHRRT 20 (7 Sep. 2012).
723. *Cook v. Manawatu Community Law Centre* [2021] NZHRRT 10 (15 Feb. 2021).
724. *L v. N* [1997] NZCRT 11 (14 Apr. 1997), (1997) 3 HRNZ 721.
725. *Ibid.*
726. *Armfield v. Naughton* [2014] NZHRRT 48 (6 Oct. 2014).
727. *Hamilton v. The Deanery 2000 Ltd* [2003] NZHRRT 28 (29 Aug. 2003).
728. *Director of Human Rights Proceedings v. Slater* [2019] NZHRRT 13 (12 Mar. 2019).
729. Human Rights Act 1993, s. 105.
730. *Mayes v. Owairaka Board of Trustees* [1996] NZCRT 54 (28 Nov. 1996), (1996) 3 HRNZ 707.

Chapter 5. Liabilities

§1. Vicarious Holding of Personal Information

705. Personal information held by a person in the capacity of an officer, employee, or member of an agency is treated as being held by the agency.[731]

706. Where an agency holds information on behalf of another agency (such as for safe custody or processing), the information is treated as being held only by the latter agency, unless the agency that is holding the information uses or discloses the information for its own purposes, in which case the information is treated as being held by both agencies.[732] It is immaterial if the holding agency is located outside New Zealand or holds the information outside New Zealand.[733] Moreover, the mere transfer of information from an agency to the agency that is holding it is not considered to be a use or disclosure of the information; similarly, the transfer of the information back and any information derived from its processing is not a use or disclosure of the information by the holding agency.[734] This provision is relevant to IPP 12 of the Act ('Disclosure of personal information outside New Zealand'), in that it clarifies that the Act does not apply to cloud services.[735]

§2. Vicarious Actions and Disclosures in Respect of Personal Information

707. An action done by or information disclosed to a person employed by, or in the service of, an agency in the performance of that person's employment is treated as having been done by, or disclosed to, the agency.[736]

708. Similarly, the actions of an employee, agent, or member of an agency are treated also as those of the employer, principal or agent, whether or not the former acted with or without the latter's knowledge or approval (in the case of an employer), or (in the case of a principal or agency) unless it was done without the principal's or agency's express or implied authority.[737] However, in any proceedings under the Act, an employer will have a defence if reasonably practicable steps were taken to prevent the act.[738]

709. In relation to liability for failure to notify data breaches, however, the position is somewhat different (below).

731. Privacy Act, s. 10(1).
732. Privacy Act, s. 11(1)–(3).
733. Privacy Act, s. 11(4).
734. Privacy Act, s. 11(5).
735. Ministry of Justice *Departmental Report, Part One, Privacy Bill* (2019), at para. 145.
736. Privacy Act, s. 12.
737. Privacy Act, s. 211(1).
738. Privacy Act, s. 211(2).

§3. Data Breach Notification

710. An agency is required to notify the Privacy Commissioner as soon as practicable after becoming aware that a notifiable privacy breach has occurred.[739] Similarly, an agency must notify an affected individual as soon as practicable after becoming aware that a notifiable breach has occurred,[740] unless an exception applies.[741]

711. The regime of general application to the liability of employers, principals, and agencies[742] does not apply to processes or proceedings under the Act relating to the notification of the Privacy Commissioner or affected individuals or members of the public of a notifiable privacy breach, but is treated separately.[743]

712. An employee or a member of an agency is not personally liable in relation to notifiable privacy breach obligations if any action or omission results in the employer or agency failing to notify the Privacy Commissioner or an affected person of a notifiable privacy breach; anything done or omitted by an employee or member of an agency is treated as done or omitted by the employer or agency.[744] Where an action or omission is due to an agent of another agency, this is treated as being done or omitted by both the agent and the principal agency, but the agent's liability is affected by whether they hold personal information that is subject of a notifiable breach.[745]

713. In relation to notifiable privacy breach obligations, anything that is known by employees, agents, or a member of an agency is treated as also known by the employer, principal agency, or agency.[746]

---

739. Privacy Act, s. 114.
740. Privacy Act, s. 115(1).
741. Privacy Act, s. 115(2); *see* s. 116.
742. Privacy Act, s. 211.
743. Privacy Act, s. 119, referring to data breach notification obligations under s 120 and s 121.
744. Privacy Act, s. 120(2)–(3).
745. Privacy Act, s. 120(4)–(5); *see also* s. 11(3) (an agent will not be considered as holding personal information of the principal agency unless it uses or discloses the information for its own purposes).
746. Privacy Act, s. 121.

Chapter 6. Penalties

§1. Failure to Comply with Access Order

714. Failure to comply with an access order is an offence carrying liability on conviction of a fine not exceeding $10,000.[747]

§2. Failure to Notify Privacy Commissioner of a Notifiable Privacy Breach

715. Failure to notify the Privacy Commissioner of a notifiable privacy breach is an offence carrying liability on conviction of a fine not exceeding $10,000.[748] Taking steps to address the privacy breach is not a defence, but it is a defence if the agency reasonably did not consider the breach to be notifiable in the circumstances.[749]

§3. Failure to Comply with a Compliance Notice

716. Failure to comply without reasonable excuse with a Tribunal order that the agency comply with a compliance notice is an offence carrying liability on conviction to a fine not exceeding $10,000.[750]

§4. Failure to Comply with a Transfer Prohibition Notice

717. Failure or refusal to comply without reasonable excuse with a transfer prohibition notice is an offence carrying liability on conviction to a fine not exceeding $10,000.[751]

§5. Other Offences

718. A fine not exceeding $10,000 may imposed upon conviction for any of the following offences:

– Obstruction, hindering, or resisting without reasonable excuse the Privacy Commissioner or any other person in the exercise of their powers under the Privacy Act.[752]

747. Privacy Act, s. 104(4).
748. Privacy Act, s. 118(1).
749. Privacy Act, s. 118(2)–(3).
750. Privacy Act, s. 133(3).
751. Privacy Act, s. 197.
752. Privacy Act s. 212(1)(a).

- Refusing or failing to comply without reasonable excuse with any lawful requirement of the Commissioner or any other person under the Act.[753]
- Making a statement or giving information to the Commissioner or other person exercising powers under the Act knowing that it is false or misleading.[754]
- Representing that that authority is held under the Act when it is not.[755]
- Misleading an agency by impersonating an individual, or falsely pretending to be someone or to be acting under their authority, for the purpose of obtaining access to that individual's personal information, or having that individual's personal information used, altered or destroyed.[756]
- Destroying any document containing personal information knowing that a request for personal information under IPP 6 has been made.[757]

753. Privacy Act s. 212(1)(b).
754. Privacy Act s. 212(2)(a).
755. Privacy Act s. 212(2)(b).
756. Privacy Act s. 212(2)(c).
757. Privacy Act s. 212(2)(d).

Part IX. Specific Processing Situations

Chapter 1. Processing for Journalistic Purposes and Academic, Artistic or Literary Expression

§1. Processing for Journalistic Purposes

719. The definitions of a 'New Zealand agency'[758] and an 'overseas agency', which are key to the application of the Act, exclude 'a news entity, to the extent that it is carrying on news activities'.[759] Journalism, therefore, both domestic and overseas based, is immune from any limitations on processing. This is on the basis of their special role in a democratic society in supporting the free flow of information to the public.[760] News entities continue to be bound by the IPPs in relation to such non-news activities as advertising, employment, and the use of subscription lists. In relation to the news activities of news entities, the Privacy Commissioner still has functions that include public statements on, and inquiries into, media practices that may affect the privacy of individuals,[761] though that is as far as the Commissioner's powers extend.

I. 'News Entity'

720. The Act defines a 'news entity' as:[762]

> an entity (including an individual) –
> whose business, in whole or in part, consists of a news activity; and
>
> (a) that is, or is employed by an employer that is, subject to the oversight of –
> (i) the Broadcasting Standards Authority; or
> (ii) the New Zealand Media Council; or

758. Privacy Act, s. 8(b)(x).
759. Privacy Act, s. 9(d).
760. Justice Select Committee, reporting the Privacy Bill 2018 (34-2) to the House of Representatives, 2019, at p. 3.
761. Privacy Act, s. 17(1)(d) and (i).
762. Privacy Act, s. 7(1).

(iii) an overseas regulator providing an independent procedure for the consideration and adjudication of privacy complaints that is accessible to complainants, including complainants residing in New Zealand; or
(iv) any other body prescribed as a regulatory body by regulations made under section 215(1)(b) for the purposes of this definition.

721. A key element to the definition is that a 'news entity' is subject to oversight, which will involve compliance with a set of standards and a complaints process. A news entity is defined as including an individual, so will cover a blogger or individual publisher or broadcaster, so long as the individual is subject to appropriate oversight.

II. Broadcasting Standards Authority

722. Although the news activities of radio and television broadcasting are not legally bound by the Privacy Act's IPPs, complaints relating to matters affecting individual privacy may be made to the Broadcasting Standards Authority. The Broadcasting Standards Authority is an independent Crown entity constituted under the Broadcasting Act 1989.[763] The Broadcasting Act provides that broadcasters are responsible for maintaining standards that are consistent with the privacy of the individual,[764] and the authority has formulated a number of privacy principles. If an individual complaint is upheld, the authority may impose sanctions, including damages of up to $5,000 for each privacy breach. There is a right of appeal to the HC., whose decision is final. There is extensive Authority case law on privacy issues.[765] In *TV3 Network Services Ltd v. Broadcasting Standards Authority*,[766] the HC remarked that the term 'privacy' in the Broadcasting Act was not an absolute concept, and that it 'should receive a fair, large, and liberal interpretation'.[767] In particular, the court held that the term 'privacy' should not be narrowly construed so as to refer to the principles of the New Zealand law of privacy, for, inter alia, the term did not have an established meaning at law when the Broadcasting Act was enacted in 1989 (or when the term was used in a similar context by the preceding legislation of 1976).[768]

723. Among the authority's functions is encouraging 'the development and observance by broadcasters of codes of broadcasting practice appropriate to the type of broadcasting undertaken by such broadcasters, in relation to … the privacy of

763. Section 20.
764. Broadcasting Act, s. 4(1)(c).
765. For older decisions, *see* Michael Stace, *Privacy: Interpreting the Broadcasting Authority's Decisions January 1990 to June 1998*, Palmerston North, Dunmore Press, 1998. More recent decisions are available online at https://www.bsa.govt.nz/decisions/all-decisions/.
766. [1995] 2 NZLR 720.
767. *Ibid.*, at 731.
768. *Ibid.*, at 727.

the individual'.[769] The codes that have been issued by the authority are the Radio Code, the Free-to-Air Television Code, and the Pay Television Code. Each contains the standards that relate to people or organisations taking part or referred to in broadcasts.[770]

III. New Zealand Media Council

724. The New Zealand Media Council is a self-regulatory industry body that deals with complaints against the print media, including complaints about breaches of privacy.[771] The Media Council is the successor of the New Zealand Press Council, which was established in 1972 by newspaper publishers and journalists. The Online Media Standards Authority, launched in July 2013, came under the jurisdiction of the Media Council in January 2017.

725. The aim of the Media Council is to uphold standards in the media industry and to promote press freedom. It has to power to hear complaints against media bodies. Its complaints procedure is not intended to supersede or supplement legal remedies, and its decisions on complaints are not legally binding on publications. The remedy is publication of the Media Council's rulings in the relevant publication. The Media Council is funded by the media industry. There is no charge for use of its complaints procedure. The Council comprises six public members (including the Chair), and five representatives from various sectors of the industry.

IV. 'News Activity'

726. A 'news activity' is defined as follows:[772]

(a) gathering, preparing, or compiling, for the purpose of publication, any:
   (i) news;
   (ii) observations on news;
   (iii) current affairs.
(b) publishing any:
   (i) news;
   (ii) observations on news;
   (iii) current affairs.

727. The concept of 'news activity' thus has two aspects: 'gathering, preparing, or compiling, for the purpose of publication', and 'publishing'. The word 'publish',

769. Broadcasting Act, s. 21(1)(e)(vii).
770. Standard 10 in each of these codes deals with standards consistent with the privacy of the individual.
771. *See* http://www.mediacouncil.org.nz/
772. Privacy Act, s. 7(1).

and the corresponding term 'publication', is defined in the Act as 'to make publicly available in any manner' and this includes by:

(a) displaying on any medium;
(b) printing in a newspaper or other periodical;
(c) broadcasting by any means;
(d) disseminating by means of the Internet or any electronic medium;
(e) storing electronically in a way that is accessible to the public.

728. The scope of what qualifies as a 'news activity' in New Zealand has been quite broad. For example, the concept of a 'news activity' has included publication of the 'rich list', a list of the wealthiest individuals and families in New Zealand;[773] a letter published in a letters-to-the-editor column in *The New Zealand Beekeeper*;[774] the conducting of personal credit checks as background to a story on ownership changes in a financial journal;[775] and the surreptitious filming and broadcasting of a television repairman's conduct in a private residence for a reality television consumer programme.[776] On this approach, the publication as a whole is the focus of the analysis, rather than the specific item containing personal information that is the subject of the complaint. In a more recent decision,[777] however, the Tribunal took a narrower, more granular, approach, holding that 'the personal information must itself qualify as news, observations on news or current affairs before the news medium exemption applies'.[778] In relation to blogs in particular, the Tribunal held:[779]

> Whether a blogger is exempt from application of the information privacy principles is a question to be determined blog by blog, item of personal information by item of personal information. Only if the particular item of personal information comes within the definition of news activity is exemption from the Privacy Act triggered in relation to that particular item.

729. As noted earlier, however, under the Privacy Act 2020, the entity concerned (which includes an individual), or the entity's employer must still be subject to the oversight of a regulatory authority.[780]

773. *Talley Family v. National Business Review* [1997] NZCRT 23 (29 Aug. 1997), (1997) 4 HRNZ 72.
774. *Wallingford v. National Beekeepers Association of NZ* [2001] NZCRT 4 (26 Mar. 2001), [2001] NZAR 251.
775. *Case Note 48423* [2002] NZPrivCmr 6 (1 May 2002).
776. *Case Note 38197* [2003] NZPrivCmr 24 (1 Sep. 2003). The Privacy Commissioner investigated the repairman's complaint and suggested the complainant was entitled to lodge a complaint for breach of broadcasting standards under the Broadcasting Act 1989.
777. *Director of Human Rights Proceedings v. Slater* [2019] NZHRRT 13 (12 Mar. 2019).
778. *Ibid.*, at para. 78.
779. *Ibid.*, at para. 174.
780. Privacy Act, s. 7(1)(b), definition of 'news entity'.

§2. Processing for Academic, Artistic, and Literary Expression

730. Freedom of expression is recognised as an important right in the New Zealand Bill of Rights Act 1990, which provides that 'Everyone has the right to freedom of expression, including the freedom to seek, receive, and impart information and opinions of any kind in any form.'[781] While this is a fundamental right in New Zealand law, it can be overridden by other legislation, such as the Privacy Act, where there is an inconsistency. Freedom of expression is also incorporated into the Privacy Commissioner's exercise of his statutory powers, for example, when investigating a complaint about breach of the IPPs, issuing public statements, or making submissions on proposed legislation. The Act requires that the Commissioner must 'have regard to the privacy interests of individuals alongside other human rights and interests, including ... the desirability of facilitating the free flow of information in society'.[782] This requirement, while not imposed on the Tribunal, permits the Commissioner some flexibility in the conciliation of complaints in a pragmatic way.

731. The Act does not present barriers to academic, artistic, or literary expression where the subject is deceased, as the IPPs do not generally apply to deceased persons.[783] Academic, artistic, and literary expression are otherwise subject to the IPPs in the Privacy Act. Use and disclosure of personal information in these contexts, however, would ultimately depend on the purpose for which the information was used or disclosed, and whether any exceptions provided for under the Act would apply in the circumstances. The principal control over the disclosure of personal information for academic, artistic, or literary expression is the common law tort of defamation, under which the disclosure must be both untrue and likely to lower the individual's reputation in the minds of right-thinking people.[784]

732. Particularly relevant to the academic context are the exceptions to IPP 10 on use, and IPP 11 on disclosure. These exceptions allow an agency to use or disclose personal information in a form in which the individual concerned is not identified, or the information is used or disclosed for statistical purposes and not published in a form that could reasonably be expected to identify the individual.[785] In relation specifically to health information, personal information may be collected from a source other than the individual concerned and used (if collected for another purpose) for research or statistics purposes so long as the health agency reasonably believes that the research has been approved by an ethics committee, if required, and that the research will not be published in a form that could reasonably be expected to identify the individual concerned.[786] There is also an exception relating to the assignment of unique identifiers in the health information area. A health

781. Section 14, which incorporates Art. 19 of the UN Covenant on Civil and Political Rights.
782. Privacy Act, s. 21(a)(i).
783. *See* Part II, Ch. 2, 2.2.1 and 2.2.2.
784. *See* Part I, Ch. 4.5.3.1.
785. Privacy Act, s. 22, IPP 10(1)(b)(i) and (ii), and IPP 11(1)(h)(i) and (ii).
786. Health Information Privacy Code 2020, r. 2(2)(g)(iii) and r. 10(1)(e)(iii).

agency is not allowed to assign to an individual a unique identifier that, to the agency's knowledge, is the same unique identifier as has been assigned to that individual by another agency unless 'it is to be used by the agency for statistical or research purposes and no other purpose'.[787]

733. In relation to artistic expression, photographs and illustrations published by a news entity in the course of carrying out its news activities would fall outside the application of the Act, but photographs and illustrations published for other purposes, such as advertising or purely artistic purposes,[788] would not, unless an exception to the IPP 11 exception on disclosure applies. Relevant exceptions might include the agency reasonably believing that disclosure was one of the purposes with which the information was obtained or is directly related to that purpose;[789] disclosure is authorised by the individual;[790] the source of the information is a publicly available publication and in the circumstances of the case, it would not be unfair or unreasonable to disclose the information;[791] or the information is to be used in a form in which the individual is not identified.[792]

787. Health Information Privacy Code 2020, r. 13(2)(b).
788. Privacy Commissioner, 'Photographer may change hats' (1998) *Private Word* No 21, (4 Jan. 1998).
789. Privacy Act, s. 22, IPP 11(1)(a).
790. Privacy Act, s. 22, IPP 11(1)(c).
791. Privacy Act, s. 22, IPP 11(1)(d).
792. Privacy Act, s. 22, IPP 11(1)(h)(i).

Chapter 2. Comparison with Public Access to Official Documents

§1. Introduction

734. There is close relationship between the Privacy Act and New Zealand's two freedom of information statutes, the Official Information Act 1982 and the LGOIM Act. 'Official information' is information held by a public sector agency. There are interconnections among the three enactments in subject matter, jurisprudence, background, and administration, so much so that they each may be viewed as complementary components of the same overall statutory scheme.

§2. Subject Matter and Jurisprudence

735. New Zealand's freedom of information legislation protects individuals' privacy in relation to the disclosure of public sector information to third parties. This is in accordance with one of the purposes of the Official Information Act, which is 'to protect official information to the extent consistent with the public interest and the preservation of personal privacy'.[793] In particular, one of the exceptions to the Act's presumption of availability of official information is that withholding the information is necessary to 'Protect the privacy of natural persons, including that of deceased natural persons',[794] where there is no countervailing public interest in disclosure.

736. In addition to protecting privacy, both the Privacy Act and the freedom of information regime deal generally with the same conceptual currency: 'information'. Moreover, many of the provisions in the Privacy Act that deal with access to and correction of personal information are based on analogous provisions in the freedom of information legislation. The jurisprudence of the Privacy Act therefore inevitably draws in large part upon the long-standing jurisprudence of the earlier freedom of information statutes in this connection.

§3. Historical Relationship and Development

737. The Privacy Act is in a sense an 'offspring' of freedom of information legislation, as both deal, or have dealt, with access to and correction of personal information. The Privacy Act 1993 took over an important aspect of the official information regime through its coverage of all official information relating to natural, as opposed to legal, persons, along with the new addition of private sector personal information. Information held by public sector agencies about legal persons

793. Long title to the Official Information Act 1982; *see also* s. 4(c) ("Purposes"). The Local Government Official Information and Meetings Act 1987 contains similar provisions.
794. Official Information Act 1982, s. 9(2)(a); Local Government Official Information and Meetings Act 1987, s. 7(2)(a).

remain covered by the official information regime.[795] The entitlements contained in IPPs 6 and 7 thus have their origins in the official information legislation. The transfer of jurisdiction over official information concerning natural persons to the Privacy Act was relatively seamless, as the procedural provisions and reasons for refusal in the Privacy Act 1993 were nearly identical to the older statutes.

738. Although personal rights of access in the public sector did not substantively change in the transfer from the official information statutes to the Privacy Act regime, the number of access complaints rose substantially, presumably due to the higher profile of rights granted under the Privacy Act. Another change was the involvement of the HRRT in granting compensation, something that was not provided for in complaints handled by the Ombudsmen under the official information statutes. Interestingly, the first Privacy Act case to reach the Tribunal was an access case involving a public sector respondent.[796] Compensation of $500 was awarded, marking the change from an 'ombudsmen complaint' model of redress to a 'hybrid ombudsman-litigation' model. A fuller break from the Ombudsmen roots of access law would wait a further quarter-century when the Privacy Commissioner would be vested with determination powers under the Privacy Act 2020.

§4. Overlaps in Jurisdiction and Roles

739. The Ombudsmen, appointed under the Ombudsmen Act 1975, oversee the freedom of information regime. There are a number of areas where the Ombudsmen and the Privacy Commissioner have overlapping roles and duties of mutual consultation. For example, a common issue is dealing with access to 'mixed' information, that is, official information that is about both the requestor and a third party, whether living or dead. The matter would fall primarily in the Privacy Commissioner's jurisdiction, but because it also involves access to information about a third party, the Ombudsman would need to be consulted with a view as to whether granting access to the requestor would be 'unwarranted' in terms of section 53(b) of the Privacy Act. Such issues naturally arise where there is a relationship or interaction between two or more people, one of whom is the individual making the access request. Where the 'evaluative material' exception for refusing access is dealt with under the Privacy Act,[797] it falls under the Privacy Commissioner's jurisdiction; but where such evaluative material is relied upon for a decision affecting a person and it is comprised in information held by a public sector agency, it may alternatively be dealt with under the Ombudsmen's investigative jurisdiction in respect of people's entitlement to reasons for decisions affecting them.[798]

795. Parts 4 of the Official Information Act and the Local Government Official Information and Meetings Act.
796. *Mitchell v. Police Commissioner* [1994] NZCRT 13 (4 Nov. 1994); [1995] NZAR 74; (1994) 1 HRNZ 403 (4 Nov. 1994).
797. Section 50.
798. Official Information Act, s. 23, and Local Government Official Information and Meetings Act, s. 22 ('Right of access by person to reasons for decisions affecting that person').

740. The Privacy Commissioner and the Ombudsmen are also required to consult with one another where either receives a complaint that relates to an area under the other's jurisdiction.[799] Each is also empowered to consult the other about any function relating, in the case of the Privacy Commissioner, to the Commissioner's function under the Privacy Act, or, in the case of the Ombudsmen, to the functions of the Ombudsmen, and may do so without breaching their respective requirements of confidentiality.[800] Moreover, both of the freedom of information acts require the Ombudsmen to consult with the Privacy Commissioner before forming an opinion concerning a complaint arising from a public sector agency's refusal to disclose information on the grounds of protecting personal privacy.[801]

799. Privacy Act, s. 75(1)(a) and Ombudsmen Act 1975, s. 17A.
800. Privacy Act, s. 208(1)(a), and s. 21 of the Ombudsmen Act, s. 21A.
801. Official Information Act, s. 29A, and Local Government Official Information and Meetings Act, s. 29A.

Chapter 3. Processing of the National Identification Number

§1. General

741. New Zealand does not have a national identification number in the sense of a single official identifier that a citizen will carry throughout their life for transacting with the government.

742. However, New Zealand does have a variety of government systems which assign unique identifiers to individuals for use for various roles, including in some cases identifiers of general application possessed by most adults in the country. Those systems are sometimes subject to specific laws that govern their operation and may provide safeguards for individuals against misuse. Other systems are established administratively and have no specific statutory basis.

743. The Privacy Act 2020 includes a specific IPP, IPP 13, devoted to unique identifiers. This principle in part seeks to address the risk that a system of unique identifiers might become a de facto national identifier through diffusion beyond its original remit across multiple settings in the public and private sectors. IPP 13 also addresses other data protection risks relating to unique identifiers such as misidentification and identity fraud.

§2. Rationale for Unique Identifiers Principle

744. The forerunner of IPP 13 in the Privacy Act 1993 (Principle 12 of the 1993 Act) was a response to concerns about the accuracy and use of personal information where a unique identifier is assigned. In particular, there is a danger that if one unique identifier, such as an Inland Revenue Department (IRD) number (also referred to as the Tax File Number (TFN)), is used for a wide variety of authentication and identification purposes in both the public and private sectors, this would amount to a de facto universal identifier. De facto universal identifiers have been viewed as undesirable because they are both potentially unreliable and a threat to individuals' privacy.

745. Since a de facto universal identifier is not designed to be a true universal identifier, such an identifier can be technically unreliable and vulnerable to falsification or error. True universal identifiers are unique to each individual and individuals will each have only one identifier that they will carry throughout their lives and that will not be reused after their deaths. Moreover, such identifiers should contain internal features that allow incidental bureaucratic errors in their communication or transcription to be readily detected.

746. Moreover, from a rights perspective, any unique identifier that facilitates the exchange and matching of personal information held by different agencies and within different record systems might be perceived to be a threat to privacy. It is thought to be socially undesirable to enable public and private agencies to compile composite profiles of individuals, where any and every aspect of their lives is open to potential scrutiny by the government or private enterprise.

747. In addition, it was feared that if a de facto universal identifier were to emerge, this could ease the way towards the requirement of a national identity card or document. Among the concerns raised about such proposals are that the data collected within such a system may be inaccurate, incomplete, misleading or irrelevant, and that personal data may be misused, whether by authorised or unauthorised users. Furthermore, for some, the idea of a national identity card or document conjures up the spectre of a police state, where identification can only be authenticated and entitlements only made available upon presentation of the card, and where the loss, lack or confiscation of such a card renders the individual a 'non-person'.

748. Refinements to the unique identifier principle made by the 2020 Act were addressed to risks of identity fraud as well as seeking to ease compliance.

§3. IPP 13: Unique Identifiers

749. The Privacy Act 2020 regulates 'unique identifiers' through IPP 13. It defines 'unique identifier as:

> *unique identifier*, in relation to an individual, means an identifier other than the individual's name that uniquely identifies the individual.

750. IPP 13 provides:

> *Unique identifiers*
>
> (1) An agency (A) may assign a unique identifier to an individual for use in its operations only if that identifier is necessary to enable A to carry out 1 or more of its functions efficiently.
> (2) A may not assign to an individual a unique identifier that, to A's knowledge, is the same unique identifier as has been assigned to that individual by another agency (B), unless –
>   (a) A and B are associated persons within the meaning of subpart YB of the Income Tax Act 2007; or
>   (b) the unique identifier is to be used by A for statistical or research purposes and no other purpose.
> (3) To avoid doubt, A does not assign a unique identifier to an individual under subclause (1) by simply recording a unique identifier assigned to the individual by B for the sole purpose of communicating with B about the individual.
> (4) A must take any steps that are, in the circumstances, reasonable to ensure that –
>   (a) a unique identifier is assigned only to an individual whose identity is clearly established; and

(b) the risk of misuse of a unique identifier by any person is minimised (for example, by showing truncated account numbers on receipts or in correspondence).

(5) An agency may not require an individual to disclose any unique identifier assigned to that individual unless the disclosure is for one of the purposes in connection with which that unique identifier was assigned or is for a purpose that is directly related to one of those purposes.

751. Accordingly, IPP 13 is intended to promote data quality and impose an important form of control on the transfer and linking of individuals' personal information. IPP 13(1) is intended to control the use of unique identifiers and define when it will be legitimate for an agency to assign them.

752. IPP 13(2) and (3) control the reassignment of unique identifiers, and thereby aid in promoting data quality and discourages illegitimate profiling and data matching of individuals.

753. IPP 13(4) is directly concerned with data quality in that agencies must take all reasonable steps to verify the identity of individuals who are assigned unique identifiers and minimise the risk of their misuse. IPP 13(4)(a) requires agencies to take reasonable steps in the circumstances to ensure that unique identifiers are only assigned to individuals whose identity is clearly established.

754. IPP 13(4)(b) requires agencies to take reasonable steps in the circumstances to ensure that the risk of misuse by any person of a unique identifier is reduced or minimised. This requirement was a new feature in the 2020 Act that responded to heightened concerns at identity crime. The policy behind the change was to reduce identity theft by requiring measures that control the publication of unique identifiers and more clearly apply to the display of unique identifiers (for example, where they are printed on receipts). Examples of such measures include truncation (e.g., of credit card numbers on receipts) and encryption.

755. Finally, IPP 13(5) controls the use of unique identifiers by restricting their use to the purposes in connection with which they were assigned, or a directly related purpose, and by requiring agencies not to require disclosure otherwise of unique identifiers. This is intended to discourage the illegitimate use of unique identifiers and their collection for linking or profiling purposes. It also indirectly promotes data quality, since restricting the spread of individuals' unique identifiers makes it less likely that incorrect, inaccurate or outdated personal information will later be used.

§4. Other Privacy Act Provisions Related to Unique Identifiers

756. In addition to IPP 13, the Privacy Act regulates unique identifiers in two further ways through:

(1) codes of practice; and
(2) information matching rules.

757. Codes of practice issued under Part 3 Subpart 2 of the Privacy Act can do various things including prescribing more stringent standards in relation to IPP 13 or exempting an action or agency from the IPP.

758. Several codes exempt a class of agencies from the prohibition on reassigning a specified unique identifier or type of unique identifier already assigned by another agency. The exemptions that have been issued have been given for public interest reasons such as to legitimise a practice that predated the Privacy Act and where the reassignment brings public benefits or supports the interests of the individuals concerned. Examples of exemptions by code from the prohibition on reassignment of unique identifiers have included are set out in the following paragraphs.

759. The Health Information Privacy Code 2020 exempts a wide number of health service providers from the prohibition on reassignment of the NHI Number (*see* Health Information Privacy Code 2020, rule 13(3) and Schedule 2). The NHI number is a universally issued unique identifier that is assigned to everyone in the country who access health services. (The code also exempts registration bodies from the prohibition on reassigning practitioner numbers and common provider numbers issued by the Ministry of Health. However, these are not numbers of general application and so do not raise issues akin to a national identification number.)

760. The Justice Sector Unique Identifier Code 2020 exempts certain agencies in the justice sector from the prohibition on reassigning the identifiers used by other justice sector agencies (*see* Justice Sector Unique Identifier Code 2020, rule 13(3) and Schedule 1). The code regularises long-standing practices that existed before the Privacy Act was enacted and that help ensure that individuals are correctly identified as they pass through different organisations in the justice system from investigation through prosecution and punishment. As well of a variety of departmental numbers of significance to the agencies concerned, the code applies to the driver licence number, which is an identifier assigned to most adults in the country.

761. The Credit Reporting Privacy Code 2020 permits certain use of the driver licence number in the credit reporting system. The permitted use is limited and subject to stringent conditions (refer Credit Reporting Privacy Code 2020, rules 8, 11, 12 and 13 and Schedules 3 and 6). The driver licence number is not strictly a unique identifier as it identifies a document rather than an individual. However, given the fact that each licence relates to a specific individual and is a class of document held by most adults that is required to be carried and produced on occasion, the identifier carries many of the same privacy risks as a true unique identifier.

762. A number of government data matching programmes are regulated as 'authorised information matching programmes' under Part 7 Subpart 4 of the Privacy Act 2020. These programmes are required to be operated in accordance with information matching agreements that give effect to the statutory 'information matching rules' set out in Schedule 6 of the Privacy Act.

763. Information matching rule 2 provides:

> **Use of unique identifiers**
>
> Except as provided in any other enactment, unique identifiers may not be used as part of any authorised information matching programme unless their use is essential to the success of the programme.

764. A number of programmes are authorised to use identifiers of general application such as the TFN.

§5. ENACTMENTS RELATING TO SELECTED IDENTIFIERS OF GENERAL APPLICATION

765. Most systems for assigning unique identifiers are established administratively and do not have special legislative authorisation. Such administrative systems must be operated in accordance with IPP 13 and other IPPs. However, some systems of identifiers are underpinned by legislation. This is especially the case with systems involving government identifiers of general application where it may be mandatory for agencies or individuals to use the identifier. Where such legislation exists some departure for the requirements of the IPPs is allowed (*see* Privacy Act, section 24). Some such legislation is brief and simply provides for mandatory use of an identifier. In other cases, the legislation provides substantial detail about establishment and limits on use and disclosure and may add additional safeguards. A selection of core legislative provisions applying to various identifiers of general application follows.

766. Section 3(1) of the Tax Administration Act 1994 includes the definition:

> *tax file number* means an identification number that the Commissioner allocates to a person

767. All taxpayers have a tax file number and tax legislation makes use of the identifier mandatory in various circumstances.

768. An NHI number is assigned to each patient at their first use of New Zealand's health and disability services. The NHI computer system has been in place since the 1990s as the system used to issue NHI numbers and record patient identity and demographic information. The NHI number is the primary key used to associate patients with their health information. A person's NHI number is stored on the NHI along with that person's demographic details. The NHI and associated NHI numbers are used to help with the planning, coordination, and provision of health and disability support services across New Zealand. The NHI number is not underpinned by special legislation.

769. A system of National Student Numbers (NSN) is authorised under Schedule 24 of the Education and Training Act 2020, which continues provisions enacted in 2006 in the former Education Act 1989. An NSN is assigned to a child when first enrolled with an education provider (including an early childhood service, school or tertiary education organisation. The purpose of Schedule 24 is to authorise the use by specified users of NSNs for specific purposes, in order to facilitate the accurate use and transfer, by specified users, of information relating to individual students. The schedule includes provisions relating to both the assignment of NSNs and the use of NSNs.

770. The New Zealand Business Number (NZBN) is unusual in having an entire statute devoted to it. The NZBN Act 2016 Act 2016 establishes the NZBN, with its supporting register, as a means for eligible entities in New Zealand to interact more easily with government. While most businesses are corporate bodies outside the scope of privacy law, sole traders can also obtain an NZBN. While the identifier system has been established on the basis that obtaining an NZBN is voluntary, provision has been made for regulations to be made authorising a government agency to require an eligible entity, or a class of eligible entity, to which the agency provides services to register for an NZBN and provide that NZBN to the agency (*see* NZBN Act 2016, section 29). Before recommending such regulations, the minister must consult with the Privacy Commissioner (NZBN Act 2016, section 29(2)).

§6. Comparison to EU GDPR

771. Article 87 of the EU GDPR states:

> **Processing of the national identification number**
>
> Member States may further determine the specific conditions for the processing of a national identification number or any other identifier of general application. In that case the national identification number or any other identifier of general application shall be used only under appropriate safeguards for the rights and freedoms of the data subject pursuant to this Regulation.

772. New Zealand does not have a 'national identification number' but it may be said to have several 'identifiers of general application'. Principal among those identifiers of general application would be:

- the TFN assigned by the IRD to all taxpayers;
- the NHI number assigned by the Ministry of Health to everyone accessing health services.

773. Most New Zealanders will be in both those systems and the identifiers will be in use multiple times every year throughout their lives.

774. By contrast some of the other national systems have less general application. For instance, the NSN system will capture all New Zealanders as they enter the education system and will continue to be relevant throughout their years of education. However, the system is comparatively new and will neither have captured older New Zealanders nor will it have any relevance to most individuals past their years of formal education. Similarly, the NZBN will, as the name implies, only cover those in business.

775. The standards set by the GDPR anticipate two matters. First that the state determines 'the specific conditions for the processing of any identifier of general application' and, second, that an identifier of general application must be used 'only under appropriate safeguards for the rights and freedoms of the data subject'.

776. It is perhaps surprising that there are not more explicit statutory safeguards surrounding both the TFN and NHI number as there is, for example, with the NSN. However, in common with all unique identifiers, there are safeguards contained in IPP 13 of the Privacy Act which seek to provide safeguards for the rights and freedoms of the data subject.

Chapter 4. Processing in the Context of Employment

§1. Introduction

777. Privacy interests often raise difficult issues in the workplace. The collection of information about workers in relation to both their private lives and their on-the-job conduct constitutes a common flashpoint at the employment law/privacy law interface, and this has increased as technology has developed new ways of collecting and analysing such information. The importance of regulating employer control over the private lives and conduct of workers has never been greater, when the growth of the service industry sector and the spread of professionalism rests on a foundation of public image,[802] and when technological developments have opened up new possibilities for the way we work and the ways in which workers can be monitored both on and off the job. The Privacy Act, however, neither contains any provisions that specifically deal with processing in the context of employment, nor is there is a relevant code of practice in the area. The Act's IPPs must apply to the workplace sector as they stand.

778. For its part, employment law in New Zealand has sometimes used the Privacy Act's IPPs to inform decisions on whether an employer's actions have been fair and reasonable, even though the specialist employment institutions do not have the jurisdiction to interpret the IPPs or apply them directly.[803] The Employment Court, however, has recognised that 'The Privacy Act's provisions may be said to represent current community standards and expectations',[804] which are considerations that are relevant in deciding whether or not an employer's actions are justifiable. For example, an employment law case drew upon the Privacy Act's collection principles to assist in determining that an employer unjustifiably dismissed an employee for misrepresentation by not volunteering health information in an overly wide pre-employment application form for a sales position that it was not entitled to collect in the first place.[805] The Employment Relations Authority's determination was upheld on appeal in the Employment Court, which remarked that the company's question was 'inappropriate' and imposed no obligation on the job

802. *See*, for example, Ronald McCallum, *Employer Controls over Private Life*, Sydney, 2002.
803. The earliest employment law case drawing on the principles of the Privacy Act was *Graham v. Christchurch Polytechnic* [1993] NZEmpC 129 (14 Sep. 1993), which was decided just a few months after the Act came into force. In *NZ Amalgamated Engineering Printing and Manufacturing Union Inc v. Air New Zealand Ltd* [2004] NZEmpC 32 (13 Apr. 2004), [2004] ERNZ 614, (2004) 7 HRNZ 539, at para. 218, the Court observed that 'the Privacy Act 1993 does not give rights or impose obligations that are enforceable in this or any other Court of law. Questions of statutory privacy are to be dealt with by a discrete and exclusive procedure involving, among others, the Privacy Commissioner and the Human Rights Review Tribunal'.
804. *NZ Amalgamated Engineering Printing and Manufacturing Union Inc v. Air New Zealand Ltd* [2004] NZEmpC 32 (13 Apr. 2004), [2004] ERNZ 614, (2004) 7 HRNZ 539, at para. 221.
805. *Attwood v. Imperial Industries* [2001] NZERA 183 (25 Oct. 2001).

applicant to disclose all of her medical problems. Therefore, the employee could not be justifiably dismissed because of this failure to disclose the information concerned.[806]

§2. The Employment Law/Privacy Act Interface

779. As might be expected in an institutional setting such as the workplace, the individual as job applicant or employee tends to be in a position of relative weakness in relation to an employer who wants to acquire or use personal information. While individuals may in law consent to, or acquiesce in, intrusions into their personal sphere, refusal is not usually an option because of the power dynamics between the parties. The nature of the employment relationship, even within the current legal framework for enforcing privacy rights, means that employees often have few realistic options other than to comply with the employer's requirements. Some of the IPPs that might be expected to confer some privacy protection in the workplace allow for derogations, so that, for example, individuals can waive their application where personal information is collected from a third party (IPP 2); used (IPP 10) or disclosed (IPP 11). The benefit of protection by the other IPPs cannot by waived or contracted out of by individuals, so these non-derogable principles ought to have the strongest force in the workplace. In practice, however, some of these non-derogable principles, such as IPP 1 on purpose limitation in relation to the collection of personal information, offer imperfect protection in the workplace context because the employer is usually considered to be the best judge as to its own informational needs. The most important of the non-derogable principles is the IPP 6 right to access one's personal information. This right is often invoked when an employee is being disciplined or has been dismissed, so its utility is largely realised when the employment relationship has broken down or coming to an end. But it may also be invoked by a job applicant as proxy for an employer via what is known as 'procured access', where personal information is requested by the individual at the direction of a prospective employer so that it may be vetted by a third party, such as the police or a professional body.

780. Balanced against any workplace privacy rights, and largely weighted against them, is the employer's contractual right to manage. Managerial prerogative allows the employer to collect and use worker's personal information, but always within the limits of what is fair and reasonable at employment law. The latter limitations stem from three sources: the implicit statutory prohibition against unjustifiable conduct, which can be sanctioned pursuant to the statutory personal grievance

806. *Imperial Enterprises Limited v. Attwood* [2002] NZEmpC 206 (18 Dec. 2002), [2002] 2 ERNZ 740, at para. 59.

jurisdiction;[807] the statutory duty of good faith;[808] and the implied common law contractual term importing mutual trust, cooperation, and fair dealing into the employment relationship.

781. Managerial prerogative is recognised in the Privacy Act, whereby the Privacy Commissioner is required to have 'regard to the privacy interests of individuals alongside other human rights and interests, including ... government and business being able to achieve their objectives efficiently'.[809] This consideration is evident in the Commissioner's generous approach to information that an agency regards as 'necessary' to collect for its purposes under IPP 1,[810] supported in turn by the HRRT's interpretation of the term 'necessary' as meaning 'reasonably necessary'.[811] The Commissioner also tends to avoid forming views on the application of employment law, even though IPP 4(a) of the collection limitation principle requires that personal information be collected by 'lawful' means.[812]

782. Employment legislation contains several provisions that relate to access to information. Unions and employers have rights to be provided with 'information that is reasonably necessary to support or substantiate claims or responses to claims made for the purposes of the bargaining',[813] but this does not override individuals' rights in respect of their personal information under the Privacy Act, which can relate an individual's terms and conditions.[814] Another key provision relating to access to information concerns an employer's decision that will, or is likely to have, an adverse effect on the continuation of an employee's employment. In such circumstances, the employees affected must be provided with 'access to information, relevant to the continuation of the employees' employment, about the decision',[815] as well as an opportunity to comment on the information to their employer before the decision is made.[816]

§3. Job Applicants

783. Without legal protection, job applicants are ordinarily not in a position to refuse to disclose information requested by a prospective employer or employment agency. New Zealand, like many other jurisdictions, has remedies for discriminatory hiring practices.[817] Whether or not the collection of particular information is

807. Employment Relations Act, s. 103(1)(a) (the 'unjustifiable dismissal' grievance) and (b) (the 'unjustifiable disadvantage' grievance).
808. Employment Relations Act, s. 4.
809. Privacy Act, s. 21(a)(ii).
810. Privacy Act, s. 22, IPP 1. *See* discussion at Part III, Ch. 1.3.2.
811. *Lehmann v. Canwest Radioworks Limited* [2006] NZHRRT 35 (21 Sep. 2006).
812. *See* for example, *Case Note 33623* [2003] NZPrivCmr 5 (February 2003), discussed below at 4.6.
813. Employment Relations Act, s. 32(1)(e).
814. Employment Relations Act, s. 34(8).
815. Employment Relations Act, s. 4(1A)(c)(i).
816. Employment Relations Act, s. 4(1A)(c)(ii).
817. Human Rights Act 1993, Part 2, which deals with acting on the basis of particular prohibited grounds of discrimination. In particular, s. 23 of the Act makes it unlawful 'to use or circulate any

'necessary' in terms of IPP 1 when considering job applicants is largely left to the employer's judgment of what is required in the circumstances. The views of the Privacy Commissioner on a number of complaints indicate that the test in IPP 1 involves a low threshold that is not usually difficult for an employer to satisfy. For example, the Privacy Commissioner has found that personality testing of job applicants is permissible under the Act, even for a sales position.[818] The Commissioner did not address the intrusiveness of the test's numerous questions or its relevance to the particular position applied for by the complainant. The employer, however, ought to have borne the burden of proving that the test was indeed 'necessary'.

784. In relation to job interviews, a pre-Privacy Act case that fell under the Ombudsman's jurisdiction illustrates the utility of the extended concept of 'information' to cover mentally processed information in the employment context.[819] The complainant, an unsuccessful job applicant, requested the interview notes of an appointment panel. The panel had destroyed the notes after the employment decision was made, but the Ombudsman asked the individual panel members 'each to supply a written statement of reasons why the other candidates had been considered better suited, or the requester considered less suited, for the position'.[820]

§4. Covert Recording

785. In New Zealand, there are few legal controls on surreptitious video or audio recording in the workplace. In the early years of privacy legislation, there were a few cases brought by complainants but none of them were successful, the Privacy Commissioner having found workplace surveillance to be a permissible practice on the facts.

786. In the earliest case,[821] the Commissioner dealt with a complaint about the surveillance of a work changing room. The purpose of the surveillance was to detect theft. The Commissioner found that the employer was not obliged to take reasonable steps to ensure, in accordance with IPP 3, that the employee was aware that the surveillance was being undertaken. This was on the basis of a number of exceptions to that principle that illustrate the difficulty in imposing control over workplace surveillance activities. The Commissioner found that it was not reasonably practicable to disclose the surveillance to the complainant, as its purpose was to film covert and unlawful conduct;[822] and disclosure prior to the surveillance would have prejudiced

form of application for employment or to make any inquiry of or about any applicant for employment' that suggests that a decision will be made on the basis of a prohibited ground of discrimination.

818. *Case Note 2418* [1999] NZPrivCmr 6 (Aug. 1999).

819. *See* above, Part II, Ch. 3.1.3.

820. Ombudsman's *Case No 794* (1987) 8 CCNO 66, a public sector case dealt with under the Official Information Act 1982; after 1993, it would have been dealt with in a similar manner by the Privacy Commissioner under the Privacy Act.

821. *Case Note 0632* [1994] NZPrivCmr 27 (Aug. 1994).

822. *See* now IPP 3(4)(d).

the purpose of the collection of personal information.[823] Moreover, the Commissioner found that the manner of collecting personal information through surveillance was both lawful, fair, and did not intrude to an unreasonable extent into the individual's personal affairs in terms of IPP 4. This was on the basis that the use of the video camera was lawful; steps had been taken to minimise the extent of the surveillance; the locker room was not a private space intended for the removal of clothing; the complainant was only filmed removing his outer clothing; and the surveillance was not unfair because it was necessary to identify the source of the stolen property and the filming was used solely for this purpose. In a similar subsequent case,[824] a union unsuccessfully complained on an employee's behalf that a video camera had been installed in a locker room. The Commissioner considered that none of the IPPs had been breached. The purpose of the surveillance was to identify the persons responsible for thefts from the lockers. A notice was displayed at the entrance to the worksite, advising that hidden cameras might operate there. The Commissioner, however, was of the view that the sign at the worksite warning employees generally of hidden filming was insufficient to alert employees that there was a hidden camera in the locker room, as employees would not expect that. However, an exception to the requirement of notification applied in the circumstances, in that the employer reasonably believed that compliance would prejudice the purposes of the collection. The Commissioner also did not find that the filming was unreasonably intrusive into workers' privacy, despite it taking place in a locker room. This was because the camera was activated only by movement near the target locker; it was necessary that the camera be able to record faces so as to identify the thief; and the camera was to be in operation only until the culprit was identified.

787. In another workplace case,[825] the Commissioner found it acceptable for an employee to surreptitiously film a colleague with a cell phone. Both worked as caregivers for young people with disabilities, and the worker was concerned about the complainant's conduct towards clients, which could be abusive and inappropriate. Believing it posed a safety risk, he gave the recordings to their employer, who used them in disciplinary proceedings against the worker that resulted in a warning. The Commissioner considered that the recordings provided the employer with the best evidence against the employee. At the same time, the Commissioner acknowledged that 'covert recording is intrinsically intrusive, and needs strong justification for its use'. In this case, the Commissioner observed that the intrusion was justified in light of the safety reasons for collecting clear evidence of wrongdoing, particularly as the victims were not in a position to complain of mistreatment on their own account. Accordingly, the Commissioner observed that 'On balance, this was one of the rare occasions where it will be acceptable for an onlooker to make a covert recording to ensure that evidence of what was said is accurately captured.' As IPP 4 does not provide for any exceptions, the reasoning in this case must depend on the Commissioner's duty under the Act to balance privacy against other important social

823. *See* now IPP 3(4)(c).

824. *Case Note 32277* [2003] NZPrivCmr 25 (Sept. 2003).

825. *Case Note 101213* [2008] NZPrivCmr 4 (Mar. 2008).

interests.[826] The Tribunal, however, is not bound by the same requirement. If the complaint had been taken further, the result may not have been the same.

788. The Privacy Commissioner, however, did not find it acceptable to surreptitiously tape-record an interview with an employee suspected of stealing stock without later informing him of the recording.[827] The employee was dismissed, but only found out about the recording in the course of proceedings contesting his dismissal. The Commissioner found that the employer had not breached the collection principle that covered the lawfulness and necessity for collecting the information, as collecting information and evidence relevant to a possible termination of employment was lawful and reasonably necessary for a business. However, the employer breached the requirement that the individual be informed under IPP 3 concerning the collection of personal information. The Commissioner commented that 'The fact of recording an interview on tape, rather than merely relying upon written notes and memory, is a matter that the individual should be made aware of.' The Commissioner also found that the collection of the information was unfair in terms of IPP 4, since the individual would not be aware of all 'the minute details of what was said and how it was said' that could be recorded by taping, as opposed to recording by hand or through one's memory. The individual might also have responded to questions differently if he was aware of the recording. The Commissioner added that the nature of the relationship between the parties, being an employment relationship, and the circumstances in which the recording took place, also contributed to the unfairness.

§5. Collection of Personal Information from Workplace Computers

789. There are a few cases involving the collection by employers of information from workplace computers, but with one exception, the Privacy Act plays no significant role in these. Underlying such cases is the technical issue whether an employer who gathers information about an employee's Internet use is actually 'collecting' personal information in strict terms of the Privacy Act. This is because the employer already 'holds' this information in its computer system, which is a prerequisite for its use. Therefore, the rules relating to individual notification in IPP 3, and the requirement that the retention, use, and disclosure of such information must relate to the original purpose for collecting it, are not straightforward in their application. Any rights that an employee has in this area in respect to the collection of personal information therefore arguably stem from employment law, not from the Privacy Act. There is only one reported Privacy Commissioner's case on the collection of personal information from a worker's computer by means of monitoring software,[828] and it proceeded on the basis that the employer was indeed 'collecting'

826. The case was considered when s. 14(a) of the Privacy Act 1994 was in force. That provision has now been re-enacted as s. 21(a).
827. *Case Note 16479* [2001] NZPrivCmr 6 (June 2001).
828. *Case Note 229558* [2012] NZPrivCmr 1 (31 May 2012).

the information in terms of the Privacy Act. The monitoring took place in the context of an employment investigation, and the information collected included emails and key stroke logs for the computer. The key stroke logs were used to access the worker's personal web-based email account. The Commissioner considered that the collection of information directly from the work computer did not breach the Privacy Act since computer monitoring was provided for in both the employment agreement and work rules. The key stroke logging, however, was not covered, and this was a breach of IPP 3, which requires making an individual aware of the fact that information is being collected. The Commissioner found that access to a significant number of emails sent over a number of years 'was unnecessary and disproportionate to the employer's needs';[829] and workers were not notified that the employer could use keystroke logging to obtain their passwords to collect further personal information about them that was not held on the work computer.[830] Moreover, given that there was a high expectation of privacy in a password-protected account, 'it would require exceptional circumstances to justify an employer directly accessing it'. As there were no such circumstances here, 'this method of collection was unreasonably intrusive'.[831] This complaint was subsequently settled through mediation.

790. The workplace cases tend to turn on the justifiability of subsequent disciplinary action. There are no privacy rights *per se* in respect of employees' workplace email or other Internet use, but the justifiability in terms of employment law of any disciplinary action for misuse may turn on whether the employee had a reasonable expectation of privacy in the circumstances, and other factors. For example, there have been cases that involved the issue whether there have been employer training and policies regarding Internet use,[832] the nature of the use (messages containing sexual innuendoes and surfing the net for pornography being particularly frowned upon),[833] length of service,[834] and rights of free expression during industrial negotiations.[835] The emphasis has been on fairness and due process, rather than reliance on the Privacy Act.

§6. Workplace Drug and Alcohol Testing

791. With the testing of bodily substances, one encounters a conceptual difficulty: are bodily fluids and cells 'personal information', or are they merely, and literally, disembodied data that, when analysed scientifically, yield information, but

829. There was therefore a breach of IPP 1.
830. There was therefore a breach of IPP 3.
831. There was therefore a breach of IPP 4.
832. *Clarke v. Attorney-General* [1997] NZEmpC 119 (4 Jun. 1997), [1997] ERNZ 600.
833. *Ibid.*, and *Allerton and Offord v. Methanex (NZ) Ltd* [2000] NZEmpC 59 (28 Mar. 2000), [2000] 1 ERNZ 242.
834. *Ibid.*
835. *Howe v. The Internet Group Ltd (IHUG)* [1999] NZEmpC 147 (27 Jun. 1999), [1999] 1 ERNZ 879.

are not themselves information? Unless legislation specifically includes bodily substances in a definition of 'personal information', then the notion can become contestable.[836] New Zealand privacy law is silent on the issue, except in relation to health information as covered in the Health Information Privacy Code. This code applies to information provided by a person in the health system in connection with the donation of body parts or substances, or derived from the testing or examination of these.[837]

792. The Privacy Commissioner has opposed random drug testing in the workplace,[838] but there have been no published Privacy Act complaints on the issue.[839] Assuming that collecting a bodily sample such as urine would amount to the collection of 'personal information', then the testing would have to be for a lawful purpose connected with a function or activity of the employer and be necessary for that purpose (IPP 1), and carried out fairly and not intrude unreasonably into the individual's personal affairs (IPP 4). Workplace testing could generally be viewed as reasonably necessary by employers in so far as it ostensibly addresses productivity and health and safety issues. Moreover, in principle at least, testing is a consensual activity, despite the likelihood that an unreasonable refusal to undergo testing will mean losing one's employment.

793. The legitimacy of drug and alcohol testing, therefore, has turned on employment law rather than on privacy law. Unless specifically provided for in an employment agreement,[840] however, an employer would be faced with real difficulties if an employee refused to submit to a test, particularly random testing when

---

836. *See* Lee Bygrave, 'The body as data? Reflections on the relationship of data privacy law with the human body', conference paper, Office of the Victorian Privacy Commissioner, Melbourne, 8 Sep. 2003; B Alston, *Blood rights: the body and information privacy*, 426 J. Law Med. 12 no. 4 (2005); Rohan J. Hardcastle, *Law and the Human Body: Property Rights, Ownership and Control* (Hart Publishing, Oxford, 2007, 98).

837. Health Information Privacy Code 2020, cl. 4(1)(d).

838. Bruce Slane, *The Privacy Implications*, in *Drug Testing. The Sporting Experience: the Employment Possibility* 89–92 (Legal Research Foundation, Auckland April 1995), and 'Critical Privacy Issues for Employers and Employees,' Address to IIR's 10th Annual Industrial Relations Conference, 19 Mar. 1996.

839. For discussion of how the Privacy Act might apply, *see* John Edwards, 'Workplace drug testing' (1995) 1(1) HRLP 43; Michael Webb, 'Workplace drug testing: Another perspective' (1995) 1(3) HRLP 131; John Edwards, 'Privacy Updates - Notes on Recent Developments', (1996) 1(4) HRLP 187, at pp. 187–188; Cordelia Thomas, 'Drug Testing in the Workplace' (1997) 22(2) NZJIR 159; and Paul Roth, 'The Privacy Act 1993: Workplace testing, monitoring, and surveillance' (1997) 3(2) HRLP 113.

840. In an early case concerning the legality of testing, a collective agreement providing for unrestricted random testing was found by the Employment Court to be 'harsh and oppressive' under now-repealed industrial legislation: *Harrison v. Tuckers Wool Processors Ltd* [1998] NZEmpC 207 (30 Sep. 1998), [1998] 3 ERNZ 418. On appeal, the Court of Appeal remitted the matter to the Employment Court to reconsider in light of 'statistical, research or other empirical material in support of the proposition that particular terms of the contract are or are not "harsh and oppressive:"' *Tucker Wool Processors Limited v. Harrison* [1999] 1 ERNZ 894; [1999] 3 NZLR 576, para. 79. The Employment Court found that the requirement to undergo drug and alcohol testing on an undefined fair and reasonable basis was among a number of provisions which in combination rendered the contract 'exceptionally burdensome': *Harrison v. Tuckers Wool Processors* [2000] 1 ERNZ 572,

there is no reasonable cause for conducting it. The employer cannot physically compel the worker to undergo testing, and could only take disciplinary action if a refusal to be tested was unreasonable in the circumstances. If the employer decides to dismiss the worker, the issue then becomes whether or not the employer was substantively and procedurally justified in doing so. The Privacy Act does not provide any guidance as to what would be fair and reasonable in such circumstances. Like employment law, it simply requires that any collection of personal information be reasonably necessary and undertaken in a fair and reasonable manner.[841] The only thing added by the Privacy Act is the background of upholding the societal value of an individual's freedom from unreasonable intrusion into personal affairs unless there are sufficiently important countervailing considerations.

794. Drug testing has been upheld in an early interim reinstatement case,[842] where the Employment Court did not find anything wrong where drug testing was carried out in a procedurally fair manner and in a safety-sensitive context. The Privacy Act was not cited. In the absence of a contractual entitlement to require testing, it is more common for employers to carry out tests on job applicants rather than on current employees. The permissibility of introducing a drug and alcohol testing regime for existing workers was first determined by the Employment Court in 2004,[843] when the full court found that an employer would be justified in introducing such a regime where health and safety were legitimate concerns. Although the Privacy Act was cited by opponents to the unilateral changes, the dominant considerations in this case were the employer's statutory and common law obligations in respect of workplace health and safety. These, together with its right to manage, empowered the employer to promulgate relevant policies. In a subsequent case on workplace drug and alcohol testing,[844] the Employment Court held that the employer's intended introduction of a drug and alcohol policy would not breach collective and individual agreements covering union members and would be otherwise lawful. Such testing policies 'must meet the twin tests of lawfulness and reasonableness if they are to be enforceable.'[845]

§7. Workplace Biometrics

795. There is one case where the Privacy Commissioner investigated but rejected a union complaint about the introduction of finger-scanning technology for an employer's payroll system.[846] The union claimed that a system of time sheets and

paras 63–64. The court commented that some of the provisions 'could only have provided the satisfaction of exercising domination over the persons of others'.

841. IPPs 1 and 4 respectively.

842. *Philson v. Air NZ Ltd* [1996] NZEmpC 118 (3 Jul. 1996).

843. *NZ Amalgamated Engineering Printing and Manufacturing Union Inc v. Air New Zealand Ltd* [2004] NZEmpC 32 (13 Apr. 2004), [2004] 1 ERNZ 614.

844. *Maritime Union of New Zealand Inc v. TLNZ Ltd* [2007] NZEmpC 168 (21 Dec. 2007).

845. *Ibid.*, para. 126.

846. *Case Note 33623* [2003] NZPrivCmr 5 (Feb. 2003).

clock cards was sufficient, and that the introduction of the new system was 'overkill'. The company, however, claimed that a scanner had become 'necessary' in terms of the IPP 1 collection principle because of employee dishonesty in completing time sheets. The Commissioner, however, agreed that finger-scanning was necessary for the company's purposes in the circumstances. The union also claimed that the use of finger-scanning technology for hospital cleaners involved an unlawful, unfair, or unreasonably intrusive means of collecting information in terms of IPP 4. In particular, there was no express or implied term in the employment contract requiring employees to consent to the physical contact involved in having their fingers measured by sensors. The Commissioner, however, disagreed, and he declined to consider the contractual issue on the basis that it fell within the exclusive jurisdiction of the specialist employment law court and it would have been 'quite improper' to usurp it. Given that IPP 4(a) prohibits agencies from collecting personal information 'by unlawful means', the refusal to consider whether finger-scanning breached employees' contracts amounted to a concession to the employer, who ought to have borne the burden of proof. In effect, the Commissioner endorsed the lawfulness of the practice under the contract by declining to consider whether or not it was unlawful.

796. The union fared better before the Employment Court.[847] The court found that the introduction of finger-scanning was unlawful in the circumstances because the employer breached contractual and statutory requirements to consult the employees concerned, who were hospital cleaners. The employees objected to having their fingerprints scanned, and advised that they would not comply until the dispute was resolved. The company maintained that its direction to the employees was lawful, and it sought a declaration to that effect. The court found that the employees concerned were not breaching their contracts because the instructions they had been given were themselves unlawful. The court held that the employer had a statutory good faith obligation to consult on changes in workplace practices.[848] The court remarked that the requirement of consultation will depend on the context. The context here – and this was the key factor upon which this case turned – was that most of the nearly fifty employees concerned were Samoan. The evidence indicated that these particular workers regarded the introduction of the new technology as culturally offensive because it implied that like criminals, they were not to be trusted. Expert evidence was introduced to show that the technology raised issues relating to Samoan beliefs concerning the sacredness of parts of the body and the concept of *Va Fealoia*, 'the sacred space which governs and manages all relationships between people including employers and employees'. The court also noted that the legislation requires employers in the public health sector to be 'good employers'.[849]

847. *OCS Ltd v. Service and Food Workers Union Nga Ringa Tota Inc* [2006] NZEmpC 86 (31 Aug. 2006), [2006] ERNZ 762.

848. Employment Relations Act 2000, s. 4(1A)(b) requires that 'parties to an employment relationship to be active and constructive in establishing and maintaining a productive employment relationship in which the parties are, among other things, responsive and communicative'.

849. Employment Relations Act, cl. 5 of Sch. 1B. There was also a specific statutory requirement (via s. 6(1) of the New Zealand Public Health and Disability Act 2000 and s. 118(2)(f) of the Crown Entities Act 2004) to recognise 'the cultural differences of ethnic or minority groups'.

Chapter 5. Processing for Scientific Research, Public Archiving and Statistical Purposes

§1. GENERAL

797. New Zealand law includes derogations from various of the Privacy Act's requirements for scientific research, public archiving, and statistical purposes. These derogations are found in various places within the legislation including as exceptions to the IPPs themselves, overriding requirements in various enactments and the tightening of standards in codes of practice.

798. The derogations from the Privacy Act's requirements for research, archiving, and statistical purposes are generally limited and subject to safeguards. The derogations for statistical or research purposes generally require that personal information will not be published in a form that could reasonably be expected to identify the individual concerned. In relation to archiving, standards issued under the Public Records Act 2005 seek to ensure that privacy protection requirements are incorporated in business process and systems design and that access restrictions accord with Privacy Act requirements.

§2. EXCEPTIONS TO IPPS FOR RESEARCH OR STATISTICAL PURPOSES

799. IPPs 2, 3, 10, 11, and 13 each contain an exception for research or statistical purposes.

800. The exceptions in IPP 2(2)(g)(ii), 3(4)(e)(ii), 10(1)(b)(ii) and 11(1)(h)(ii) are in essentially identical terms and provide that it is an exception to the applicable principle if the information to be collected, used or disclosed:

> is to be used for statistical or research purposes and will not be published in a form that could reasonably be expected to identify the individual concerned.

801. The exception in IPP 13(2)(b) is a derogation only from the prohibition on reassignment of unique identifiers in IPP13(2) and not to the other requirements of IPP 13. The exception simply provides that in respect to the identifier to be assigned to the individual:

> the unique identifier is to be used … for statistical or research purposes and no other purpose.

§3. Exceptions to IPPs for Research Purposes Modified by Health Information Privacy Code 2020

802. A code of practice issued under section 33 of the Privacy Act 2020 may, among other things, modify the application of one or more of the IPPs by prescribing more stringent standards. This has occurred with respect to research involving access to health information held by health agencies. The Health Information Privacy Code 2020, continuing the requirements of a 1994 code, has added additional safeguards for health research. The principal change made by the code affects the four rules that replace the IPPs containing research exceptions.

803. The first change affects the three rules that replace IPPs 2, 10, and 11. Rules 2, 10, and 11 that provide that that it is an exception to the applicable rule if the health information to be collected, used or disclosed:

> will be used for research purposes (for which approval by an ethics committee, if required, has been given) and will not be published in a form that could reasonably be expected to identify the individual concerned.

804. The additional requirement, not found in the IPPs, is that the use if for research 'for which approval by an ethics committee, if required, has been given'.

805. Clause 3 of the Health Information Privacy Code contains the following definition:

> *ethics committee* means –
>
> (a) the Ethics Committee of the Health Research Council of New Zealand or an ethics committee approved by that committee; or
> (b) the National Advisory Committee on Health and Disability Support Services Ethics; or
> (c) an ethics committee required to operate in accordance with the currently applicable Operational Standard for Ethics Committees promulgated by the Ministry of Health; or
> (d) an ethics committee established by, or pursuant to, any enactment

806. The requirement for ethics committee approval is not found in the code itself but in external requirements of funding bodies or of professional regulators. The Health Research Council, a funding body, has, for example, released guidance for health researchers and ethics committees on health research and privacy.

807. It may be noted that there will be instances of health research where approval by an ethics committee may not be required. Such instances would principally arise where no external funding body is involved and might typically involve an agency using its own records for the purpose for which they were created.

808. In relation to the other IPP having a research exception, IPP 3, the exception has been omitted entirely from the replacement rule 3(4). The effect is that the matters that an agency is required to make individuals aware of under Rule 3(1) must be provided in the case of health research. Accordingly, there is greater transparency required in the collection of health information by health agencies for research than is the case with agencies engaged in research.

809. Given that there is no specific exception relating to research in the code it is possible to consider the possible application of other general exceptions or exemptions in this context (although such reliance might be scrutinised by an ethics committee). Examples include 'prejudice to the purposes of collection' (Rule 3(4)(a)(ii)) or 'not reasonably practicable' (Rule 3(4)(a)(ii)).

810. For the sake of completeness, it may be noted that section 22H of the Health Act 1956, which prevails over the Health Information Privacy Code, allows for the supply of 'anonymous health information':

> **Anonymous health information**
>
> Notwithstanding any enactment, rule of law, or other obligation, any person may supply to any other person health information that does not enable the identification of the individual to whom the information relates.

§4. Privacy Act Exemption from IPP 7 for Statistics New Zealand

811. Section 29(2) provides that:

> IPP 7 does not apply to personal information collected by Statistics New Zealand under the Statistics Act 1975.

812. Pursuant to the Statistics Act 1975, Statistics New Zealand is the department of state formerly known as the Department of Statistics and is headed by the Government Statistician.

§5. Reason for Refusing Access to Personal Information under IPP 6: Material Placed in Archive

813. Section 53 of the Privacy Act provides that an agency may refuse access to any personal information requested if:

> the disclosure of the information, being information contained in material placed in any library or museum or archive, would breach a condition subject to which that material was placed.

814. Under the Privacy Act there is a right of access to personal information contained in a library or museum. This is to be contrasted to the position under the other freedom of information statutes, where 'information contained in library or museum material made or acquired and preserved solely for reference or exhibition purposes' was excluded from the definition of 'official information': *see* section 2(1)(e)(i) of the definition in the Official Information Act 1982 and section 2(1)(b)(i) of the definition in the LGOIM Act. Under the Privacy Act, such information is available as personal information, except where disclosure of it would breach a condition under which the material was placed in the institution.

§6. Other Relevant Enactments: Research Purposes

815. The IPPs are subject to provisions in other enactments. Section 24 of the Privacy Act provides:

Relationships between IPPs and other New Zealand law

(1) Nothing in IPP 6, 11, or 12 limits or affects –
  (a) a provision contained in any New Zealand enactment that authorises or requires personal information to be made available; or
  (b) a provision contained in any other New Zealand Act that –
    (i) imposes a prohibition or restriction in relation to the availability of personal information; or
    (ii) regulates the manner in which personal information may be obtained or made available.

(2) An action taken by an agency does not breach IPPs 1 to 5, 7 to 10, or 13 if the action is authorised or required by or under New Zealand law.

816. There are several provisions of the Health Act 1956 that have the effect of authorising the disclosure of health information for, among other purposes, health research.

817. Section 22D requires district health boards to provide information to the Ministry of Health for health research:

Duty to provide health information

(1) The Minister may at any time, by notice in writing, require any district health board to provide, in such manner as may from time to time be required, such returns or other information as is specified in the notice concerning the condition or treatment of, or the services provided to, any individuals … for the purposes of … health research.

(2) Subject to subsection (3), it is the duty of a district health board to provide the returns or other information specified in a notice given to it under subsection (1) within such time, and in such form, as is specified in the notice.

(3) No information that would enable the identification of an individual may be provided under this section unless –

(a) the individual consents to the provision of such information; or
(b) the identifying information is essential for the purposes for which the information is sought.

(4) For the purposes of subsection (3)(a), consent to the provision of information may be given –

(a) by the individual personally, if he or she has attained the age of 16 years; or
(b) by a representative of that individual.

818. As can be seen, section 22D(3) adds a safeguard requiring that information not identify any individual unless consent has been obtained or that obtaining information in identified form is 'essential'.

819. On a more specific context, Health Act allows for release from the National Cervical Screening Programme register of information that identifies a woman for the purpose of research (refer section 112J(4)(c)).

§7. Other Relevant Enactments: Public Archiving Purposes

820. The key legislation in relation to public archives is the Public Records Act 2005. This enactment creates a comprehensive scheme for retaining, maintaining, and classifying public archives and allowing for public access. The Act prevails over the IPPs. Standards issued under the Public Records Act 2005 seek to ensure that privacy protection requirements are incorporated in business process and systems design and that access restrictions accord with Privacy Act requirements.

§8. Other Relevant Enactments: Statistical Purposes

821. The key legislation in relation to statistics is the Statistics Act 1975. This law makes provision for official statistics, provides the statutory basis for the Government Statistician and Statistics New Zealand and provides for the five-yearly census of population and dwellings among other things. The Act prevails over the IPPs.

822. There are several provisions of the Health Act 1956 that have the effect of authorising the disclosure of health information for, among other purposes, statistical research.

823. Section 22C (2)(g)(ii) of the Health Act authorised employees of the Ministry of Health to disclose health information for 'compiling statistics for health purposes'.

824. Section 22D of the Health Act requires district health boards to provide information to the Ministry of Health for statistical purposes:

Duty to provide health information

(1) The Minister may at any time, by notice in writing, require any district health board to provide, in such manner as may from time to time be required, such returns or other information as is specified in the notice concerning the condition or treatment of, or the services provided to, any individuals in order to obtain statistics for health purposes … .

(2) Subject to subsection (3), it is the duty of a district health board to provide the returns or other information specified in a notice given to it under subsection (1) within such time, and in such form, as is specified in the notice.

(3) No information that would enable the identification of an individual may be provided under this section unless –

(a) the individual consents to the provision of such information; or

(b) the identifying information is essential for the purposes for which the information is sought.

(4) For the purposes of subsection (3)(a), consent to the provision of information may be given –

(a) by the individual personally, if he or she has attained the age of 16 years; or

(b) by a representative of that individual.

825. As can be seen, section 22D(3) adds a safeguard requiring that information not identify any individual unless consent has been obtained or that obtaining information in identified form is 'essential'.

826. In a more specific context, the Health Act allows for release from the National Cervical Screening Programme register of information that identifies a woman for the purpose of research (refer section 112J(4)(c)).

§9. Comparison with Requirements in European Instruments in Relation to Research, Archiving and Statistical Purposes

827. Article 89 of the GDPR states:

GDPR Safeguards and derogations relating to processing for archiving purposes in the public interest, scientific or historical research purposes or statistical purposes

1. Processing for archiving purposes in the public interest, scientific or historical research purposes or statistical purposes, shall be subject to appropriate safeguards, in accordance with this Regulation, for the rights and freedoms of the data subject. Those safeguards shall ensure that technical and organisational measures are in place in particular in order to ensure respect for the principle of data minimisation. Those measures may include pseudonymisation provided that those purposes can be fulfilled in that manner. Where those purposes can be fulfilled by further processing which

does not permit or no longer permits the identification of data subjects, those purposes shall be fulfilled in that manner.

2. Where personal data are processed for scientific or historical research purposes or statistical purposes, Union or Member State law may provide for derogations from the rights referred to in Articles 15, 16, 18 and 21 subject to the conditions and safeguards referred to in paragraph 1 of this Article in so far as such rights are likely to render impossible or seriously impair the achievement of the specific purposes, and such derogations are necessary for the fulfilment of those purposes.
3. Where personal data are processed for archiving purposes in the public interest, Union or Member State law may provide for derogations from the rights referred to in Articles 15, 16, 18, 19, 20 and 21 subject to the conditions and safeguards referred to in paragraph 1 of this Article in so far as such rights are likely to render impossible or seriously impair the achievement of the specific purposes, and such derogations are necessary for the fulfilment of those purposes.
4. Where processing referred to in paragraphs 2 and 3 serves at the same time another purpose, the derogations shall apply only to processing for the purposes referred to in those paragraphs.

828. Article 11 of the COE provides:

Article 11 – Exceptions and restrictions

(1) No exception to the provisions set out in this Chapter shall be allowed except to the provisions of Article 5 paragraph 4, Article 7 paragraph 2, Article 8 paragraph 1 and Article 9, when such an exception is provided for by law, respects the essence of the fundamental rights and freedoms and constitutes a necessary and proportionate measure in a democratic society for:
  (a) the protection of national security, defence, public safety, important economic and financial interests of the State, the impartiality and independence of the judiciary or the prevention, investigation and prosecution of criminal offences and the execution of criminal penalties, and other essential objectives of general public interest;
  (b) the protection of the data subject or the rights and fundamental freedoms of others, notably freedom of expression.

(2) Restrictions on the exercise of the provisions specified in Articles 8 and 9 may be provided for by law with respect to data processing for archiving purposes in the public interest, scientific or historical research purposes or statistical purposes when there is no recognisable risk of infringement of the rights and fundamental freedoms of data subjects.

(3) In addition to the exceptions allowed for in paragraph 1 of this article, with reference to processing activities for national security and defence purposes, each Party may provide, by law and only to the extent that it constitutes a necessary and proportionate measure in a democratic society to

fulfil such aim, exceptions to Article 4 paragraph 3, Article 14 paragraphs 5 and 6 and Article 15, paragraph 2, litterae a, b, c and d.

This is without prejudice to the requirement that processing activities for national security and defence purposes are subject to independent and effective review and supervision under the domestic legislation of the respective Party.

829. It is useful to break the European requirements into the component requirements which might be summarised in simplified form as:

(a) Scientific research, public archiving, and statistical purposes should be subject to appropriate safeguards to protect individual privacy rights. GDPR Article 89.1; COE Article 11.1.
(b) Derogations to certain individual privacy rights in relation to scientific research, public archiving and statistical purposes may be established by law; those rights being subject access, rectification, restriction on processing and right to object plus, in respect of archiving only, notification following rectification and portability right, GDPR Article 89.2; transparency and rights of data subject, COE Article 11.2.
(c) Derogations for scientific research, public archiving, and statistical purposes not permissible in relation to other rights and requirements not articulated such as proportionality and lawfulness requirements, special categories, security, cross-border transfers, mandatory notification, etc. GDPR Article 89.3; COE Article 11.1.
(d) Derogations for scientific research, public archiving, and statistical purposes should not be arbitrary or absolute but be justified by risk and provided in a proportionate manner. GDPR Articles 89.2 and 89.3; COE Article 11.2.

830. The New Zealand law broadly accords with the European approach although it could be said to fall short in some respects.

831. With respect to (a) New Zealand privacy law does, as a general starting point, provide that research, public archiving, and statistical purposes will be subject to privacy law subject to exceptions to several privacy principles. However, New Zealand law is not as specific as GDPR with Article 89.1 requiring that 'safeguards shall ensure that technical and organisational measures are in place in particular in order to ensure respect for the principle of data minimisation'.

832. With respect to (b) derogations are made to selected New Zealand privacy rights by law. Generally, these are directed only in relation to research and statistical purposes and not to archiving. The New Zealand exceptions refer to 'research' which conceivably may be wider than the European term 'scientific research'. The research and statistical purposes exceptions appear to be in area that are seen as permissible in the European instruments although the exception to IPP 3 reduces the transparency right: a derogation that appears to be prohibited in the GDPR but permissible under the COE.

833. With respect to (c), the New Zealand approach broadly accords with the European approach. However, as other enactments can override the IPPs it is possible that outside the confines of the Privacy Act itself there may be legislation that derogates from privacy rights in this area.

834. With respect to (d) the exceptions contained in the IPPs would appear to be carefully selected and limited to ensure that the derogations are proportionate to the risks and have appropriate safeguards.

Part X. Specific Data Protection Regimes

Chapter 1. Obligations of Professional Secrecy

§1. General

835. New Zealand has adopted specific provisions that set out the powers of the Privacy Commissioner during investigations to require persons to give evidence, answer questions or provide information, documents, or things notwithstanding that those persons are subject to an obligation of obligation of secrecy or non-disclosure. The relevant provisions are set out in sections 88 to 90 of the Privacy Act 2020 (continuing the position formerly contained in sections 94 to 96 of the 1993 Act).

§2. Disclosure of Information May Be Required Despite Obligation of Secrecy

836. Section 88 of the Privacy Act provides that, subject to any privilege a person might choose to invoke pursuant to section 89, a person bound by any enactment not to disclose particular information may be required to supply that information to the Privacy Commissioner, in which case the disclosure will not constitute a breach of the relevant enactment.

837. The Privacy Commissioner may not require the information where the Prime Minister certifies that disclosure might prejudice certain security, defence or international relations interests, or where the Attorney-General certifies that disclosure might prejudice law enforcement interests or injure the public interest through the disclosure of confidential Cabinet matters.

§3. Protection and Privileges of Persons Required to Provide Information, Etc.

838. Section 89 of the Privacy Act provides that, with the exception of a claim of public interest immunity, the same privileges as would apply in legal proceedings apply in relation to the giving of information to the Privacy Commissioner and his or her employees. Moreover, a person will enjoy immunity from prosecution if, in supplying information to the Commissioner pursuant to section 87 or section 88, such compliance constitutes an offence under any enactment. However, if the giving of information constitutes an offence against section 212 of the Privacy Act (e.g., because the information is false or misleading), the immunity does not apply. The section also limits the Commissioner's use and disclosure of privileged information received.

839. When an individual who is denied access by an agency to information requested under IPP 6 complains to the Privacy Commissioner, the first thing the Commissioner's office does is request from the agency the documents that have been withheld to review whether the request was properly refused. Some agencies are reluctant to let the Commissioner have the documents, and have to be compelled under section 87 to do so.

840. In the case of *Jeffries v. Privacy Commissioner* [2010] NZSC 99, [2011] 1 NZLR 45, a lawyer was unwilling to provide the Commissioner with information and asserted that he could refuse because he claimed the information was legally privileged. The Supreme Court said such information must be provided to the Privacy Commissioner if it is requested under section 91 of the 1993 Act (equivalent to section 87 of the Act).

§4. Disclosed Information Privileged

841. Section 90 of the Privacy Act provides that that any information, document or thing provided to the Privacy Commissioner is privileged as if given in court proceedings.

842. The Privacy Commissioner, Commissioner's staff and Director of Human Rights Proceedings cannot be compelled to give evidence in court as to matters that came to their knowledge through performing their functions (subject to certain criminal proceedings under the Crimes Act 1961).

843. For the purposes of the law relating to the defence of qualified privilege under the Defamation Act 1992, any report made under the Privacy Act by the Privacy Commissioner is deemed to be an official report.

Chapter 2. Churches and Religious Associations

§1. General

844. New Zealand has no special data protection rules in relation to churches and religious associations. Churches and religious associations are 'agencies' for the purposes of the Privacy Act 2020 and subject to the IPPs and the supervision of the Privacy Commissioner.

§2. Case Examples: Complaints to the Privacy Commissioner

845. One reported case involving a church or religious organisation that was taken to the Privacy Commission involved an employee of the church.

846. In *Case Note 18541* [2002] NZPrivCmr 8 the Privacy Commissioner reported that the pastor of a church was having marriage difficulties and was receiving counselling through elders of the church. The elders prepared a statement that was read at a public meeting of the church. It explained the couple's difficulties at some length, and asked the congregation to pray for them.

847. The pastor complained that the elders had divulged personal and sensitive information about him in the statement and had violated his privacy. He also said that the statement contained inaccuracies that misrepresented his situation. The complaint raised issues under the accuracy and disclosure principles (IPPs 8 and 11 of the 1993 Act).

848. In responding to the complaint, the church said it was not a body to which the Privacy Act applied. It also argued that the New Zealand Bill of Rights Act 1990 gave a church the right to manage its internal affairs, free from state interference. Finally, it maintained that because the statement had been read out within the church, it was not a disclosure under the Privacy Act. The Privacy Commissioner considered the church's arguments in preliminary investigations but did not need to form a final opinion on the issues as the parties reached a settlement.

849. The first issue was the definition of 'agency'. The 1993 Act defined an agency as 'any person, or body of persons, whether corporate or incorporate and whether in the public or private sector … '. It listed a number of exceptions but churches and religious organisations were not among them. The church was an agency to which the Privacy Act applied.

850. The Privacy Commissioner also considered the New Zealand Bill of Rights Act 1990. The church's view was that the freedom of expression and freedom of worship guaranteed in sections 13 and 15 of the New Zealand Bill of Rights Act included the right of any church to manage its own affairs free from state control and interference. The church quoted section 6: 'whenever an enactment can be given a meaning that is consistent with the rights and freedom contained in this Bill of Rights, that meaning shall be preferred to any other meaning'. However, the Commissioner noted that section 4 stated:

> **Other enactments not affected**
>
> No court shall, in relation to any enactment (whether passed or made before or after the commencement of this Bill of Rights), –
>
> (a) hold any provision of the enactment to be impliedly repealed or revoked, or to be in any way invalid or ineffective; or
> (b) decline to apply any provision of the enactment –
>
> by reason only that the provision is inconsistent with any provision of this Bill of Rights.

851. The Privacy Act came into effect in July 1993, three years after the Bill of Rights, and contained twelve IPPs covering all aspects of how personal information is dealt with. The principles provide additional rights to individuals in respect of information held about them. Section 69 of the Privacy Act required the Commissioner to investigate complaints arising under the privacy principles. The Commissioner expressed the view that the Privacy Act had to be construed in terms of section 4 of the New Zealand Bill of Rights Act, but that the Bill of Rights did not override the Privacy Act's provisions.

852. A further issue concerned disclosure within an agency. The church considered that it was not possible to breach IPP 11 by disclosing information within the same agency. Assuming for the purposes of this argument that church attendees are within that agency, the Commissioner nevertheless took the view that it was possible to breach IPP 11 by disclosure to persons within the same agency. IPP 11 prohibits disclosures 'to a person or body or agency'. A person who is in some way within the disclosing agency may be singularly inappropriate to be a recipient of certain personal information held by the agency. For instance, it may be appropriate to discuss an alleged staff impropriety with a director or manager in order to carry out disciplinary action, but it may not be appropriate for every employee in the agency to be informed of the matter. It would require clear wording to exclude that sort of situation from the purview of Principle 11.

853. The Commissioner was mindful of a decision by the Complaints Review Tribunal in 2000 that suggested disclosure by an agency to one of its employees is not a disclosure caught by IPP 11, but as the point was not canvassed in the hearing or covered by any legal submissions the Commissioner did not consider himself bound by the Tribunal's comments on that point and considered the disclosure in the case was covered by IPP 11.

854. The church advised the Commissioner that it accepted that it was covered by the Privacy Act. It did not wish to pursue legal arguments on the other points any further, but instead wished to settle the matter. The pastor and the church agreed on a statement which was read at a public meeting of the church. Copies were sent to members who would have been present at the earlier meeting. The church also paid the pastor's legal expenses.

855. In another case, albeit not a complaint but merely the grant of an exemption, the Privacy Commissioner reported that an application for an exemption from IPP 11 was granted to a church which wanted to locate individuals for whom money on deposit was being held. The church had tried other means of contact, but without success, and proposed placing notices in the church's national and local newspapers. The Privacy Commissioner took the view that the benefit to the individuals concerned outweighed any interference with their privacy that might occur from the publication (*see Report of the Privacy Commissioner for the year ended 30 June 2001* Appendix to the Journals of the House of Representatives A.11 at 40).

§3. Case Examples: Human Rights Review Tribunal

856. In the case of *W v. Director-General of Social Welfare* [1998] NZCRT 11 and 12, reported at (1998) 5 Human Rights Reports of New Zealand 580, the plaintiff alleged that the defendant breached Principle 5 of the Privacy Act 1993 in that it failed to ensure that personal information about her was protected from unauthorised disclosure. The proceedings not taken against a church but rather the church was the recipient of personal information at the centre of the case.

857. The plaintiff was in receipt of a social security benefit. She moved to a small town, and as she had no accommodation, sought help from the local Methodist church. A member of the church's congregation, Mrs F, undertook to help the plaintiff find accommodation. Mrs F, acting under mistaken advice from the local council, visited the Income Support Service office in order to obtain reimbursement for $500 advanced from the church's welfare fund to pay the bond for the plaintiff's accommodation. Mrs F was unaware of the correct procedure, which was that the service would require an application for a bond advance from the plaintiff, and that before such an application was granted or rejected, it would be considered in the light of other information which the service held about the plaintiff. Mrs F alleged that when she asked about the criteria that would be used to determine the plaintiff's application, she was told that the plaintiff had already been granted an advance of this kind within the previous year. The service officer denied that she disclosed this particular information at the time, but maintained that the disclosure was made in the course of a telephone call three or four days later, after it was reasonable to assume that Mrs F was acting as the plaintiff's agent. The plaintiff alleged that she felt embarrassed and humiliated that this information was disclosed to Mrs F, and she felt unable to remain in the town. She returned to her prior town of residence, thereby incurring further expense.

858. The legal issues at stake in this case did not concern the church and so were not further discussed here. However, it may be noted that the Tribunal found that the plaintiff suffered humiliation, loss of dignity and injury to her feelings as a result of this breach, and also that she incurred costs. Accordingly, the Tribunal ordered that the defendant write a letter of apology to the plaintiff, and that the defendant pay $1000 to the plaintiff.

859. The case of *Director of Human Rights Proceedings v. The Catholic Church for New Zealand* [2006] NZHRRT 22 (13 June 2006) involved an application by defendant to state case concerning preliminary issue to HC as to whether the Catholic Tribunal is a 'tribunal' within definition of 'agency' in the Privacy Act.

860. This decision related to the defendant's application for a case to be stated to the HC under section 122 of the HR Act. The case stated concerned the preliminary issue whether or not the Catholic Tribunal, the adjudicative entity operating under the auspices of the Catholic Church of New Zealand, was a 'tribunal' within the meaning of the definition of 'agency' in section 2(1)(b)(viii) of the Privacy Act 1993. The Catholic Tribunal was neither an incorporated body, nor was it created or recognised in any relevant way by any statutory provision (at [1]). Section 2(1)(b)(viii) provides that an 'agency' for the purposes of the Privacy Act does not include 'in relation to its judicial functions, a tribunal'.

861. The Director of Human Rights Proceedings brought this case on behalf of a complainant who claimed that the Church breached Principle 6, in that it failed to respond to her requests for access to her personal information. The Catholic Tribunal had been involved here in issuing a decree for the annulment of a marriage that had been solemnised by the Church. The Church claimed that the Privacy Act did not apply to it because the information was held by the Catholic Tribunal. The Tribunal summed up the preliminary issue here as whether 'the word "tribunal" in section 2(1)(b)(viii) is intended to include only those tribunals that are either created, or which are in some relevant way recognised, by statute – or whether the word in intended to include "tribunals" of other kinds as well' (at [4]). This was a question of law.

862. The Tribunal also identified a second issue, which would arise even if the Catholic Tribunal fell outside the definition of an agency in terms of section 2(1)(b)(viii), since that exception only applied to a Tribunal 'in relation to its judicial functions'. The Director contended that the complainant's access requests did not relate to matters that fell within the Catholic Tribunal's judicial functions. The HRRT held that this was a mixed question of law and fact.

863. The Tribunal may, at any time, before or during the hearing or before delivering its decision, on the application of any party to the proceedings or on its own motion, state a case for the opinion of the HC on any question of law arising in any proceedings before the Tribunal. The Tribunal remarked that it was having to deal with 'two powerful but conflicting pressures' (paragraph 23). On the one hand, dealing with such preliminary issues of law was 'part of the Tribunal's core business' but on the other hand, 'there is the powerful pragmatic point that it would be unfortunate to commit these parties to a course of litigation in the Tribunal when the whole exercise might effectively prove to be empty if in due course the Tribunal's decision on the preliminary issues is not upheld by the High Court' (at [24]).

864. The Tribunal held that:

- The question of whether or not the word 'Tribunal' in section 2(1)(b)(viii) of the Privacy Act includes non-statutory tribunals ought to be remitted by way of the case stated procedure provided for in section 122 of the Human Rights Act for determination by the HC in the first instance, but
- The question as to whether what occurred in this case falls within the phrase '... in relation to its judicial functions...' ought not to be so remitted, but should be decided by the Tribunal in the first instance when and if it becomes appropriate to do so (at [30]).

865. In the result, the HC held that the Catholic Tribunal was not a 'Tribunal' in the sense intended by paragraph (1)(b)(xiii) of the section 2 definition of 'agency'. Such tribunals had to be statutory in nature, as the context suggested that only public sector tribunals were exempted from the definition of 'agency' (*see* below).

§4. Case Example: High Court

866. Director of Human Rights Proceedings v. Catholic Church for New Zealand [2008] NZHC 156, [2008] 3 NZLR 216 was a case stated by the HRRT under section 122 of the HR Act. The question that the HC was asked to answer in relation to the definition of 'agency' in section 2 of the Privacy Act 1993 was:

> Whether the word 'tribunal' in s. 2(1)(b)(viii) of the Privacy Act 1993 is capable of applying to a non-statutory tribunal and, if so, what criteria (if any) must such a non-statutory tribunal satisfy (apart from the exercise of judicial functions) so as to qualify as a 'tribunal' under that provision?

867. The background to the case involved a proceeding commenced by the Director of Human Rights Proceedings on behalf of an individual who had had dealings with the Catholic Tribunal in relation to the annulment of a marriage. The Catholic Church had denied her request for access personal information on the basis that the information was held by the Catholic Tribunal, and as a 'Tribunal', it fell outside the definition of an 'agency' under the Privacy Act, and so did not have any of the Privacy Act obligations of an agency under the Act.

868. The Catholic Tribunal is an entity within the Catholic Church for New Zealand, but it is neither an incorporated body, nor is it an entity that is either created or recognised by any statutory provision. The issue of whether or not this Tribunal was a 'Tribunal' that was exempted from the section 2 definition of 'agency' was a threshold question in relation to the case that had been brought before the HRRT (*see* above). As the HRRT put it, the issue was 'whether or not the word "Tribunal" ... is intended to include only those tribunals that are either created, or which are in some relevant way recognised, by statute – or whether the word is intended to include "tribunals" of other kinds as well' (at [4]).

869. The relevant part of the definition of 'agency' is as follows:

> agency –
>
> (a) means any person or body of persons, whether corporate or unincorporate, and whether in the public sector or the private sector; ... but
> (b) does not include – ...
> (viii) in relation to its judicial functions, a tribunal

870. The court noted that the word 'Tribunal' also appears in IPPs 2, 3, 10, and 11, where in each case it appears as part of an exemption from the particular principle concerned. For example, the exemption in principle 2(2)(d)(iv) provides that non-compliance is necessary 'for the conduct of proceedings before any Court or Tribunal (being proceedings that have been commenced or are reasonably in contemplation)'.

871. The court commented that the question raised by the case stated was 'not one which has an obvious answer, or at least not one which is to be easily arrived at' (at [49]). The court found that there was merit in both parties' arguments, and that 'In the end, it is the accumulation of a number of considerations rather than any one which is of decisive significance' that led it to favour the plaintiff's arguments.

872. The court noted that paragraph (a) of the definition of 'agency' was 'very broad' (at [51]). It went on to note that 'The list in paragraph (b) of the definition is, I think, distinguished by its emphasis on public bodies or organs of the executive or government' (at [52]). The only departure from this general characteristic is in sub-paragraph (xiii), which refers to the news media, which could be either publicly or privately owned. The court concluded that:

> Consequently, although sub-paragraph (viii) looked at in isolation might arguably be thought to extend to tribunals which were both public and private in their constitution, that is not the result that one naturally arrives at when the sub-paragraph is viewed in the context of paragraph (b) as a whole.

873. Moreover, the use of the term 'Tribunal' elsewhere in the Privacy Act, in connection with principles 2, 3, 10, and 11, appeared in the context of 'matters that necessarily related to the public sector' (at [55]). The court went on to remark:

> I would go further, however, and discern in the four sub-paragraphs a clear emphasis on public law. The matters mentioned are avoiding prejudice to the maintenance of the law by any public sector agency, the enforcement of a law which imposes a pecuniary penalty, protection of the public revenue, and finally the conduct of proceedings before any Court or tribunal. I regard it as unlikely that by the time the word 'tribunal' was reached at the end of these

> series of provisions, the legislature intended what would have been a change of course, so as to embrace both publicly and privately constituted tribunals. Indeed, I think it more likely that, had that been Parliament's intent, there would have been an expanded reference to tribunals either here, or within paragraph (b) of the definition of 'agency' in s 2(1), to make that plain. It should also be noted that after sub-paragraph (viii) the list continues to refer to public offices of various kinds right until the final sub-paragraph.

874. The court reasoned on the basis that 'Plainly, the word "Tribunal" must carry the same meaning in all these principles, and also have the same meaning in the definition of "agency"' (paragraph 56). Accordingly, the court concluded that:

> most of the indications in the text of the relevant provisions of the Privacy Act favours the conclusion that the word 'tribunal' is used so as to refer to bodies with a judicial function which are recognised by law and likely therefore to be created either directly by a statute or pursuant to a statute (at [57]).

875. The court also found that this approach was consistent with wider considerations of statutory interpretation. The court noted that the Privacy Act 1993 aims to protect and promote privacy and establish certain principles relating to the collection, use, and disclosure of personal information by public and private sector agencies. In addition, the Act's purpose includes establishing rights of access by individuals to their personal information held by public and private sector agencies. The wording used in the Act's long title emphasises the application of the IPPs to information held by both public and private sector agencies. Paragraph (a) of the section 2 definition of 'agency', the court observed, 'is consistent with the statutory purpose by virtue of its breadth' (paragraph 59). Accordingly, the court considered that 'an interpretative approach which confines the scope of the exclusions to the definition of "agency" within narrow grounds will best advance the purposes of the Act'. Such an approach was also consistent with the various international instruments that underpinned the Privacy Act, particularly the OECD Guidelines.

876. The court did not accept the defendant's argument that Parliament would not have intended to subject disciplinary committees or 'tribunals' of professional bodies to the Privacy Act. It commented that it considered the reverse to be true. It remarked that 'It is certainly not difficult to imagine circumstances in which information about a person might be given to such a body with the resultant creation of a very real and legitimate interest in that individual to know what the information is' (at [63]). In relation to the position of disciplinary committees of associations and members' clubs, the court could not see any policy reason why such bodies should not fall under the section 2 definition of 'agency'. The court commented that 'In this case too it is not difficult to imagine situations where it might be of vital interest to an individual to know what information such a body is holding in relation to them' (at [64]).

877. In relation to Church tribunals, the court did not consider that there were any real policy justifications for excluding them from the ambit of the definition of 'agency'. The court acknowledged that under the common law, courts have traditionally declined to become involved in matters relating to the private or domestic procedures of religious organisations, particularly ecclesiastical disputes and disputes involving matters of faith and doctrine. However, courts have been prepared to intervene 'where civil, economic or proprietary rights are alleged to have been infringed', as Randerson J observed in *Marshall v. National Spiritual Assembly of the Baha'is of New Zealand Inc* [2003] 2 NZLR 205, at [31].

878. The court then went on to comment:

> It is but a small step from that recognition to a situation such as the present where what is at stake is the application of general provisions aimed to protect the privacy of individuals by, amongst other things, entitling those individuals to have access to information held about them (IPP 6) and in appropriate cases to request its correction (Principle 7). It is unclear to me how making a body such as the Catholic Tribunal subject to the provisions of the Privacy Act would raise any issue of doctrine or belief, or in any real sense hamper the proper functioning of that body (at [66]).

879. Similarly, the court could not see how section 15 ('Manifestation of religion and belief') of the New Zealand Bill of Rights Act 1990 could be invoked on the facts:

> As I see the case, a person's right to manifest his or her religion or belief in 'worship, observance, practice or teaching' would not be threatened in any way by application of the provisions of the Privacy Act. This means that there can be no resort to s. 6 of the New Zealand Bill of Rights Act to bolster the defendant's interpretative argument, either (at [68]).

880. Accordingly, the court concluded as follows:

> there is no compelling argument of policy which should place 'church tribunals' in a special position any more than there is such an argument favouring the exclusion of the disciplinary bodies of professions or other private associations. The conclusions that I have earlier expressed based upon the wording of the statute and its purpose all favour the inclusion of such bodies within the definition of 'agency', and tend against their exclusion as 'tribunals' under paragraph (b)(viii) (at [69]).

881. The court went on to comment on another issue that had not been raised in argument in the case, but which supported the court's conclusion. This was that the defendant's argument depended on a distinction being drawn between the defendant and the Catholic Tribunal as an entity. The court noted that a similar distinction would have to be drawn between an incorporated society, and a committee of such an organisation that was set up to deal with special tasks, such as expulsion from membership or some other disciplinary matter. The court commented:

> If what might be termed the 'parent' organisation is itself captured by the broad definition of 'agency', it is unclear what justification there might be for isolating out and treating as a separate entity a body set up within that overall entity for the purpose of performing a particular function. There is no doubt that paragraph (a) of the definition of 'agency' would extend to such a body. The defendant's argument has it first being caught by paragraph (a), and then excluded by paragraph (b). Apart from the requirement that that body perform 'judicial functions', expressed in paragraph (b)(viii) of the definition, there would be no other limitation on the ability of the parent body to carve out a segment of its affairs for exemption from the provisions of the Privacy Act. It seems to me that would be wrong as a matter of principle. Further, I cannot see how it can be legally achieved by resort to private rule-making powers. In my view, if the parent organisation is within the definition of 'agency', then so must the entities that it establishes under its aegis, given that they are not separate corporate entities (at [71]).

882. In the result, the court found that the term 'Tribunal' in paragraph (b)(viii) of the definition of 'agency' in section 2(1) of the Privacy Act is not capable of applying to a non-statutory Tribunal.

Chapter 3. Law Enforcement Agencies

§1. General

883. New Zealand has a single national police service. The New Zealand Police was established as the Police Force under the Police Force Act 1886 and currently operates under the Policing Act 2008. Many public bodies have responsibilities to enforce the law in some capacity but some of the core government departments primarily responsible for law enforcement include, in addition to the New Zealand Police, the Serious Fraud Office, New Zealand Customs Service, New Zealand Immigration Service, Department of Corrections, New Zealand Transport Agency, and Ministry of Justice.

884. The IPPs in the Privacy Act apply to all law enforcement agencies as they do for all other agencies. However, the special needs of law enforcement are recognised in various ways throughout the Act including:

- Exceptions to the IPPs addressed to law enforcement matters (section 22).
- Overriding provisions in other laws (s. 24).
- Codes of practice (sections 32–38).
- Applicable reasons for refusing access to personal information (section 53).
- Approved information sharing agreements (sections 136–161).
- Access to identity information (sections 162–172).
- Law enforcement information sharing (sections 169–173)
- Authorised information matching programmes (sections 174–191).

885. In addition, it may be noted that there are some laws in addition to the Privacy Act addressed to protecting privacy interests in such areas as criminal history information.

§2. 'Maintenance of the Law' Exceptions to the IPPs Addressed to Law Enforcement Matters

886. There is an exception in each of IPPs 2, 3, 10, and 11 in relation to collection, use or disclosure of personal information where non-compliance is necessary in order to 'avoid prejudice to the maintenance of the law by any public sector agency' including 'prejudice to the prevention, detection, investigation, prosecution, and punishment of offences'.

887. The maintenance of the law exceptions have been considered numerous times by the Privacy Commissioner and HRRT. In one case, the matter was considered by the Supreme Court.

888. The Supreme Court case of *R v. Alsford* [2017] NZSC 42 dealt with the prosecution of the defendant for cannabis cultivation. The aspect of the case that is relevant to the Privacy Act is the police request for personal information about the defendant's electricity consumption from his power company without a warrant or production order. The police collected the information pursuant to the IPP 2(2)(e)(i) exception of the 1993 Act (equivalent to IPP 2(2)(e)(i) of the 2020 Act), in that the police reasonably believed that non-compliance was necessary to avoid prejudice to the maintenance of the law. However, the police had failed to provide detailed reasons to the company for its request for information.

889. The majority in the Supreme Court dealt first with whether there was an unreasonable search in terms of section 21 of the New Zealand Bill of Rights Act. The question whether the defendant had a reasonable expectation of privacy in respect of his electricity consumption information was answered by applying the test from *Hamed v. R* [2011] NZSC 101 at [163]. On this test, the majority held that the defendant did not have such a reasonable expectation. For example, it did not reveal any intimate details of the defendant's lifestyle or personal choices.

890. The majority noted that the police were not required to seek power consumption data through a production order, but they could ask the power company to voluntarily give this information to them. Such consent searches were not prohibited, but they still had to comply with the requirements of the Privacy Act. The agency from which the information was requested also had to comply with its Privacy Act obligations relating to the disclosure of personal information. The majority found that IPP 11(e)(i) was breached because the police had provided insufficient information upon which the company could form a reasonable belief that non-compliance was necessary to avoid prejudice to the maintenance of the law. The request was generalised and did not contain sufficient detail.

891. There are additional exceptions to the IPPs that are not confined to law enforcement purposes but which may be commonly invoked by law enforcement agencies. An example would be the exception to prevent or lessen a serious threat to the life of an individual.

§3. Overriding Provisions in Other Laws

892. Section 24 of the Privacy Act sets out the relationship between the IPPs and other New Zealand law. The IPPs are generally subject to other law. IPPs 6, 11, and 12 (access and disclosure) are subject to the provisions of other law that deals with the availability of personal information. An agency does not breach IPPs 1–5, 7–10 or 13 if its action is authorised or required by or under New Zealand law.

893. Law enforcement agencies all operate under statutes that contain powers that may prevail over the IPPs.

§4. Codes of Practice

894. Section 32 provides for the Privacy Commissioner to issue codes of practice. A code of practice may modify the application of the IPPs by prescribing standards that may vary from those provided by the IPPs or by exempting particular actions from the IPPs. A code may also prescribe how the IPPs are to be applied or complied with.

895. A code of practice may apply to: any specified information or class of information; any agency or class of agency; any activity or class of activity; or any industry, profession or calling or class of industry, profession or calling. It may also regulate information matching in the private sector, set guidelines in respect of charges and make provision for various administrative and mechanical aspects of that code of practice.

896. The Justice Sector Unique Identifier Code 2020 seeks to assist in the effective administration of justice by enabling core law enforcement authorities to share and reassign the unique identifiers assigned to individuals. The code modifies IPP 13 by allowing, in accordance with a schedule, reassignment of certain justice sector unique identifiers by identified justice sector agencies for stated purposes.

897. In particular, the NZ Police take steps to establish the true identity of a person at the time of entering the criminal justice system. Once a person's identity is established, they may have their fingerprints and photograph taken which is then linked to the originating identity. On charging an offender, police will assign a PRN to that person that can then be used and shared by other justice sector agencies.

§5. Applicable Reasons for Refusing Access to Personal Information

898. Sections 49–53 provides for all of the other good reasons on the basis of which an agency may refuse an access request under IPP 6(1)(b). Section 59(c) provides that an agency may refuse access to any personal information requested if:

> the disclosure of the information would be likely to prejudice the maintenance of the law by any public sector agency, including –
>
> (i) the prevention, investigation, and detection of offences; and
> (ii) the right to a fair trial.

§6. Approved Information Sharing Agreements and Authorised Information Matching Programmes

899. Under subparts 1 and 4 of Part 7 there is provision for approved information sharing agreements and authorised information matching programmes. These arrangements are not limited to law enforcement purposes and may, for example, have objectives relating to social services or electoral enrolment. However, a number of agreements and programmes do operate between law enforcement agencies and these will prevail in the event of any conflict with the IPPs.

§7. ACCESS TO IDENTITY INFORMATION

900. Subpart 2 of Part 7 of the Privacy Act authorises 'accessing agencies' (which are public bodies with functions connected with law enforcement), when carrying out specified functions, to verify the identity of an individual by accessing identity information held about that individual by certain specified public bodies referred to as 'holder agencies'.

901. The subpart enables confirmation of identity to be based on unalterable information such as fingerprints and facial recognition rather than paper records which allows agencies to have access to the driver licence photo database and birth, death, and marriages-related information of offenders and mental health patients subject to the criminal justice system. A single shared record of photos, fingerprints, and facial recognition is intended to equip New Zealand law and border enforcement agencies with the best tools to identify offenders and absconders.

§8. LAW ENFORCEMENT INFORMATION SHARING

902. Subpart 3 of Part 7 of the Privacy Act authorises specified public sector agencies to have access to specified law enforcement information held by other specified agencies about identifiable individuals.

§9. ADDITIONAL PRIVACY PROTECTIVE LAWS

903. The Criminal Records (Clean Slate) Act 2004 establishes a clean slate scheme to limit the effect of an individual's convictions in most circumstances (subject to certain exceptions) if the individual satisfies the relevant eligibility criteria. In addition, the Criminal Records (Expungement of Convictions for Historical Homosexual Offences) Act 2018 creates a scheme for the expungement of convictions for a historical homosexual offence.

Chapter 4. National Security Services

§1. Overview

904. Following amendments made to the Privacy Act 1993, carried over into the 2020 Act, nearly all the IPPs apply to New Zealand's intelligence and security agencies.

905. Therefore, the starting point should be that, for the most part, New Zealand's intelligence and security agencies are bound to comply with the same information privacy obligations as other agencies and individuals may expect the same privacy rights with respect to intelligence and security agencies as with other agencies.

906. However, the picture is less clear-cut than might at first appear. In fact, the privacy compliance obligations are weaker for intelligence and security agencies and individuals are not in a strong position to assert their usual rights. In particular it may be noted:

- IPPs 2, 3 and 4(1)(b) do not apply to information collected by an intelligence and security agency: accordingly key principles requiring transparency and prohibiting unfair or unduly intrusive means of collection of personal information do not apply.
- A looser standard applies for the use of personal information by intelligence and security agencies than that which applies more generally to other agencies.
- There is a wide exception to IPP 11 and IPP 12 for disclosures to enable an intelligence and security agency to perform any of its functions.
- Cases cannot be taken against intelligence and security agencies to the HRRT by either an individual or the Privacy Commissioner, all that is available is an Ombudsman-like complaint to the Commissioner.
- National security concerns can be relied upon to refuse subject access requests, withhold breach notification or silence the Privacy Commissioner.
- Subject access cases are routinely refused on a neither confirm nor deny basis and this approach has been endorsed by the Privacy Commissioner.

§2. New Zealand's Intelligence and Security Agencies and Wider Intelligence Community

907. The Security Intelligence Service (NZSIS) is New Zealand's primary national intelligence agency with responsibilities for both national security (including counterterrorism and counterintelligence) and foreign intelligence. The NZSIS headquarters is based in Wellington with regional offices in Auckland and Christchurch, and some staff based overseas.

908. The GCSB is the signals intelligence and information security agency of New Zealand. Its main activity is the interception, decryption, and translation of the communications of foreign governments, including both satellite and radio signals. It is responsible for defending the New Zealand government against similar attempts by other countries, and from attempts at electronic eavesdropping. GCSB has two communications interception stations: a high frequency radio interception and direction-finding station at Tangimoana, near Palmerston North, and a satellite communications interception station at Waihopai, near Blenheim. The National Cyber Security Centre (NCSC) has been located within the GCSB since 2011. The NCSC provides enhanced services and advice to government agencies and critical infrastructure providers to assist them to defend against cyber-borne threats.

909. Both the NZSIS and GCSB operate under the Intelligence and Security Act 2017 which replaced the NZSIS Act 1969 and GCSB Act 2003. NZSI and GCSB are defined as 'intelligence and security agencies' in the Privacy Act.

910. The NZSIS and GCSB are core agencies of the New Zealand Intelligence Community along with the National Assessments Bureau in the Department of the Prime Minister and Cabinet.

911. The New Zealand Defence Force also has intelligence capabilities in the Directorate of Defence Intelligence, in GEOINT New Zealand, and in the individual services. There are also intelligence units in the New Zealand Police, the New Zealand Customs Service, and INZ.

912. New Zealand is a member of the UKUSA Agreement, a multilateral agreement for SIGINT cooperation. This international partnership is also referred to as the 'Five-Eyes'.

§3. Application of IPPs to Intelligence and Security Agencies

913. The expression 'intelligence and security agency' is defined in section 7(1) of the Privacy Act 2020 as the NZSIS and the GCSB.

914. Section 28 provides that IPPs 2, 3, and 4(1)(b) (relating to the collection of personal information) do not apply to information collected by an intelligence and security agency. Accordingly, IPP 1 and part of IPP 4, in relation to the collection principles, apply to intelligence and security agencies as do all of the other IPPs governing security, subject access and correction, accuracy, retention, use, disclosure of personal information, and unique identifiers.

> The Intelligence and Security Act 2017 had earlier amended the Privacy Act 1993 so that all of the privacy principles apply to the intelligence agencies, except 2, 3, and 4(b), and the 2020 Act continued this unchanged. Previously only IPPs 6 and 7 had applied under the 1993 Act.

§4. Application of IPP 10 to Intelligence and Security Agencies

915. IPP 10(2) provides that in addition to the exceptions to IPP 10 set out in IPP10(1), an intelligence and security agency that holds personal information that was obtained with one purpose may use that information for another purpose if it reasonably believes that this secondary purpose is necessary for the agency to perform its functions. The secondary purpose need not be 'directly related' to the original purpose, as required in IPP 10(1)(a).

916. IPP10(2) thereby allows a looser standard for the use of personal information under IPP 10 by intelligence and security agencies than that which applies more generally. IPP 10(1)(a) provides that an agency may use personal information if it reasonably believes that 'the purpose for which the information may be used is directly related to the purpose in connection with which the information was obtained'. IPP 10(2), provides a wider exception in this respect for intelligence and security agencies, in that 'an intelligence and security agency that holds personal information that was obtained in connection with one purpose may use the information for any other purpose (a secondary purpose) if the agency believes on reasonable grounds that the use of the information for the secondary purpose is necessary to enable the agency to perform any of its functions'.

§5. Exception to IPP 11 for Disclosure to Intelligence and Security Agencies

917. IPP 11(1)(g) provides that an intelligence and security agency may disclose personal information if it reasonably believes that the disclosure is necessary for it to perform its functions.

918. This wide exception was included in the disclosure principle when IPP 11 was first applied to intelligence and security agencies by amendments to the Privacy Act 1993 by the Intelligence and Security Act 2017.

§6. Special Complaints and Investigation Procedure Relating to Intelligence and Security Agency

919. Section 95 of the Privacy Act provides for a special procedure to be followed when the Privacy Commissioner is of the opinion that the privacy of an individual has been interfered with by an intelligence and security agency.

920. If, after completing an investigation involving an intelligence and security agency, the Commissioner is of the view that action should be taken, the Commissioner is to report his or her opinion and recommendations (if any) to the intelligence and security agency. Where the Commissioner requests the agency to notify him or her, within a specified time, of the steps that the agency proposes to take to give effect to the recommendations, and where, after a reasonable amount of time, no adequate and appropriate action has been taken, the Commissioner may, after inviting the agency to comment, send a copy of the report to the Prime Minister. The Prime Minister in turn may then lay before the House of Representatives a copy of all or part of the report.

§7. Inquiry Functions of the Inspector-General of Intelligence and Security

921. Part 6 of the Intelligence and Security Act 2017 provides for the appointment of an Inspector-General of Intelligence and Security in order to increase the level of oversight and review of intelligence and security agencies.

922. Among the Inspector-General's relevant functions provided for under section 158(1) are the following:

(a) to conduct an inquiry into any matter relating to an intelligence and security agency's compliance with New Zealand law, including human rights law, if that inquiry is requested by:
   (i) the minister responsible for the intelligence and security agency; or
   (ii) the Intelligence and Security Committee;
(b) to conduct an inquiry into any matter where it appears that a New Zealand person has been or may be adversely affected by an act, omission, practice, policy, or procedure of an intelligence and security agency, if that inquiry is requested by:
   (i) the minister responsible for the intelligence and security agency; or
   (ii) the Intelligence and Security Committee;
(c) to conduct an inquiry into the propriety of particular activities of an intelligence and security agency, if that inquiry is requested by:
   (i) the minister responsible for the intelligence and security agency; or
   (ii) the Intelligence and Security Committee; or
   (iii) the Prime Minister;
(d) to conduct an inquiry of the type referred to in paragraph (a), (b), or (c) on the Inspector-General's own initiative.

923. Thus, although the activities of an intelligence and security agency that interfere with an individual's privacy interests may not fall under the purview of the Privacy Act, the Inspector-General of Intelligence and Security may inquire into them. Section 161(3)(c) of the Act provides that the Inspector-General may consult with the Privacy Commissioner in relation to any matter relating to the functions set out in section 158, and that for the purposes of any such consultation the Inspector-General may disclose such information as may be considered necessary for that purpose.

924. Conversely, section 75(1)(c) of the Privacy Act 2020 provides for consultation by the Privacy Commissioner with the Inspector-General in relation to complaints under Part 5 of the Act that the Commissioner considers to more properly fall, in whole or in part, within the jurisdiction of the Inspector-General. Section 208(1)(c) of the Privacy Act 2020 provides that the Commissioner may at any time consult with the Inspector-General of Intelligence and Security about any matter relating to the Commissioner's functions.

§8. National Security Exceptions in the Privacy Act

925. There are several provisions in the Privacy Act that provide national security grounds to limit an individual's rights or an agency's obligations or to restrict the Privacy Commissioner's actions.

926. Section 51 provides that an agency may refuse an access request under IPP 6(1)(b) for reasons relating to the security and defence of New Zealand, as well as its international relations, and those of its dependencies and associated states.

927. Section 116(1)(a) provides that an agency is not required to notify an affected individual or give public notice of a notifiable privacy breach if the agency believes that the notification or notice would be likely to 'prejudice the security or defence of New Zealand or the international relations of the Government of New Zealand'.

928. Section 206(3)(a) limits the Privacy Commissioner's powers to make a matter public if that matter 'might prejudice the security, defence, or international relations of New Zealand (including New Zealand's relations with the government of any other country or with any international organisation)'.

§9. Case Examples: Complaints to Privacy Commissioner

929. In *Case Note 0635* [1994] NZPrivCmr 15 (31 January 1994), a very early case following the enactment of the Privacy Act 1993, the complainant alleged that the NZSIS had disclosed personal information about him some time ago which he believed was both inaccurate and misleading. In September 1993 the complainant requested a copy of any file concerning himself held by the service for possible correction pursuant to IPPs 7 of the Act. In response the service issued a notice pursuant to section 32 of the 1993 Act (equivalent to section 47 of the 2020 Act) neither confirming nor denying the existence or non-existence of any information held about the complainant. However, copies of correspondence between the complainant and the Prime Minister were made available.

930. The complainant asked the Privacy Commissioner to investigate the service's decision to issue the notice. Following discussions with the NZSIS the Commissioner formed the opinion that the issuing of the notice was necessary in the circumstances of this particular case. The Commissioner advised the complainant that he could neither draw the conclusion from the negative result of his complaint that the service did hold information about him and that there was a good reason to withhold such information, nor could he conclude that the service did not hold such information.

931. In *Case Note 219773* [2010] NZPrivCmr 25 (1 December 2010) a man-made request to the NZSIS under Principle 6 of the Privacy Act 1993 for a copy of information held by the service about him. The service responded to the man's request by neither confirming nor denying that it held information about the man, and therefore relying on section 32 of the 1993 Act (equivalent to section 47 of the 2020 Act).

932. The 1993 Act provided that in certain circumstances the agency dealing with a request may where the interest protected by certain good reasons for refusing a request would be prejudiced by the disclosure of the existence or non-existence of such information, give notice in writing to the applicant that it neither confirms nor denies the existence or non-existence of that information. The Privacy Act does not provide for a right of redress against the NZSIS in the HRRT as would apply in complaints against other agencies. As a last point of review, the Privacy Commissioner carefully scrutinises the NZSIS's decision-making in this regard.

933. As a result of discussions and correspondence with the service the Commissioner satisfied that the NZSIS had a proper basis for its decision to give notice under section 32 of the Privacy Act and closed the case. The Commissioner's case note stated:

> Section 32 enables the Service to uphold the integrity of its intelligence gathering function, which relies on discretion and the keeping of confidences. Section 32 allows that work to continue by allowing the Service to be consistent in responses to both subjects of interest and subjects of no interest when requests for information are made to it. This consistent response reduces the Service's susceptibility to orchestrated requests for information and any prejudice to security by disclosing what the Service does and does not know. This fits with the prospective nature of the Service's investigations and its need to preserve its position.

934. Case Note 284416 [2017] NZPrivCmr 5 (31 May 2017) concerned a man's request for his personal information from the NZSIS and the GCSB. He asked for 'any file and/or any information that is held in regards to myself by the New Zealand Security Intelligence Service and/or the GCSB'.

935. NZSIS and GCSB, in their separate responses, said they could neither confirm nor deny the existence or non-existence of information about him. Both said that to do so would likely prejudice the interests protected by section 27(1)(a) of the Privacy Act 1993, specifically, the security or defence of New Zealand.

936. In his complaint to the Privacy Commissioner, the man explained that he was dissatisfied with the responses. As a result, he had made a request of each agency under the Official Information Act: 'in terms of the number of requests such as mine that the NZSIS [GCSB] receives, I would like to know what percentage of such file requests receive the response that I received from you [s. 32 response]'.

937. The GCSB replied that in the two years prior to receiving his request, from October 2014 to October 2016, it had responded to 88% of all requests under the Act with a section 32 response. The NZSIS replied that it had recently analysed information over a six-month period which showed that a 'neither confirm nor deny' response was provided by the service in 50% of Privacy Act responses.

938. Principle 6 provides, in general, that where any agency holds personal information in such a way that it can be readily retrieved, the individual concerned is entitled to obtain confirmation that the agency holds the information and to have access to that information. Principle 6 is subject to section 32 of the 1993 Act (equivalent to section 47 of the 2020 Act). This section allows the NZSIS and GCSB to neither confirm nor deny the existence or non-existence of information about the person. For security reasons, the NZSIS and GCSB cannot be as open with individuals about the personal information they hold or do not hold about them, compared to other public sector agencies. Due to the sensitive nature of their work, responding to Principle 6 requests and revealing what is known or not known about a person can have national security implications. Individuals could share Principle 6 responses with each other to draw inferences about what the NZSIS and GCSB is or is not aware of. A requester may present no security risk but section 32 allows the NZSIS and GCSB to take a cautious approach to revealing whether or not it holds the personal information requested.

939. To rely on section 32, an agency has to be satisfied that disclosure of the existence or non-existence of information in response to a request would prejudice an important interest such as national security or international relations (or one of the other interests as set out in sections 27 and 28 of the 1993 Act).

940. In this case, the Commissioner accepted that both the NZSIS and GCSB did have reasons to neither confirm nor deny the existence or non-existence of the information and that section 32 had been correctly applied in the circumstances. The Commissioner concluded that the complainant had not suffered an interference with his privacy.

941. The complainant was not happy with this outcome but agreed with the Commissioner's suggestion that the Commissioner publish a case note to highlight the case.

Selected Bibliography

Court Judgments

Jeffries v. Privacy Commissioner [2010] NZSC 99, [2011] 1 NZLR 45
R v. Alsford [2017] NZSC 42
Hamed v. R [2011] NZSC 101

Tribunal Decisions

Director of Human Rights Proceedings v. Catholic Church for New Zealand [2008] NZHC 156, [2008] 3 NZLR 216
Marshall v. National Spiritual Assembly of the Baha'is of New Zealand Inc [2003] 2 NZLR 205
W v. Director-General of Social Welfare (Complaints Review Tribunal, Decision Nos 11/98 and 12/98, CRT 4/98, S C Bathgate (Chairperson), M A Smith, D B Emery; reported at (1998) 5 HRNZ 580)
Director of Human Rights Proceedings v. The Catholic Church for New Zealand [2006] NZHRRT 22
Human Rights Commission v. Eric Sides Motors Co Ltd (1981) 2 NZAR 447
McCready v. Hawkins and Hawkins Associates, unreported, Dec No 10/97, CRT 30/96
Imperial Enterprises Ltd v. Attwood [2002] 2 ERNZ 740

Privacy Commissioner Case Notes

Case Note 18541 [2002] NZPrivCmr 8
Case Note 0635 [1994] NZPrivCmr 15 (31 January 1994)
Case Note 219773 [2010] NZPrivCmr 25 (1 December 2010)
Case Note 284416 [2017] NZPrivCmr 5 (31 May 2017)

Reports

Report of the Privacy Commissioner for the year ended 30 June 2001 AJHR A.11
OECD Group of Experts on Data Barriers and Privacy Protection, *Explanatory Memorandum to the OECD Guidelines on the Protection of Privacy and Transborder Flows of Personal Data*, 1980

International Instruments

United Nations International Covenant on Civil and Political Rights

Selected Bibliography

OECD Guidelines Governing the Protection of Privacy and Transborder Flows of Personal Data, 1980 and 2013
APEC Privacy Framework, 2005 and 2015
APEC Cross-Border Privacy Rules system (CBPRs), 2011
Comprehensive and Progressive Agreement for Trans-Pacific Partnership (CPTPP), 2018
Regional Comprehensive Economic Partnership (RCEP), 2022
European Union Data Protection Directive, 1995
General Data Protection Regulation, 2016
Council of Europe Modernised Data Protection Convention

Index

The numbers here refers to paragraph numbers.

Index

Index

www.ingramcontent.com/pod-product-compliance
Lightning Source LLC
Chambersburg PA
CBHW072243240926
51846CB00012B/153
* 9 7 8 9 4 0 3 5 1 6 1 6 5 *